Katherine Mansfield and World War One

KATHERINE MANSFIELD STUDIES

Katherine Mansfield Studies is the peer-reviewed, annual publication of the Katherine Mansfield Society. It offers opportunities for collaborations between researchers with interests in postcolonial studies and in modernism in literature and the arts. Because Mansfield is a writer who has inspired successors from Elizabeth Bowen to Ali Smith, as well as numerous artists in other media, *Katherine Mansfield Studies* encourages interdisciplinary scholarship and allows for a proportion of creative submissions.

Katherine Mansfield Studies

Volume 6

Katherine Mansfield and World War One

Editors
Gerri Kimber, Todd Martin
and Delia da Sousa Correa

Guest Editors
Isobel Maddison and Alice Kelly

Editorial Assistant
Louise Edensor

EDINBURGH
University Press

Edinburgh University Press Ltd
The Tun – Holyrood Road, 12(2f) Jackson's Entry, Edinburgh EH8 8PJ

www.euppublishing.com

Typeset in 10.5/12.5 New Baskerville by
Servis Filmsetting Ltd, Stockport, Cheshire,
and printed and bound in Great Britain by
CPI Group (UK) Ltd, Croydon CR0 4YY

A CIP record for this book is available from the British Library

ISBN 978 0 7486 9534 8 (hardback)
ISBN 978 0 7486 9535 5 (webready PDF)
ISBN 978 0 7486 9536 2 (paperback)

Published with the support of the Edinburgh University Scholarly Publishing Initiatives Fund.

Contents

CREATIVE WRITING

REPORTS

List of Illustrations

Acknowledgements

The editors would like to thank the academics with expertise in the writings of World War One who judged this year's Katherine Mansfield Society essay prize. We are grateful to Professor Margaret Higonnet, Dr Santanu Das and Professor Sydney Janet Kaplan for their interest in this prize and for the generous spirit in which they engaged with the new scholarship published in this volume. Their thorough readings and detailed responses were helpful to all the entrants when revising their work and we are indebted to them.

The editors would also like to thank Sarah Pickstone for allowing us to use her painting 'Mansfield's Moth' as the cover image for this volume and Virginia King for sharing photographs of her sculpture in progress. They would also like to thank the following organisations and individuals: the Open University; the University of Northampton; Barbara Sullivan; the Alexander Turnbull Library, Wellington, New Zealand; the Harry Ransom Center, University of Texas at Austin, and in particular Rick Watson, Head of Reference Services; Tate Britain, for permission to reproduce the image of Gertler's 'Merry-Go-Round', and the National Archives of the UK for permission to publish a copy of the death report of Leslie Beauchamp.

Also available in the series:

Katherine Mansfield and Continental Europe
Edited by Delia da Sousa Correa and Gerri Kimber
Katherine Mansfield Studies, Volume 1
Hbk 978 0 7486 8470 0

Katherine Mansfield and Modernism
Edited by Delia da Sousa Correa, Gerri Kimber and Susan Reid
Katherine Mansfield Studies, Volume 2
Hbk 978 0 7486 8471 7

Katherine Mansfield and the Arts
Edited by Delia da Sousa Correa, Gerri Kimber and Susan Reid
Katherine Mansfield Studies, Volume 3
Hbk 978 0 7486 8472 4

Katherine Mansfield and the Fantastic
Edited by Delia da Sousa Correa, Gerri Kimber, Susan Reid and Gina Wisker
Katherine Mansfield Studies, Volume 4
Hbk 978 0 7486 8473 1

Katherine Mansfield and the (Post)colonial
Edited by Janet Wilson, Gerri Kimber and Delia da Sousa Correa
Katherine Mansfield Studies, Volume 5
Hbk 978 0 7486 6909 7

Frontispiece. 'Merry-Go-Round', 1916, Mark Gertler (1891–1939).
Image courtesy of Tate Modern.

Introduction: Katherine Mansfield, War Writer

Alice Kelly

> I put all the unfinished MSS I had brought with me here in a row last night and [. . .] reviewed them – & told them that none of them were really good enough – to march into the open (Ugh! No – I cant even in fun use these bloody comparisons. I have a horror of the way this war creeps into writing . . . oozes in – trickles in.)[1]

In a letter to John Middleton Murry from February 1918, Katherine Mansfield explicitly acknowledges the unintentional influence of the ongoing war on her own rhetorical structures, using the metaphors of creeping, oozing and trickling to describe its pervading effects. Her parenthetical distaste for these 'bloody comparisons' admits the disjunction between the situation she is recording (her evaluation of her literary manuscripts) and her descriptive mode. Both her deliberate and unintentional incorporation of military discourse results in a hybridised figurative language in her writing, which can tell us about the effect of the Great War on literary language more generally, as well as on Mansfield in particular.

This special issue of *Katherine Mansfield Studies* examines, in Kate McLoughlin's succinct phrase, 'what happens when war and words are brought together'.[2] It addresses Mansfield's engagement with the First World War – the 'Great War' – and its impact on her writings. Like the reclamation of women's war writings that we have already seen in relation to Woolf and others, Mansfield's literary response to the key political event of her time – one which postcolonial scholars are still demonstrating was truly global – is key to our understanding of her developing writerly style. It is in her responses to this event that we find a 'political Mansfield', commenting on the public events of her time, and the articles in this volume provide us with a greater understanding of Mansfield in her socio-historical context.[3] In providing new and different readings of Mansfield's explicit and implicit war stories, these essays refine and extend our understanding of these particular stories and their genealogy, and more broadly illuminate the specific and more general influences of the war on Mansfield's evolving technique. They jointly suggest the importance of the influence of the war on Mansfield's literary language, and simultaneously for Mansfield's own particular brand of modernism. Conversely, these articles demonstrate Mansfield's literary skill in her explicit war writings, going beyond the subject matter to provide further analysis of her narrative mode and technique. They continue to develop our ideas of what constitute war writings, and in so doing, expand the field of First World War studies, as well as Mansfield studies.

Vincent O'Sullivan has asserted that, '[f]rom any perspective, the most important public event in Mansfield's lifetime was the First World War'.[4] What were Mansfield's experiences during the war that she variously characterised as a 'terrible, tedious calamity', 'that dark place' and 'this bloody war'?[5] In February 1915, Mansfield travelled alone into the war zones to visit Francis Carco, stationed in Gray, France, which provided the inspiration for one of her best-known war stories, 'An Indiscreet Journey' (written in 1915), as well as being recounted in her notebooks and two extant letters. On her trip to visit Carco, was Mansfield, as O'Sullivan notes, 'perhaps the first to record the effects of gassing' on the men at the front, or did she, as Mary Burgan suggests, move 'in the closed circle of her own sensibility in which the actual suffering of the wounded French soldiers seen along the way [intrudes] only as so many touches of local color'?[6] Mansfield's journey to the war zone gave her a privileged perspective on the effects of the war at first hand that was not usually afforded to civilians, particularly women; as O'Sullivan observes, '[f]or a civilian, Mansfield saw a good deal of the war'.[7] Similarly, Mansfield's experience of the first air raids in Paris in March 1915, and subsequently the three-week bombardment of Paris in March and April 1918, provided her with an experience and stimulus for her writing ahead of many of her contemporaries. The accidental death of her brother Leslie (Chummie) Beauchamp in a hand-grenade accident during a training session on 6 October 1915 (the accurate date of his death, as confirmed by J. Lawrence Mitchell in this volume), as well as the deaths of a number of her close friends, including the poet Rupert Brooke in April 1915 and the writer Frederick Goodyear in May 1917, was the cause of great suffering for Mansfield. As has been noted by other critics, Murry wrote in the commentary to his Definitive Edition of her *Journal*, that 'no single one of Katherine's friends who went to the war returned alive from it'.[8] Mansfield's frequent sojourns abroad because of her illness meant that she participated in a similar isolation and distance from loved ones that characterised the civilian experience of the war. Reading through her letters, one is struck by Mansfield's acquaintance with a range of male and female figures, both publically and privately engaged with the war, who jointly covered the spectrum of political responses to it.[9]

Prominent literary and cultural histories of the war have traditionally been concerned with the male experience of battle. The Great War has been depicted as a break from the past, inaugurating, or at least being seen to inaugurate, a new 'modern' era and modes of thought. More recently, however, studies of First World War writing have broadened in their scope to examine previously neglected aspects of the conflict. There has been a surge of critical attention paid to women's First World War writing. There have also been a number of historical studies of the broad variety of women's wartime experience, and the accessibility of women's wartime writing has increased through a number of useful anthologies and new editions.

This edition of *Katherine Mansfield Studies* falls into what Santanu Das has identified as 'the "second wave" of war criticism [. . .] marked by two important trends: interdisciplinarity and diversification of concern'.[10] *The Cambridge Companion to the Literature of the First World War* illustrates this revisionist mode, as well as the entry of the genre into the critical commonplace and on to university syllabi.[11] Studies of First World War rhetoric have discussed the recruitment of authors as propagandists, or analysed the political premises inherent in language itself. A number of scholars have begun to consider the connections between First World War and modernist writing. Studies of popular culture and the war, as well as publishing histories, have broadened the field of war writing to include popular literature and magazines. The inherent problems of 'authoring war' have been discussed. Other examinations of war writing have been increasingly interdisciplinary, such as studies of the bodily, corporeal experience in wartime and its expression, and have also begun to focus on racial and colonial aspects of the war.[12] One very recent development is the increasing interest in First World War short stories, seen in the review in this issue of Ann-Marie Einhaus's *The Short Story and the First World War*, published in July 2013: a useful antidote to an otherwise surprisingly sparse subfield of First World War studies.[13] The centenary commemorations of the outbreak of the First World War, beginning in 2014, will result in the further development – even explosion – of this field in surprising and novel directions, in both the academic and popular spheres.

How does Mansfield fit into this field of First World War studies? Not very obviously, is the short answer. There has been a surprising reluctance to view Mansfield as a war writer, and the body of criticism that does so remains a very small field. This perception of Mansfield as curiously divorced from her socio-historical context is reflected in the very limited number of stories included within collections of First World War women's writing, or First World War short stories; only 'An Indiscreet Journey' and 'The Fly' are regularly anthologised.[14] Usually, Mansfield's depiction of the war is critically focused on these stories, and on her journal responses to Leslie's death.[15] Con Coroneos and Angela Smith have further provided highly original readings of these stories, and both Christiane Mortelier and Gerri Kimber have expanded our understanding of Francis Carco and wartime France.[16] Christine Darrohn and Ariela Freedman have highlighted the significance of the war in 'The Garden Party'.[17] But what about those stories which explicitly or implicitly discuss the war, stories such as 'Spring Pictures', 'Two Tuppenny Ones, Please', 'Late at Night', 'The Common Round' ('Pictures'), 'Prelude' or 'A Dill Pickle'? Or stories with titles obviously influenced by their wartime context: 'Last Words to Youth', 'The Lost Battle' or 'Love-Lies-Bleeding'? What about Mansfield's descriptions of her experiences of air raids in her letters from early 1915 and early 1918, or her descriptions of herself in militarised language throughout 1919? O'Sullivan has stressed Mansfield's understanding of the war's larger significance, placing her 'among the group of writers who understood early on how the First World War brought a permanent fragmentation of what living in Europe implied'.[18] Anne Fernihough and Lee Garver have emphasised Mansfield's political engagement, reading *In a German Pension* (1911) as satirical commentary on contemporary socio-political issues.[19] Unlike Woolf, who has been increasingly recognised in her wartime context, there have been no sustained studies of Mansfield and the war. In fact, Woolf is perceived as far more closely linked with the war than Mansfield, even though Mansfield lost an immediate family member. This perception is perhaps indicative of the dearth of criticism on First World War short stories, as opposed to Woolf's predominant medium of novels.

A number of the essays in this issue provide new readings of Mansfield's stories, tracing influences and developing previous assessments of these works. The 2013 winner of the Katherine Mansfield Society's Essay Prize, Josiane Paccaud-Huguet, illuminates Mansfield's arguably best-known war story, 'An Indiscreet Journey', putting it in a different light for readers. Drawing on Sigmund Freud, Jacques Lacan and Giorgio Agamben, and on the notion of *jouissance*, Paccaud-Huguet makes the case that this story 'mingles from the start the eroticism of love with the theme of death' and compares the form of the narrative with that of the fairy tale and the mystery play. This is a story which is both a specific war story, and not a specific war story; Paccaud-Huguet calls attention to the timelessness and the 'timeless present' of this text, which is 'the hallmark of Mansfield's contemporariness to her time'. In a series of close readings of the text, Paccaud-Huguet presents us with the means by which Mansfield encodes the action of war in the narrative, exemplified in her reading of the bottle breaking in the café: a moment which 'is surely more significant than the whole epic narrative of a battle' (19).

In a different vein, J. Lawrence Mitchell's more biographical essay challenges the idea that Mansfield and Murry were oblivious to the war, arguing instead that Mansfield 'was fully aware of what was happening around her' (28). He makes humorous the common misperception of Mansfield as unengaged, noting that it is odd that the author of a story such as 'Stay-Laces', which demonstrates her 'scorn for such wilful ignorance and such callous indifference to anything outside one's own circumscribed world' (33), could be accused of similar behaviour herself by critics. Mitchell notes 'the acuity of Mansfield's observation' (31) and her conscious attempts to educate herself about the war. He draws an admittedly speculative but none the less interesting link between Mansfield's early patriotic writing published in the newspaper and Chummie's voluntary enlistment, and provides a new genealogy of the story 'Stay-Laces', suggesting it was likely penned before, rather than after, Chummie's death. Mitchell posits a potential reading of Mansfield's relationship with her brother, suggesting a particular kind of special bond between the pair. This wide-ranging essay provides us with a scholarly example of how biographical knowledge can illuminate our understanding of the writing.

Isobel Maddison's discussion of Mansfield's 'writing game' reminds us of the importance of publication context. Focusing on the sketches that constitute *In a German Pension* (1911) and the original publication of some of them in the *New Age*, Maddison investigates the original appearance of stories that Mansfield later refused to republish. These give us an insight into the pre-war moment when fears of a war with Germany were becoming increasingly justified, as well as an important early example of Mansfield's 'flair for mimicry' (43). Maddison emphasises a number of important factors contributing to these sketches: the significant influence of A. R. Orage and Beatrice Hastings on Mansfield's 'literary apprenticeship' in the *New Age*, her own miserable personal experience in Bad Wörishofen in Bavaria, and the context of anti-invasion fiction. Maddison reminds us that many, including Orage and D. H. Lawrence, held a far more nuanced view, continuing to hold German culture in great esteem, and that the *New Age* 'became a vehicle for independent and competing discussions of German life' (45). Her readings of stories such as 'Germans at Meat' and 'Bavarian Babies' therefore complicate our understandings of these texts, as she discusses their wider publication context, such as letters from readers which object to the caricatured view of German people and culture that Mansfield presents. Maddison offers a reading of a fascinating story, 'The Breidenbach Family in England', a story that we cannot attribute without doubt to Mansfield, which provides the counter-perspective of a German family holidaying in England.[20]

Helen Rydstrand provides a more theoretical perspective on 'An Indiscreet Journey' and 'Two Tuppenny Ones, Please'. Using the ideas and terminology of Henri Lefebvre's *Elements of Rhythmanalysis*, Rydstrand is interested in 'the strange tension between the ordinary and the extraordinary in wartime' (56). She traces the concept of rhythm as an important intellectual context for Mansfield's work, demonstrating its proliferation as an idea across a variety of disciplines. Depicting the war through the everyday and the ordinary has been seen as a modernist technique, and 'Mansfield's use of rhythmic linguistic technique to explore and represent the ordinary' (62) extends our understanding of her modernism. Rydstrand also discusses the importance of the short story form, both for the immediacy of its response to the war and for its fragmentary, plotless nature: particularly fitting for the representation of an ongoing war. We then find familiar stories explained in unfamiliar ways; the victim of gassing whose eyes 'brimmed and spilled, brimmed and spilled' in 'An Indiscreet Journey' is here described as 'the permanent disturbance of this soldier's rhythm (his everyday life)' (64). Similarly, Rydstrand notes that the three-part structure of 'An Indiscreet Journey', each part reiterating the last, mimics the wartime experience of 'monotony and anxious anticipation', resulting in what Rydstrand terms 'a novel method of mimesis' (61, 66).

The next two essays both examine the development of 'The Aloe' into 'Prelude', neither of which is typically considered as a war story. Alex Moffett's essay presents us with a textual history of 'Prelude', which traces Mansfield's deletion or moderation of the militaristic language and imagery of 'The Aloe' as she developed it. Moffett suggests that in this revision, 'the war moves from a metaphorical yet tangible presence in the text, to a seeming and signifying absence' (70). An important factor in this conscious revision of imagery was the death of Mansfield's brother, Leslie, which Moffett argues 'inaugurated for her a different set of representational strategies for dealing with the First World War' (71). He suggests that after Leslie's death, the war 'most frequently asserts its presence through absence' (71), citing 'The Fly' and 'The Garden Party' as examples of this. In Mansfield's revision of the text of 'The Aloe' into 'Prelude', the war became 'an ominous undercurrent rather than a persistent metaphorical reference point' (76). One striking example is the elimination of Doady Trout, and her persistent fantasies of 'some shocking catastrophe' (77) occurring to her family members. Similarly, Moffett suggests that the excised episode of Kezia's birth in 'The Aloe' recalls Mansfield's writing about the Paris air raids. Moffett links the repression of referentiality in 'Prelude' as entirely in keeping with Mansfield's consideration of the effects of the war on literature: that it could not be mentioned '*bang out*', but that it had to be present.[21]

Working as a neat complement to Moffett's essay, Richard Cappuccio's piece suggests that '[b]y 1916 elements of the war had been integrated into the everyday lives of children' (85–6), and provides a contextual reading of wartime culture apparent in 'The Aloe'. He links Kezia's experience of walking around the empty Burnell house with the experience of civilians attempting to comprehend the erasure of home for combatants, noted by Allyson Booth. He juxtaposes Mansfield's writing with combatant narratives, comparing the fragments that Kezia observes in the home with the fragments of bodies seen in a passage in *All Quiet on the Western Front*, arguing that '[t]he two scenes [. . .] share the struggle to find coherence among arbitrary remains' (87). Similarly, Cappuccio draws attention to wartime material culture; Kezia's observation of a forgotten lump of soap is linked to Sunlight Soap, 'a product that was later advertised as particularly tied to the war effort' (87). Cappuccio offers an extended reading of this story, plus a short reading of 'Stay-Laces' and a concluding discussion of Mansfield's literary response to the death of Leslie, noting how imagery such as Pat slaughtering the duck constitutes an exploration of fate and the prefiguring of violence to sons. Cappuccio argues that 'The Aloe' is 'a tale of ominous foreboding, a tale of paternal *hubris*, and a tale of the foreshadowed tragedy of Linda's pregnancy' (94).

Finally, Erika Baldt's essay offers a reading of 'The Daughters of the Late Colonel' – a text not normally considered a war story – in the context of classical mythology. Rather than the common interpretation of the war as a break in history, Baldt highlights the continuity, rather than the division, of the war, 'drawing parallels between women's experiences of conflict through the ages to the contemporary moment' (98). In this way, 'a correlation can be found between the Great War and both classical and contemporary mythology' (100). Baldt argues that

Mansfield, like many of her contemporaries (prominently T. S. Eliot and Ezra Pound), used 'ancient texts to filter and reflect on the Great War' (100), and suggests that the particular intertexts for this story are *Titus Andronicus*, the myth of Philomela and Procne, and Aeschylus' *Agamemnon*. Baldt suggests that, much like the treatment of women in these myths, Josephine and Constantia are the victims of trauma inflicted by their military father.

The three creative pieces in this issue, a short story by Emily Perkins entitled 'After the Pictures' and two poems, one by Kevin Ireland and one by the late Seamus Heaney, which mentions Mansfield, demonstrate the inspiration she provoked and continues to provoke. Mirosława Kubasiewicz offers a thoughtful gloss on Heaney's poem. The reports in this issue further our understanding of Mansfield in a more general sense. David Bradshaw enlightens our understanding of Mansfield's relationship with J. W. N. Sullivan, an important figure who previously has been curiously absent from Mansfield studies, as Bradshaw notes. His analysis of their complex and frequently volatile relationship suggests that Sullivan may have had more affection for Mansfield than has hitherto been suggested. Gerri Kimber's report offers a comprehensive account of C. K. Stead's longstanding creative and critical engagement with Mansfield, in which his own 'war novel', *Mansfield* (2004), occupies a prominent place. She creates three tables that map 'how Stead uses Mansfield's writing to construct his novel' (145), and how he draws on the works of both Woolf and Mansfield to compose his two poems, 'Jealousy I' and 'Jealousy II'. Robin Woodward's report on Virginia King's 3.4-metre-high Mansfield monument, 'Woman of Words' (2013), in Wellington reminds us of the intense labour involved in creating this work of art. This is the only statue of Mansfield in the world, and King chose to present Mansfield '[w]rapped in her writing and defined by her own words', with '[h]er dress, hair and ribbon [. . .] all formed in text', as Woodward notes (161, 160). The intense attention to detail, such as the emphasis on Mansfield's hands because of Mansfield's frequent references to hands and gloves in her writings, is remarkable. With a regard for the labours of other writers that would have impressed Murry in his frantically dashed-off *Times Literary Supplement* reviews of 1916, no less than six reviews in this issue provide readers with an update on all that is current in Mansfield and modernist studies more generally, a particular highlight being C. K. Stead's long review of Janet Frame's 1974 novel, *In the Memorial Room*, unpublished until 2013.

Together these contributions allow, indeed urge, us to reassess Mansfield's engagement with the First World War and its impact on her writing. By providing a greater understanding of Mansfield in her socio-political context, we can extend our understanding of the genealogy of a number of her war-related and apparently non–war-related stories, and consider the profound influence of the war on her developing technique and type of modernism. One thing that we are prompted to consider whilst reading is the extent to which Mansfield's wartime experience not only influenced, but also provoked her literary experimentation: whether or not her modernism was a particular brand of 'civilian modernism', in Allyson Booth's formulation.[22] In this year of the centenary of the Great War, this issue of *Katherine Mansfield Studies* demonstrates that we should both reconsider our ideas of what constitutes war writing and reconsider Mansfield's acute renderings of 'this bloody war'. It reminds us to consider Mansfield – amongst her many other masks – as a war writer.

Notes

1. To Murry [12 and 13 February 1918], in Vincent O'Sullivan and Margaret Scott, eds, *The Collected Letters of Katherine Mansfield*, 5 vols (Oxford: Clarendon Press, 1987), Vol. 2, p. 70. Hereafter referred to as *Letters*, followed by volume and page number.
2. Kate McLoughlin, 'War and Words', in Kate McLoughlin, ed., *The Cambridge Companion to War Writing* (Cambridge: Cambridge University Press, 2009), pp. 15–24 (p. 15).
3. I take the term from Lee Garver: 'The Political Katherine Mansfield', *Modernism/Modernity*, 8 (2001), pp. 225–43.
4. Vincent O'Sullivan, '"Finding the Pattern, Solving the Problem": Katherine Mansfield the New Zealand European', in Roger Robinson, ed., *Katherine Mansfield: In from the Margin* (Baton Rouge and London: Louisiana State University Press, 1994), pp. 9–24 (p. 14).
5. Letter to Harold Beauchamp [6 March 1916], *Letters* 1, p. 252. Letter to Ottoline Morrell [16 June 1917], *Letters* 1, p. 311. Letter to Ottoline Morrell [11 August 1917], *Letters* 1, p. 324.
6. O'Sullivan, p. 18. O'Sullivan follows a suggestion by Antony Alpers, where he writes: 'her horrific portrayal of a gassed French soldier in a café [. . .] must have been based on something seen very recently, in Paris' (Antony Alpers, ed., *The Stories of Katherine Mansfield – Definitive Edition* (Auckland: Oxford University Press, 1984), p. 554). Mary Burgan, *Illness, Gender, and Writing: The Case of Katherine Mansfield* (Baltimore and London: Johns Hopkins University Press, 1994), p. 37.
7. O'Sullivan, p. 18.
8. John Middleton Murry, ed., *Journal of Katherine Mansfield: Definitive Edition* (London: Constable, 1954), p. 104.
9. These acquaintances included Rupert Brooke, Frederick Goodyear, Robert Graves and Siegfried Sassoon (whom Murry helped draft his 'Declaration' in 1917).
10. Santanu Das, *Touch and Intimacy in First World War Literature* (Cambridge: Cambridge University Press, 2005), p. 10.
11. Vincent Sherry, ed., *The Cambridge Companion to the Literature of the First World War* (Cambridge: Cambridge University Press, 2005).
12. Das, *Touch and Intimacy* (2005). *Race, Empire and First World War Writing*, ed. by Das (Cambridge: Cambridge University Press, 2011).

13. Ann-Marie Einhaus, *The Short Story and the First World War* (Cambridge: Cambridge University Press, 2013).
14. 'The Fly' is included in Trudi Tate, ed., *Women, Men and the Great War: An Anthology of Stories* (Manchester: Manchester University Press, 1995), pp. 68–72; and in Margaret R. Higonnet, ed., *Lines of Fire: Women Writers of World War I* (New York: Plume, 1999), pp. 412–16. 'An Indiscreet Journey' is included in Agnès Cardinal, Dorothy Goldman and Judith Hattaway, eds, *Women's Writing on the First World War* (Oxford: Oxford University Press, 1999), pp. 255–67. 'An Indiscreet Journey' and 'The Fly' are also included in Barbara Korte and Anne-Marie Einhaus, eds, *The Penguin Book of First World War Stories* (London and New York: Penguin, 2007), pp. 77–92, 297–302.
15. See Claire Tylee, '"The Magic of Adventure" – The Western Front and Women's Tales About the War-Zone, 1915–16 (May Cannan, Katherine Mansfield, Ellen La Motte, Mary Borden)', in *The Great War and Women's Consciousness: Images of Militarism and Womanhood in Women's Writing, 1914–64* (Iowa City: University of Iowa Press, 1990), pp. 75–102; Angela K. Smith, '"I have broken the silence": Katherine Mansfield's War', in *The Second Battlefield: Women, Modernism and the First World War* (Manchester: Manchester University Press, 2000), pp. 162–9.
16. Con Coroneos, 'Flies and Violets in Katherine Mansfield', in Suzanne Raitt and Trudi Tate, eds, *Women's Fiction and the Great War* (Oxford: Clarendon Press, 1997), pp. 197–218; Angela Smith, 'Katherine Mansfield at the Front', *First World War Studies*, 2 (2011), pp. 65–73. Christiane Mortelier, 'The French Connection: Francis Carco', in Robinson, pp. 137–57; Gerri Kimber, *Katherine Mansfield: The View From France* (Bern and New York: Peter Lang, 2008).
17. Christine Darrohn, '"Blown to Bits!": Katherine Mansfield's "The Garden-Party" and the Great War', *Modern Fiction Studies*, 44 (1998), 513–39; Ariela Freedman, 'After the Party: Woolf, Mansfield, and World War I', in *Death, Men, and Modernism: Trauma and Narrative in British Fiction from Hardy to Woolf* (New York and London: Routledge, 2003), pp. 81–102.
18. O'Sullivan, p. 16.
19. Anne Fernihough, 'Introduction', in Kathleen Murry [Katherine Mansfield], *In A German Pension* (London: Stephen Swift, 1911; repr. London: Penguin, 1999), pp. ix–xxxi; Garver (2001).
20. For a discussion of the story's attribution to Mansfield, see Gerri Kimber and Vincent O'Sullivan, eds, *The Edinburgh Edition of the Collected Works of Katherine Mansfield*, Vol. 1, *The Collected Fiction of Katherine Mansfield, 1898–1915* (Edinburgh: Edinburgh University Press, 2012), pp. 516–19.
21. *Letters* 3, p. 98 [16 November 1919].
22. Allyson Booth, *Postcards from the Trenches: Negotiating the Space between Modernism and the First World War* (Oxford: Oxford University Press, 1996), p. 5.

CRITICISM

'By what name are we to call death?': The Case of 'An Indiscreet Journey'[1]

Josiane Paccaud-Huguet

Published in the posthumous volume, *Something Childish and Other Stories* (1924), 'An Indiscreet Journey' was written in the first year of the Great War.[2] We know that the story is based on Mansfield's liaison with the French poet Francis Carco, whom she visited in the forbidden military zone at Gray near Dijon, in February 1915. The interest of the autobiographical element here is the fact that it mingles from the start the eroticism of love with the theme of death. It is the poetic seed for a unique narrative where Mansfield is observing, according to Claire Tomalin, 'nothing less than the 1914–1918 war in action, not in its heroics or horror even, but in the casualness, the muddle and confusion of the French army just behind the lines in 1915'.[3] In other words, she deals with the *real* substance of war experience, and the plotless narrative will be her medium for this:

> Almost banishing the personal and the romantic, Mansfield has drawn instead a picture of the interaction of civilian and military life in which irreverence for the great theme of war and insistence on detail captures a vanished moment of history. There are not many war stories by women: this is a little classic.[4]

It is a classic which a fellow writer, K. A. Porter, also praised for its 'curious timelessness',[5] and it is this quality, I will argue, that is the hallmark of Mansfield's contemporariness to her time, and to our own; she gets to the heart of the significance of modern war unshaped by epic semblances since, as her friend D. H. Lawrence also wrote, 'the old ideals are dead as nails'.[6] She touches on the something 'beyond the pleasure principle' which, according to Freud, binds together Eros with Thanatos and to which Lacan will later give the name of *jouissance*.[7]

In a brief essay entitled *Qu'est-ce que le contemporain?*, the philosopher Giorgio Agamben argues that the contemporary poet is the one who dips her pen in the darkness of the present time, in the blind spots of individual or collective history: a feature which no doubt characterises modernist writers.[8] Conrad, for example, declares that the modern artist who writes beyond the fairy tales of ideology has to confront the impossibility of narration: 'If in action we may admit with awe that the Impossible recedes before men's indomitable spirit, the Impossible in matters of analysis will always make a stand at some point or other.'[9] Where the substance of war is concerned, a certain anachronistic relation to time is then needed: a kind of 'active passiveness' that, according to Agamben, will enable the poet to neutralise the lights of the day in order to make the intimate darkness palpable. Such darkness is not made of inert matter; it is itself a form of light that needs time to reach us, like the gaze of stars travelling in space.[10]

The Uses of Dis-enchantment

There are many markers of the fairy tale in 'An Indiscreet Journey' but, of course, Mansfield makes her own use of its simple pleasures.[11] After reaching the war zone where she has decided to pay a visit to her lover, the female narrator flies away with him in a little cab, passing down a white street to a little house as white as the people who inhabit it: 'White as snow', her companion says (69). But the uses of enchantment in Snow White's home will be less to arouse wonder than to enhance a sense of the anachronistic, of discrepancy and irreverence.

The rhetoric of conquest underlying both the romance and the epic war story is never safe here; the soldiers are neither the stock figures going to the front *la fleur au fusil* (lightheartedly), nor is the narrator very much the lady of romance. Before leaving Paris, she has exchanged her coat with a seal collar for a friend's rather masculine old Burberry, and pertly comments: 'Lions have been faced in a Burberry. Ladies have been rescued from open boats in mountainous seas wrapped in nothing else' (63). Nothing much of the kind ever happens, however. Her journey to the front-line is an eerie rite of passage: '"Why so fast, *ma mignonne*?" said a lovely little boy in coloured socks, dancing in front of the electric lotus buds that curved over the entrance to the Métro' (63). The lotus buds here evoke less the symbol of modernity than the flower that gives access to dream and sleep. As to the little boy, he is less a character than a type, a helper in the steps of the narrator's descent into hell. He will reappear under different guises at the cafés at which she will stop.

The young woman, who has not taken a watch with her, dances and runs as if in suspended time. She conjures up her best smile to pass through the various obstacles that will lead to a kind of pre-symbolic area, where place names are just letters, X. Y. Z. (63). Gray, the name of her destination, is never mentioned except by displacement, just as in a dream: for example, in the name of the authority who has signed her passport, Sir Edward Grey. She does not even seem to remember the station where she has to change. Her passport to the forbidden zone is a false letter from an imaginary Aunt Julie, a mere simulacrum that mimics affectionate family ties in order better to conceal the nature of her illicit appointment. She is constantly afraid of muddling the French names in the letter, whose characters nevertheless seem very 'real' and 'solid' to her. Actually, they provide an ironically useful semblance for the voice of her desire that winks obliquely at her from the page: 'And then, for the first time, folding Aunt Julie's letter, I saw scrawled in a corner of the empty back page: *Venez vite, vite.* Strange impulsive woman! My heart began to beat!' (66). Who is the strange impulsive woman here, Aunt Julie or our daring heroine? The italicised message is like a whisper from the darkness, an indiscreet truth in a brief flash of insight, just like the irreverent post-scriptum that leaps to Marlow's eyes from the margins of Kurtz's philanthropic report in *Heart of Darkness* (1899).[12]

There is another letter in the story, handed out by a fellow traveller: an old woman with a black bonnet on her head, who takes the first letter received from her son to her daughter-in-law. This time the family ties are not fake, the old ideals are not dead. A figure of socially prescribed roles, the old woman is here to warn our heroine against coming too close to the soldiers, against the unbridled eroticism that is not uncommon in such extreme circumstances. But a detail in her outfit sticks out incongruously:

> [S]he wore a black velvet toque, with an incredibly surprised-looking sea-gull camped on the very top of it. Its round eyes, fixed on me so inquiringly, were almost too much to bear. I had a dreadful impulse to shoo it away, or to lean forward and inform her of its presence . . . .
>
> 'Excusez-moi, madame, but perhaps you have not remarked there is an *espèce de* sea-gull *couché sur votre chapeau.*' (66)

What does the old woman stand for? Is she the suffering and dutiful mother, the gaze of the super-ego, an old witch threatening a young woman's identity? The story will not tell. A marvellously comic piece of dialogue then follows:

> Did I or did I not detect in her voice a strange, insulting relish? '[. . .] You know what women are like about soldiers.' She raised a final hand – 'mad, completely mad. But' – and she gave a little laugh of triumph – 'they could not get into X. Mon Dieu, no! There is no question about that'.
> 'I don't suppose they even try to,' said I.
> 'Don't you?' said the sea-gull. (67)

Who speaks here? Is it a human being, a bird or both, as is always possible in fairy tales? But of course the name of the bird brings another question: who is the gull in whose game? The story will not tell either.

Thus Mansfield takes us into her favourite grey area of indetermination: on the porous edge between dream and reality, between the trivial and the holy, between beauty and the horror where the pulsing substance of the Real oozes through. A familiar place will suddenly look uncanny in the dusk. We are made to feel the proximity of a mysterious, vaguely threatening thing, the 'it' beneath the thin layer of civilisation. An old man springs out of nowhere with a pail of 'brown speckled fish, like the fish one sees in a glass case, swimming through forests of beautiful sea-weed' (65), and then he is gone with his burden, reminiscent of the fish glimpsed from a window in 'At the Bay'.[13] Inside, the forest of trees on the wallpaper rear their swollen 'mushroom heads' to the ceiling (70), very much like the poppies in the wallpaper in the Burnell home in 'Prelude'.[14] The local Blackbeard (who is not the heroine's little corporal) plays Adam to the freshly arrived Eve and declares: 'I am sure I could eat another mushroom if Madam gave it to me out of her hand' (73). In other words, the threat of orality is never far away and, of course, the semblances of romantic love quickly decompose. Our heroine 'clop-clops' in her *sabots* through the greasy mud, up a road where she meets four big boys singing a verse from a popular song of the time, 'Idylle rouge' (69). A rather lurid picture hangs on either side of the clock in the café: 'one, a young gentleman in black tights wooing a pear-shaped lady in yellow over the back of a garden seat, *Premier Rencontre*; two, the black and yellow in amorous confusion. *Triomphe d'Amour*' (70).

But inside, the place rather smacks of the sex trade, with the Madame of the house whose plump hands are folded on a red book. As usual with Mansfield, gendered divisions are not quite clear. The young lady's lover, the little corporal with long curly lashes who cannot stand strong drinks such as whisky, does not cut a virile figure; we even wonder who is the addressee of the pretty waiting boy when he brings the couple's meal with a 'V'la monsieur!' (72). There are also eerie changes in his voice: 'Sometimes his voice boomed up from his throat, deep and harsh, and then in the middle of a sentence it broke to a funny squeaking. He seemed to enjoy it himself' (70). In short, we are in the area of ungendered enjoyment, of *jouissance* where the socially coded values of good and evil have lost relevance.[15] It may be that the underlying subject of Mansfield's irreverent story, the immemorial truth which is the mark of its contemporary quality, is the *rendez-vous* with Eros and Thanatos.

'Is there such a thing as war?'[16]

Conrad Aiken was another of Mansfield's fellow writers who praised her 'unique sensibility in the modern, not in the pre-Victorian sense'.[17] He compares her to Chekhov while regretting that she did not achieve the range of the Russian writer, as if her exquisite style were her very limitation: 'Why did Miss Mansfield's extraordinary sensibilities find, as it were, so little to feed on?'[18] V. S. Pritchett also suggests that the gaps and silences in the 'plotless' short story are 'fatally limiting, if we do not detect in those silences the murmur of a containing society of other human beings'.[19] I do not think that there is little to feed on in 'An Indiscreet Journey', whose symptomatic gaps and silences are to me the very kernel of its contemporariness. They locate a blind textual spot that marks the impossibility of narration; they concern a mass of human beings trapped on the edge of a historical catastrophe whose muffled presence can be felt everywhere. We must read them, as it were, obliquely, just like Arthur Rimbaud's poem 'Sleeper in the Valley' (1870), which is another little classic. A young man, who may be just any young man, lies in the sun in a green hollow where the water gurgles:

> Il dort dans le soleil, la main sur sa poitrine,
> Tranquille. Il a deux trous rouges au côté droit.
>
> *He sleeps in the sun, with his hand on his breast*
> *At peace. There are two red holes in his right side.*[20]

Like other modernists, Mansfield tends to think of history outside chronology and teleology. For example, the soldiers who swing off the hill to their sheds seem to have taken 'the last breath of the day with them' (69), and the text skilfully plays on narrative depth of field and interpolation of the present time, with a timeless present:

> And years passed. Perhaps the war is long since over – there is no village outside at all – the streets are quiet under the grass. I have the idea this is the sort of thing one will do on the very last day of all – sit in an empty café and listen to a clock until – (70)

Like Rimbaud's poem, the fabric of the story encloses a silence that takes the reader by surprise, suddenly revealing a void of insignificance, in the liminal zone where the beautiful and the sublime are contiguous with extreme violence: 'At all the bridges, the crossings, the stations, a *petit soldat*, all boots and bayonets. Forlorn and desolate he looked – like a little comic picture waiting for the joke to be written underneath' (64). Mansfield will use the bright, coruscating detail like a little spot from which the image looks back at us, like the soldier's tin wine cup 'stained a lovely impossible pink' (65) that seems to wink at the narrator in a friendly manner. And she is indeed clairvoyant when she has the narrative voice exclaim at the sight of the troops 'winking red and blue in the light': 'But really, *ma France adorée*, this uniform is ridiculous. Your soldiers are stamped upon your bosom like bright irreverent transfers' (64). She does no less here than anticipate the criticism made in the aftermath of action against the generals who turned these 'bright irreverent transfers' into ideal targets for the enemy.

The Great War was presented in its time as a sacrifice orchestrated by the nation's political fathers. However, it soon appeared that in many cases the sacrifice that erased a whole generation and caused the brutal disappearance of the peasant class in France amounted to pointless butchery. Mansfield hints at the cruel enjoyment beneath the war machine, represented by the grotesque generals nicknamed God I and God II (67–8), before whom her narrator is ready to kneel 'without question' (67) to achieve her own purposes. Once she is in the war zone, the actual drama of suffering manifests itself obliquely again, through a trivial incident when the waiting boy puts a bottle of orange-coloured stuff on the table:

> A shout from the card-players made him turn sharply, and crash! over went the bottle, spilling on the table, the floor – smash to tinkling atoms. An amazed silence. Through it the drip-drop of the wine from the table on to the floor. It looked very strange dropping so slowly, as though the table were crying. Then there came a roar from the card players. 'You'll catch it, my lad! Now you've done it! . . . Sept, huit, neuf.' They started playing again. (71)

This little vignette is a perfect example anticipating the 'little language' which Bernard longs for in Virginia Woolf's *The Waves*,[21] when he looks for the word that will name love or death: a language made of the words of one syllable used by children and lovers. Here the images, the rhythm, the brief shout are evocative of the explosion, the sacrifice without a cause, the liminal moment when a body is being smashed into atoms – all this for the delight of uncanny father and mother figures.

The Madame cries out with relish, patting her hair: 'You wait until he finds out,' to which the boy replies 'He can't say anything, if I pay for it' (71). Who is *he*, that threatening figure without a face, that will make you pay for the spilled wine? What is this something crying, a mere table which is the bearer of an affect without a subject? For the contemporary reader, the vivid moment in the lamplight of the café on the edge of nowhere is surely more significant than the whole epic narrative of a battle.

In March 1915, when she was living in Paris on the Quai aux Fleurs, Mansfield wrote to John Middleton Murry after a bout of writing:

> The Muses descended in a ring like the angels on the Botticelli Nativity roof [. . .] Yesterday I had a fair wallow in it and then I shut up shop and went for a long walk along the quai – very far. It was dusk when I started but dark when I got home. The lights came out as I walked – and the boats danced by. Leaning over the bridge I suddenly discovered that one of those boats was exactly what I want my novel to be. – Not big, almost 'grotesque' in shape I mean perhaps *heavy* – with people rather dark and seen strangely as they move in the sharp light and shadow and I want bright shivering lights in it and the sound of water.[22]

The 'novel' in question was to be her long short story, 'Prelude'. There is ample evidence that 'An Indiscreet Journey' also has all the qualities of this writing.

The Mystery Play

According to Giorgio Agamben, the key to our understanding of the modern is hidden in the archaic and the immemorial, in the dimension of the sacred.[23] In a famous letter Conrad refers to the earth as a temple where the same ancient mystery play goes on, 'childish and poignant, ridiculous and awful enough', to which he adds: 'I've tried to write with dignity, not out of regard for myself but for the sake of the spectacle, the play with an obscure beginning and an unfathomable *dénoûment*.'[24] A mystery play is a timeless narrative, often of religious inspiration, concerning, for example, the joy of the Nativity or the passion of Christ. Mansfield's own secular version of the mystery play will celebrate both joy and a 'cry against corruption'. She often speaks in her letters of her awareness of 'joy in the silent world', of 'this mysterious something that waits – that beckons', for which she has a special gaze and to which she means to give a special voice.[25] As to the cry against corruption, it will not be a protest, but a little voice crying in the dark.

The female heroine of 'An Indiscreet Journey' has the 'clairvoyant' and 'clairaudient' qualities (Conrad Aiken) of the poet. She catches the immemorial beneath the trivial detail in the figure of the concierge, who looks to her 'like St. Anne. Yes, [. . .] Really very beautiful' (62). As she steps out on the banks of the Seine, her attention is caught by the sound of a little steamer hooting on the swirling water of the river against the tall black trees (62), reminiscent of the vision of the Quai aux Fleurs. From the train, she glimpses the village houses sealed for the night, looking '[s]trange and mysterious [. . .] in the ragged drifting light and thin rain, like a company of beggars perched on the hillside' (69). She is amazed at the beauty of this thing of light and darkness: 'These dark woods lighted so mysteriously by the white stems of the birch and the ash – these watery fields with the big birds flying over – these rivers green and blue in the light – have battles been fought in places like these?' (64). She has an ear for the uncanny detail that makes audible the void beneath semblances, like the 'ghostly chatter of the dishes' (70) at the buffet. And her own voice is a topographical blank, a dash, a *dot dot dot* in the exchanges with the collector or with the old woman in the train.[26]

A mystery play is also a darkly illumined drama whose stage is a place of intimate exteriority. Here it will be the archetypal Mansfieldian café, so reminiscent in its details of Van Gogh's 'Café de nuit' (1888); the buffet at the station is 'a green room with a stove jutting out and a table. On the counter, beautiful with a coloured bottle, a woman leans, her breasts in her folded arms,' and the blue and red coats of the eating men hang upon the wall (65). Angela Smith has usefully compared Mansfield's art of the vivid detail to the fauvist period, of which Van Gogh was a representative[27] and we know that Mansfield was deeply impressed by his 'Sunflowers'.[28] Her stories, Smith observes, focus on 'luminous details which resonate within the story and gain significance in the reader's mind in retrospect'.[29] Thus her narrator *is* the exploring gaze glimpsing behind the scenes, but not the voyeur enjoying the horror of a scene of battle and death. And, of course, in this context, very much like the context of *Heart of Darkness*, the luminous will be ominous.

We remember that there was an old woman carrying her son's letter in the train carriage. The son, who was at the front, mysteriously asked his mother for some handkerchiefs (64), a detail which now gains full significance at the arrival of the next mystery in the café, 'a weed of a fellow':

> In his white face his eyes showed, pink as a rabbit's. They brimmed and spilled, brimmed and spilled. He dragged a white cloth out of his pocket

> and wiped them. 'It's the smoke,' said someone. [. . .] His comrades watched him a bit, watched his eyes fill again, again brim over. The water ran down his face, off his chin on to the table. He rubbed the place with his coat-sleeve, and then, as though forgetful, went on rubbing, rubbing with his hand across the table, staring in front of him. (71)

The narrative remains silent as to the reason for this spilling of tears, presented like mere organic water, but in retrospect we know that Mansfield here is among the first to describe the effects of chlorine gas, which the Germans first used in combat in April 1915. There is no human cause for the soldier's crying, and such a brimming and spilling from an anonymous human body is raised to the dignity of a pure affect against a 'big black hole'.[30]

The story ends on an epiphanic *punctum* that puts a question but provides no answer. The question concerns an impossible knowledge binding, again, sexuality with beauty and death. Dessert has been served out of plates painted with 'blue parrots and horned beetles' (73), and by the usual Mansfieldian chain of associations linking food with voracious sexuality and a vaguely deadly threat, strange things happen to the signifier *parrot*, out of which the idea of rot, decay detaches itself. Blackbeard declares, 'I love you, ma petite *pair-rot.* You are sweet, you are blonde, you are English. You do not know the difference between whiskey and *mirabelle*' (73).[31] He goes on saying that, after the war, he means to marry a little Englishwoman 'with her pair-rot' (74). The blue-eyed soldier then mimics the pleasure of tasting *mirabelle*, perhaps the orange-coloured stuff spilled on the table earlier in the story:

> *Cluck* he went with his tongue. '*E-pa-tant!*' [. . .] he felt with his hand for the word – 'finer, sweeter perhaps, not so sharp, and it leaves you feeling gay as a rabbit next morning'.
>
> [. . .] 'Mirabelle!' He rolled the word round his mouth, under his tongue. 'Ah-ha, that's the stuff'. (72)

And the little company made up of Blackbeard, the little corporal, the blue-eyed soldier and the narrator sets out in the night in order to find some of the forbidden golden liquor, at the risk of being caught by the police. As always with Mansfield, the sublime and subliminal moment takes place against the background of a moonlit garden, on the edge of a silent abyss.[32] The group reaches the *Café des Amis*, which seems to be awaiting them for some ancient pagan rite or some last supper to take place:

> We ran up the four wooden steps, and opened the ringing glass door into a low room lighted with a hanging light, where about ten people

were dining. [. . .] The faces lifted, listening. 'How beautiful they are!' I thought. They are like a family party having supper in the New Testament. (74)

The owner of the house ushers them into a 'dark smelling scullery full of pans, of greasy water, of salad leaves and meat bones', another place of orality, rottenness and death, as also suggested by the oblique reference to skulls in *scullery*. The man pours the liquor into four glasses and tells them to drink and go. And then the blue-eyed soldier's happy voice trickles through the dark: 'Isn't it just as I said? [. . .] A taste of ex-cellent whiskey?' (75).

Here, then, comes the moment of delicious rottenness, of subversive knowledge binding together Eros and Thanatos: the inactual tale beneath the war story. Through the work of poetic metamorphosis, Mansfield puts forth the immemorial beneath the historical; she transfers an individual emotion like joy or a cry into a universal affect; she makes the truth of corruption shine against the darkness. We remain with the mystery play of the word *mirabelle* revolving like a dormant seed, a star-like gaze and voice beckoning to us from the text. The contemporary poet is the one able to convey the vivid moment of encounter, of shared ecstatic knowledge of the real stuff rolled in the soldier's mouth, conjoining beauty with horror. The enigmatic *mirabelle* is certainly part of Mansfield's little language, to name both love and death.

Notes

1. Such is the question raised by Bernard, the persona of the writer, in Virginia Woolf's *The Waves*:

   > What is the phrase for the moon? And the phrase for love? By what name are we to call death? I do not know. I need a little language such as lovers use, words of one syllable such as children speak when they come into the room and find their mother sewing and pick up some scrap of bright wool, a feather, or a shred of chintz. I need a howl; a cry. [. . .] I have done with phrases. (Virginia Woolf, *The Waves* (London: Flamingo Modern Classics, 1994), p. 220)

2. Katherine Mansfield, 'An Indiscreet Journey', in Vincent O'Sullivan, ed., *Katherine Mansfield. Selected Stories* (New York: Norton Critical Edition, 2006). All subsequent references are to this edition.
3. Claire Tomalin, 'Dreams and Danger', in *Selected Stories*, p. 378.
4. Tomalin, p. 378.
5. Katherine Anne Porter, 'Life into Art', in *Selected Stories*, p. 344.
6. D. H. Lawrence, *Women in Love* (Harmondsworth: Penguin, 2004), p. 243.
7. In his famous post-war essay, 'Beyond the Pleasure Principle', Freud considers the case of patients suffering from traumatic neurosis. He observes that their dreams tend repeatedly to bring 'the patient back into the situation of his accident, a situation from which he wakes in another fright'. Considering the 'wish-fulfilling tenor

of dreams', he links such dreams to the 'compulsion to repeat' unpleasant experiences, and to a 'mechanical agitation [which] must be recognized as one of the sources of sexual excitation' (James Strachey, ed., *The Standard Edition of the Complete Psychological Works of Sigmund Freud,* Vol. XVIII (London: Hogarth Press, 1971), pp. 14 and 33.

8. The contemporary poet 'is the one who keeps his gaze fixed on his own time in order to perceive not its lights, but its darkness. All times are dark for those who feel their contemporaneity. The contemporary is the one who sees through this darkness, who is able to dip his pen in the darkness of the present time in order to write. (Giorgio Agamben, *Qu'est-ce que le contemporain?* (Paris: Rivages, 2008), p. 19; my translation)

9. Joseph Conrad, Author's Note to 'A Personal Record', in *The Mirror of the Sea and A Personal Record* (Oxford: Oxford Classics, 1995), p. vi.
10. Agamben, p. 23.
11. Mansfield, 'An Indiscreet Journey', pp. 62–75.
12. Marlow discovers the report written by Kurtz for a philanthropic society, a remarkable piece of propaganda:

> This was the unbounded power of eloquence – of words – of burning noble words. There were no practical hints to interrupt the magic current of phrases, unless a kind of note at the foot of the page, scrawled evidently much later, in an unsteady hand, may be regarded as the exposition of a method. It was very simple, and at the end of that moving appeal to every altruistic sentiment it blazed at you, luminous and terrifying, like a flash of lightning in a serene sky: 'Exterminate all the brutes!' The curious part was that he had apparently forgotten all about that valuable postscriptum. (Joseph Conrad, *Heart of Darkness and Other Tales* (Oxford: Oxford University Press, 1996), p. 208)

13. 'Perhaps if you had waked up in the middle of the night you might have seen a big fish flicking in at the window and then gone again' ('At the Bay', in *Selected Stories,* p. 250).
14. Linda Burnell is aware of the poppy in the wallpaper with its stem and leaf and 'fat bursting bud', which suddenly seems to swell out with the sap of life under her tracing finger: 'Things had a habit of coming alive like that [. . .] They listened, they seemed to swell out with some mysterious important content and when they were full she felt that they smiled [. . .] their sly secret smile' (p. 91).
15. According to Jacques Lacan, *jouissance* belongs to the realm of that which is forbidden, that which escapes the nets of the symbolic order of culture.
16. Mansfield, 'An Indiscreet Journey': 'Is there such a thing as war? Are all these laughing voices really going to the war?' (p. 64).
17. Conrad Aiken, 'The Short Story as Colour', in *Selected Stories,* pp. 339–42.
18. Aiken speaks of

> the evidence, luminous, colourful, and resonant everywhere, of a tactilism extraordinarily acute and individual. One was inclined to question, even, whether this perpetual coruscation, this amazing sensitiveness to rhythms and sounds and almost shuddering awareness of texture, was not symptomatic of a sort of febrility which would, sooner or later, impose on Miss Mansfield's work its very definite limitations [. . .] Clearly, this sort of febrility, clairvoyant and clairaudient, is enough, if one wants, in one's fiction, only and always an ecstatic awareness. (p. 339)

19. V. S. Pritchett, 'Who Are These People?', in *Selected Stories*, pp. 344–7.
20. Arthur Rimbaud, *Œuvres complètes* (Paris: Gallimard, Bibliothèque de la Pléiade, 1963), p. 66; my translation.
21. 'How tired I am of stories, how tired I am of phrases that come down beautifully with all their feet on the ground! Also, how I distrust neat designs of life that are drawn upon half-sheets of note-paper. I begin to long for some little language such as lovers use, broken words, inarticulate words, like the shuffling of feet on the pavement. I begin to seek some design more in accordance with those moments of humiliation and triumph that come now and then undeniably.' (Woolf, *The Waves*, p. 233)
22. Mansfield to Murry [25 March 1915], in Vincent O'Sullivan and Margaret Scott, eds, *The Collected Letters of Katherine Mansfield*, 5 vols (Oxford: Clarendon Press, 1984), Vol. 1, p. 168. Hereafter referred to as *Letters*, followed by volume and page number.
23. 'Historians of art and literature know that there is a secret appointment between the archaic and the modern [. . .] essentially because the key to the modern is hidden in the immemorial and the prehistorical' (Agamben, p. 34; my translation).
24. Joseph Conrad to Arthur Symons [29 August 1908], in Laurence Davies, ed., *The Collected Letters of Joseph Conrad*, Vol. 4, (Cambridge: Cambridge University Press, 1999), p. 113.
25. Mansfield to Murry [18 October 1920], *Letters* 4, p. 75.
26. Mansfield, 'An Indiscreet Journey', pp. 63 and 64:

    '[. . .] You must change at X.Y.Z.'
    'At –?'
    'X.Y.Z.'
    Again I had not heard. (63)

    '[. . .] I am taking it to my daughter-in-law.'
    '. . .?'
    'Yes, very good [. . .]' (64)

27. Angela Smith, 'Capture and Imagination', in *Selected Stories*, pp. 421–4.
28. In a letter to Dorothy Brett [5 December 1921], she recalls seeing Van Gogh's 'Sunflowers' at the Grafton Galleries in London in 1912:

    Yellow flowers – brimming with sun in a pot? [. . .] That picture seemed to reveal something that I hadn't realised before I saw it. It lived with me afterwards. It still does – that and another picture of a sea captain in a flat cap. They taught me something about writing, which was queer – a kind of freedom – or rather, a shaking free. (*Letters* 4, p. 333)

29. Angela Smith, 'The Secret Self', in *Selected Stories*, p. 418.
30. In 'At the Bay', Kezia asks her grandmother about Uncle William, who went to the mines and died of a sunstroke. As Mrs Fairfield muses over the death of her son, Kezia sees 'a little man fallen over like a tin soldier by the side of a big black hole' (*Selected Stories*, p. 219).
31. *Mirabelle* is the fruit from a type of plum tree. Interestingly, the etymology of the word is rather mysterious: it is related to feminine beauty (*belle*) and to admiration (the Latin *ad-mirare*): as it were, the reverse of the insult contained in 'ma petite pair-rot'.
32. Mansfield, 'An Indiscreet Journey', p. 73:

Outside, stars shone between wispy clouds, and the moon fluttered like a candle-flame over a pointed spire. The shadows of the dark plume-like trees waved on the white houses. Not a soul to be seen. No sound to be heard but the Hsh! Hsh! of a far away train, like a big beast shuffling on his feet.

Figure 1. Photo of Leslie Beauchamp, 1915. © Gerri Kimber.
Photo courtesy of Gerri Kimber.

Katherine Mansfield's War

J. Lawrence Mitchell

The War will leave none of us as it found us.

May Sinclair[1]

There is a case to be made that, despite the unfortunate interlude involving the death of her brother in 1915, Katherine Mansfield did her best to ignore the 1914–18 war, the 'Great War'. Jeffrey Meyers makes the case forcefully:

> she too was oblivious to the cataclysm until it affected her personal life – and even afterwards. Though the battle of Verdun was raging while Katherine and Murry lived blissfully in Bandol, they felt the War was merely a personal inconvenience and never mentioned it.[2]

At first glance, a brief summary of the facts would seem to support Meyers's contention. Not only did Mansfield have the temerity to dissemble and bluff her way into the war zone in France for a tryst with her lover-in-waiting, Francis Carco, in early February 1915, but also she returned to Paris twice within three months – in March, when she seemed entranced by the sight of a Zeppelin, and again in May.[3] Then, in mid-November and little more than a month after the death of her brother, Leslie, she hurried off to the South of France (Marseilles, Cassis, then Bandol), where she settled until the end of March 1916. Her final, and longest, visit to France during the war began on 8 January 1918 and lasted well over three months until 11 April 1918.

In his autobiography, *Between Two Worlds* (1935), John Middleton Murry seems to confirm at least their *indifference* to the war. After describing a solemn farewell visit from Elliott Crooke, an Oxford friend in the Special Reserve, who arrived with his kit and sword, he writes:

> We were neither for war, nor against it. To be for or against a thing, it must belong to one's world; and this was not in ours [. . .] We stood, clasping hands, by the railings of Green Park, late at night, while a Highland Regiment – someone said the Black Watch – marched to the station.[4]

Though Murry feels empowered to speak both for himself and for Mansfield, the evidence of her letters, notebooks and stories belies both his confident claim about their attitude to the war and the indictment by Meyers. As she once wrote to S. S. Koteliansky, 'Dont believe the conjugal "we".'[5] Anyway, Mansfield was fully aware of what was happening around her; she wrote to her father from the Villa Pauline on 6 March 1916:

> If only this war would end and make the Atlantic safer. It is a terrible, tedious calamity. [. . .] the papers are full of the news of the awful battle of Verdun and they seem to agree that the German offensive is only beginning![6]

Moreover, very few families emerged unscathed from a war that saw nearly nine million people mobilised throughout the British Empire; some thirty-six percent of these would become casualties, including more than 900,000 who were killed.[7] As Cicely Hamilton observed in *Senlis* (1917), in modern warfare 'the non-combatant ceases to exist'.[8] The morale of those on the home front thus became an important aspect of managing the war – not so easy, given the enormous number of dead and wounded being recorded daily in the newspapers.

Soon after war was declared on 4 August 1914, Murry, in an uncharacteristic burst of patriotism, enlisted in the Army – specifically the 25th (County of London) Cyclist Battalion – at the urging of his Oxford chum, Hugh Kingsmill (1889–1949). They were sent home until it was time for their medical – time enough for Murry to regret his impulse and to find a doctor willing to diagnose him with pleurisy and possibly tuberculosis. He had 'good reason to believe that that conjectural diagnosis was mistaken', as he freely admits in his autobiography, but 'simply welcomed it as a release from my overhasty enlistment'.[9] He was thus able to take his planned holiday in Cornwall with Mansfield, where 'we lived on cream, and blackberry jam and eggs'.[10] His change of heart was reinforced, if not precipitated, by reading of the defeat of the British Expeditionary Force at the Battle of Mons on 23 August 1914. How different the future might have been for the couple had Murry honoured his original commitment, as Kingsmill did – who served courageously until taken prisoner in France in 1917. Yet Murry insisted that he had no time for those who espoused war resistance or conscientious objection![11] Later, in July 1916, depressed at the possibility of conscription looming, he found a job in the War Office as a translator, a job that extended into editing the *Daily Review of the Foreign Press*; later, in a different branch of M.I.7, he became Chief Censor. His German had been good enough at the beginning of the war for him to be a regular reader of *Kölnische Zeitung* and to knock off an overnight review of the two-volume *Deutschland und der nächste Krieg* for the *Westminster Gazette*. For his 'services in connection with the War' he was awarded an O.B.E. on 1 April 1920. None the less, his own post-war comments show that he had few illusions about this 'service', though he still adopts an irritatingly passive stance:

> Why was it that the War had passed me by? In the last resort because I had, as I told Katherine in a letter, 'a very timid, girlish, love-seeking soul'. If I had had the positive will to enter it, doubtless I could have done.[12]

Quite an admission!

Mansfield reveals *her* patriotic streak in a letter of 21 September 1914 to Laura Bright, her mother's friend and later her father's second wife. Her well-honed powers of description serve her well, of course – the 'big white trains painted with the red cross'; 'the boys in khaki cheering and singing on their way to the front'; the searchlights sweeping the sky; and the Belgian refugees – but she has also internalised, and here relays, the official view that 'England is fighting for something beyond mere worldly gain and power' and that 'people are become more brave and generous than one could have believed in days of peace'.[13] Such a stirring and effective piece of propaganda could not be allowed to go to waste and it was duly published in the Wellington *Evening Post* on 6 November 1914, albeit without Mansfield's knowledge. It is intriguing to ponder even the *possibility* that this piece from the other side of the world – yet from 'Home', as loyal colonials still called it – might have been a factor in her younger brother's decision to sail for England at the end of December to join the British Army. Indeed, the date of Leslie's enthusiastic letter announcing his pending departure accords with just such a possibility: 'Off at last! Father gave in this morning,' he wrote on 6 December 1914.[14] In his *Reminiscences and Recollections* (1937), Harold Beauchamp recalls his son insisting, 'Dad, I must go to the war. All my schoolmates are volunteering,' and then making the arrangements for him to sail 'in one of the Tyser [Line] steamers' (Harold Beauchamp was on the board) – the S.S. *Indrabarah*.[15]

Leslie's youthful enthusiasm and patriotism could hardly have been more different from Murry's shameful cravenness. Little wonder that Mansfield had become increasingly disenchanted with Jack, as she called him, though it was his unremitting self-absorption that troubled her most. She had begun to correspond with Francis Carco, Murry's Paris contact, who had by then enlisted in the French Army and wooed her with Gallic fervour. She contemplated with alarm the prospect of him leaving soon for the front while savouring his every word: 'Vous êtes et vous serez toute ma vie.'[16] How open and unrestrained he must have seemed to her from across the Channel beside the diffident Jack! One cannot read her increasingly urgent notes about 'F'[rancis] without recognising that he had succeeded, had found a chink in her armour. So even as she makes love to Murry – her 'adieu submission'[17] – she feels she is betraying her true love and 'when I think of him at the front I am simply numb'.[18] Her reading and rereading of Colette's autobiographical and wildly eventful novel, *L'Entrave*, could only have encouraged her dissatisfaction with the *status quo*, though she notes 'but I'm not Colette' (18 December [1914]).[19] She is also rereading Carco's novel of the Parisian underworld, *Jésus la Caille* (1914); exchanging photographs with him; praying, 'Oh, God save me from this war and let us see each other soon' (23 January 1915);[20] and exclaiming, 'Francis Francis I cannot stand the war any longer' (2 February [1915]).[21] In short, she is behaving exactly like the quintessential soldier's sweetheart, 'the girl he left behind'. Postcard manufacturers reaped the benefit of just such circumstances throughout the war. But Mansfield did not fit the stereotype; headstrong she may have been, but she was not about to let a war get in the way of love and keep *her* home. So she made plans to visit her newfound *amour*, no matter the wartime impediments – he was, to be sure, stationed in the restricted war zone (*la zone des armées*).

According to Beatrice Campbell in *Today We Will Only Gossip* (1964), the original plan – wisely abandoned – was to pretend she was Carco's pregnant wife[22]; but her final cover story about a sick aunt, or perhaps it was her singular appeal, carried her through and she was whisked away from the train station by her 'petit soldat' with his unromantic postman's bag on his back. In the few days she was in Gray, the little town by the Saône river, she had a close-up view for the first time of what it meant to be at war – the wounded coming down the hill 'all bandaged up', including one man who 'looked as though he had 2 red carnations over his ears'; even some prisoners – 'not at all funny'; and the enigmatic 'soldier with the strange eyes'.[23] In time, her adventure was elaborated into 'An Indiscreet Journey' – a first-person story never published in her lifetime – with Carco now identified only as 'the little corporal' and the intimacies of love-making suppressed. Here, however, the 'strange eyes' are more explicitly 'pink as a rabbit's' and watering[24] – the after-effects, it would seem, of temporary blindness, caused quite possibly by tear-gas, already in use by the French in late 1914. There are other tellingly compressed details within the story – details that speak once again to the acuity of Mansfield's observation: cemeteries full of soldiers' graves; wounded men sitting in the sun outside Red Cross stations; a soldier's coat 'fastened with some rusty safety-pins'; and a woman train passenger with two prominent mourning rings, who struggles to digest the contents of a letter. Incidentally, Mansfield had caught a disquieting glimpse of what might await her brother at the front.

But why did she borrow money – ten pounds, allegedly – from Chummie, as Leslie was sometimes called in family circles? He was newly arrived in England and no doubt eager to spend time with his closest relative there – whom he liked to call 'Katie'. After all, she had a decent enough allowance from her father, and Alexander Kay, London manager at the Bank of New Zealand and an informal advisor, could be relied upon when necessary. Kay himself confirmed his role in a letter of 28 May 1927 to *T. P. and Cassells Weekly*, stating that he paid 'large sums for medical and other expenses', which later were approved by her father 'without demur or comment'.[25] We can only speculate about her motives: she may have wanted to humiliate Murry and / or to gain her brother's implicit approval by having him finance the trip. He had, not incidentally, travelled first-class on the voyage over, as she probably knew. And, on the evidence of the letter he sent home at the time, she used him to convey a reassuring message about the stability of her relationship and about her anticipated journalistic war work. If one of her motives was to annoy the complacent Murry, it worked – 'That was a bitter blow to my pride, or my vanity,' he recalled years later.[26]

Some of Mansfield's offhand comments in her letters do suggest that she had been consciously educating herself about the war and its causes – reading *and* observing – perhaps in optimistic anticipation of that elusive role as a correspondent. Was she not a published author and a contributor to the *New Age*? She mentions, for example, in her letter of 15 December 1914 to her father that she had been reading *The Times* and, it would seem, the French 'Yellow Book' – an official, albeit propaganda-driven, compilation of pre-war diplomatic letters designed to show that French efforts to avert war had been undermined by German intransigence. She also offers her father a couple of amusing anecdotes based upon a conversation with a wounded soldier 'just returned from the front' – a conversation she no doubt initiated to hone her reportorial skills.[27] The same day she wrote to her mother of the 'delicate' position of Frieda Lawrence, the daughter of a German baron, and asserted that the war was 'the fault of the Prussians and not those simple warm-hearted Bavarians'.[28] So either she had read Ford Madox Hueffer's just-published *When Blood Was Their*

Argument (1914), a volume of propaganda that makes that very distinction between Prussians and Bavarians, or she had perhaps read a review of the book. Anyway, she was already familiar with Paris, having lived there for a short time with Murry; and her friend Beatrice Hastings, by then involved with Modigliani, had been writing 'Impressions of Paris' under the name 'Alice Morning' – first from Montparnasse and then from Montmartre – for the *New Age* since August 1914.

The characterisation of Hastings's wartime articles as 'strongly pro-war in their tone' hardly seems warranted.[29] The articles were largely personal, but factual. She wrote of food shortages (*New Age*, 8 October 1914); of everyday military funerals, in which 'the bodies of English, French, and Prussians were all being buried together' (*New Age*, 15 October 1915); and of how the authorities 'make us shut up all shutters at night for fear of Zeppelins' (*New Age*, 28 January 1915). In the opinion of Stephen Gray, in *Beatrice Hastings: A Literary Life* (2004), her contributions were widely admired and 'mark her unique place in the British journalism of the Great War'.[30] So Mansfield had undoubtedly been reading – and perhaps envying – her friend's journalistic accomplishments. There was nothing at all implausible, then, about her own expressed desire to report on the war. She may have been guilty of wishful thinking, but surely not of calculated lies.

In fact, her story, 'Stay-Laces', which appeared in the *New Age* issue of 4 November 1915, may have bumped one of Hastings's pieces that week. It is in the satirical vein that Orage admired and seemed to expect of Mansfield. It pokes fun at the vacuous conversations of middle-class Englishwomen on their way to Selfridges to shop for corsets ('stays') and at their crass attitude to the war: 'I *love* the wounded, don't you? [. . .] and their sweet blue and red uniforms are so cheerful and awfully effective, aren't they?'[31] Given the date of this piece – not a month after the death of Mansfield's brother in October 1915 – Alpers's view that 'the crudity of its satire can only be explained as a savage reaction to the war's destruction of her brother' must carry some weight.[32] But it is just as likely that it was penned *before* Leslie's death. After all, Mansfield's last letter to him was written on Selfridge's stationery, almost certainly on Wednesday 22 September (the day he expected to leave for the Front) – not on 25 August – and she may well have been building on snatches of gossip overheard there.[33] Moreover, the same tone permeates the much later story, 'Two Tuppenny Ones, Please', published in the *New Age* on 3 May 1917 – by which time one might reasonably expect a more muted response. Again we have a dialogue between two self-indulgent middle-class women who see themselves as heroically self-sacrificing. One of them explains her presence on public transport by proclaiming that both her cars are 'on war work'; yet she hastens to explain that she can get a lift to the theatre from a friend who has managed to keep a car, adding nonchalantly 'her chauffeur's been called up [. . .] Killed by now, I think.'[34] They are both unconscionably, but hilariously, vague about many vital details of the wartime world – the rank (Major / Colonel / Brigadier-General?) and unit (company / battalion / regiment?) of a relative, perhaps even a husband – and both also appear to be quite confused about what 'over the top' means in the context of the war. 'I trot out the wounded every Tuesday,' the archetypal 'Lady' boasts, albeit merely by allowing the cook to 'take them to the Zoo, or some place like that'.[35] In representing so acutely and exquisitely the denizens of London 'society', Mansfield reveals her scorn for such wilful ignorance and such callous indifference to anything outside one's own circumscribed world. It is odd indeed that critics should accuse her of similar behaviour.

Less than a month after her foolhardy trip to the war zone, and ensconced in Carco's flat at 13 Quai aux Fleurs, near Notre Dame in Paris, Mansfield had her chance to do a little reporting of sorts, if only in a letter to Murry of 21 March 1915. She had already foreseen the threat of Zeppelins – a new kind of weapon that brought the war to the home front – in her letter to her father of 15 December 1914: 'I am sure the Kaiser will not be satisfied until Zeppelin has flown over London and dropped a few bombs into the palaces and baby carriages there.'[36] Here, then, she provides a vivid account of a Zeppelin raid over Paris – a first experience that, oddly enough, elicits at first an aesthetic rather than a disapproving response from her – and so implicitly condemns herself as one of those she would later satirise in stories like 'Stay-Laces'.

> The night was bright with stars . . . then there came a loud noise like doo-da-doo-da repeated hundreds of times. I never thought of Zeppelins until I saw the rush of heads & bodies turning upwards as the Ultimate Fish ... passed by, flying high with fins of silky grey. It is absurd to say that romance is dead when things like this happen.[37]

Carco got a similar description in French. But following the next night's raid (22 March), reality has sunk in: 'These raids after all are *not* funny. They are extremely terrifying and one feels such a horror of the whole idea of the thing [. . .] to glide over the sky like that and hurl a bomb.'[38] Later that year, Mansfield and Murry 'stared at the first Zeppelin sailing over London' from her attic study in 5 Acacia Road and were scolded by special constables for failing to put out the lights.[39]

From the beginning of the war, there had been a good deal of discussion about the potential threat of Zeppelin attacks in *The Times* and

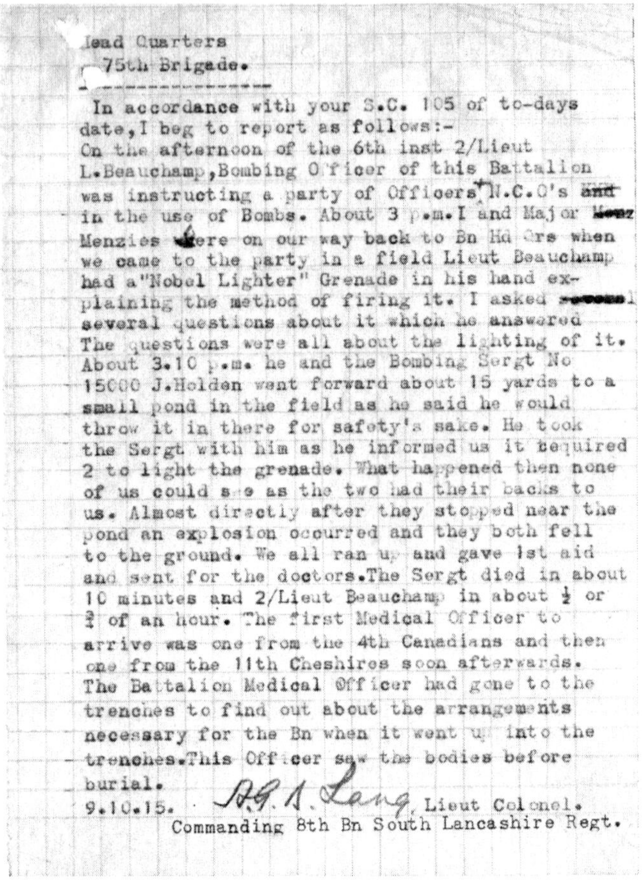

Head Quarters
75th Brigade.

In accordance with your S.C. 105 of to-days date, I beg to report as follows:-
On the afternoon of the 6th inst 2/Lieut L.Beauchamp, Bombing Officer of this Battalion was instructing a party of Officers + N.C.O's ~~and~~ in the use of Bombs. About 3 p.m. I and Major ~~Menz~~ Menzies were on our way back to Bn Hd Qrs when we came to the party in a field Lieut Beauchamp had a "Nobel Lighter" Grenade in his hand ex-
plaining the method of firing it. I asked several questions about it which he answered The questions were all about the lighting of it. About 3.10 p.m. he and the Bombing Sergt No 15000 J.Holden went forward about 15 yards to a small pond in the field as he said he would throw it in there for safety's sake. He took the Sergt with him as he informed us it required 2 to light the grenade. What happened then none of us could see as the two had their backs to us. Almost directly after they stopped near the pond an explosion occurred and they both fell to the ground. We all ran up and gave 1st aid and sent for the doctors. The Sergt died in about 10 minutes and 2/Lieut Beauchamp in about ½ or ¾ of an hour. The first Medical Officer to arrive was one from the 4th Canadians and then one from the 11th Cheshires soon afterwards. The Battalion Medical Officer had gone to the trenches to find out about the arrangements necessary for the Bn when it went up into the trenches. This Officer saw the bodies before burial.
9.10.15. Lieut Colonel.
Commanding 8th Bn South Lancashire Regt.

Figure 2. Incident report on the death of 2nd Lieut. Leslie H. Beauchamp. Courtesy of the National Archives.

elsewhere. An early article entitled 'German Airships: Raiding and Its Effects' of 6 August 1914 attempts to offer reassurance against 'airship scares' but admits that it is hard to say what a Zeppelin could do, 'if she were to come'. By the end of the month, however, the answer was delivered by a special correspondent in Antwerp; he reported five people killed, a hospital partly destroyed, and 'profound indignation among the entire population' at warfare 'directed against non-combatants'.[40] By early 1915, it was England's turn and there were raids from London to Yorkshire. Under the headline 'The Zeppelin Raids', a letter to the editor of *The Times* on 20 April 1915 protests against the tone of official comments on two recent raids, dismissed as 'fiascos' – no doubt for reasons of morale. The writer encourages 'everyone with a rifle or even a shotgun' to give the airships 'as warm a reception as possible', since 'the Zeppelins are out for murder, not warfare.' The war had come at last to the 'Home Front', but civilians were not cowed and effective counter-measures (including incendiary ammunition) were gradually developed, though Zeppelin raids continued into 1918.

Leslie Heron Beauchamp – 'Bogey' or 'Chummie' among family – arrived in England from Wellington on 5 February 1915, quickly found a regiment to join (the 8th Battalion, the South Lancashire Regiment, a unit of Kitchener's 'New Army'),[41] attended Officer's Training at Balliol College, Oxford, had further training on Salisbury Plain, and finally spent six days qualifying as a bombardier on Clapham Common. After unexpected delays, the regiment left for Flanders on 26 September 1915 just as rainy weather set in, to face 'the attendant discomforts and steady drain of casualties' characteristic of trench warfare.[42] The few days Leslie had spent at 5 Acacia Road with sister 'Katie' in August were precious to both of them, and provided sustained inspiration for her future stories – from 'Autumns II' (later reworked into 'The Wind Blows') in 1915, through to 'Prelude' in 1917 and 'The Garden Party' in 1921, to her last two stories, 'The Fly' and 'The Canary' in 1922.

Leslie's death changed everything. It occurred on 6 October 1915 – and was, in early official correspondence, mistakenly dated 7 October – but she learned about it on 11 October in a telegram from Alexander Kay, who had received the official notification the previous day. She had just bought Leslie's regimental 'Ich Dien' badge as a gesture of solidarity. There were no tears at the telegram, but she turned white and exclaimed: 'I don't believe it; he was not the kind to die,' according to John Carswell,[43] drank some wine to steady her nerves, and rushed off to learn more from Kay. There would be no more information for some time. The death was an accident and so recorded in *The Times* 'Roll of Honour' for 26 October 1915, where Leslie's death was one of 99 casualties listed that day – 32 dead, 6 missing, 61 wounded. That was also the day that Leslie's friend, Jamie Hibbert, wrote the first of two letters to Mansfield, intended to satisfy the natural hunger of the bereaved for consolation of some sort. It noted that Leslie had been buried 'in a quiet part of the wood' – something she would remember. The official account by Lieutenant-Colonel A. G. B. Lang (see above) was recorded in the obligatory incident report – a document she almost certainly never saw. But she did learn that he had died from the premature explosion of a grenade; so when Beatrice Campbell (later Beatrice Lady Glenavy) saw his photo on her desk and asked after him, Mansfield looked at her 'in a queer wild way' and said 'Blown to Bits'.[44]

There is some disagreement among biographers and critics about Mansfield's response to her brother's death at the front. In *The Brother–Sister Culture in Nineteenth-Century Literature* (2002), Valerie Sanders argues that 'in fact, the signs are that the closeness of the relationship was invoked posthumously [. . .] It was at best a patchy relationship.'[45] Cherry Hankin offers perhaps the earliest and most extended elaboration of this claim in a chapter entitled 'Death of Little Brother' in *Katherine Mansfield and Her Confessional Stories* (1983). She sees Mansfield's response to the death of her brother as 'an extreme reaction [. . .] hardly justified by the actual relationship between Katherine and her brother'.[46] Hankin adduces as evidence the six-year age gap between the siblings; an offhand remark by Margaret Woodhouse (née Wishart), her friend from Queen's College ('the little brother was too young then to interest her much except as a charming child'); and the dubious testimony of Murry, who airily opined that 'Her brother was not so supremely important to Katherine Mansfield. He was a symbol and a part of that world of innocence and Truth and Beauty which only love could comprehend.'[47] In her introduction to *The Katherine Mansfield Notebooks* (1997), Margaret Scott, by contrast, says:

> There are evidences here – unpublished until now – that Leslie was always important to Mansfield. Without these evidences one had been left with a suspicion that in Mansfield's extreme reaction to his death she may have been over-dramatising him and herself and the significance of his death for her. It can now be seen that this was not so. All the pain and grief she described were truly felt.[48]

This counter-testimony is consistent with what most of those who knew her believed. Indeed, Beatrice Campbell was amazed by Mansfield's *reticence* after she got the awful news. She had evidently asked Murry and Koteliansky not to speak of it: 'It was as if the knowledge of his death was too terrible and unbelievable a fact to share with other people until she had had time to face up to it alone and in some way accept it.'[49] Even in December 1915, when she was settled in Bandol, she had a 'vivid dream' in which she betrayed Leslie by speaking English when the two of them were together 'in Berlin without passports', and then being attacked by a German soldier.[50] This is evidence of genuine, not feigned, emotion, and is recounted in a private letter. Curiously, it was not until late December that Mansfield heard anything from D. H. Lawrence, then resident in Hampstead, in reaction to her loss. What he offered was hardly consolation; it was characteristically direct, though possibly helpful to her as an artist:

> Do not be sad. It is one life which is passing away from us, one "I" is dying; but there is another coming into being, which is the happy creative you. I knew you would have to die with your brother; you also, go down into death and be extinguished.[51]

But the key to understanding the special bond between Mansfield and her brother is surely to be found in what they alone in the family shared – an androgynous nature. Mansfield had often expressed her passion for Oscar Wilde – what he wrote and what he represented – and in a confidential letter to an unnamed friend, perhaps the faithful Ida Baker, she is more direct. Within a rudely constructed 'envelope', labelled 'Never to be read, on your honour as my friend, while I am still alive,' she has enclosed a confession of sorts, replete with such loaded terms as 'decadence' and 'degradation'. Self-dramatising the document may be, but it reflects the kind of guilt visited by society upon those who knew 'the love that dare not speak its name'. 'In New Zealand,' she testifies, 'Wilde acted so strongly and terribly upon me that I was constantly subject to exactly the same fits of madness as those which caused his ruin and his mental decay. When I am miserable now – these recur.'[52] Antony Alpers was also the first biographer to point out Leslie's 'strong resemblance' to his sister and how he was even mistaken for her at a fancy-dress ball. More daringly, and on the strength of testimony from Walter Nathan's daughter, he identifies Leslie as 'what would nowadays be called a pansy'.[53]

It may have been known within the family – by some of his sisters at least – that he was not really interested in members of the opposite sex as future life partners. But the hyper-masculine Harold Beauchamp – so well depicted as Stanley Burnell – could never have coped with the knowledge that his son, his *only* son, was homosexual or, more likely, bisexual like his sister. So 'little brother's secret' was not, in fact, as in the poem of that name, merely the surprise sugar tree he planted for his sister's birthday; rather it was something more momentous that he surely shared with 'Katie'. For this argument to hold, 'Little Brother's Secret' must have been composed *after* Leslie's death, as, in fact, Vincent O'Sullivan carefully documents. He identifies it as one of a group of nine poems 'written on identical paper and [. . .] clipped together as a group' that were written after her brother's death'.[54]

In Acacia Road – with a short period of mutual recollection intensified by Leslie's imminent deployment to the front in Flanders – the emotional stage was set for an exchange of intimacies with his sister – and not just memories of childhood. He certainly knew about some of her indiscreet and even flagrantly promiscuous behaviour by Wellington society standards and she may have admitted to earlier entanglements with Maata Mahupuku and Edie Bendall in 1907. It is not hard to imagine, then, that in the course of this family reunion, Leslie felt brave enough to bare his soul, to share with his sister his own dual nature or at least to confirm it for her. He was going to war and knew the dangers, especially – given his recent training – for soldiers who handled the notoriously unstable grenades, of which there were so many varieties. Did Katie and Chummie then realise – had they already realised – that they were far more alike than either could have had reason to suspect? That they were, in a very real sense, twins – mirror images of one another in taste, temperament and sexual inclination? Mansfield registers awareness in her semi-fictional representation of her brother and herself in 'Autumns II', where 'Bogey's Ulster is just like mine' and 'we have the same excited eyes and hot lips'.[55] By rewriting the story in the third person and presenting herself as Matilda in 'The Wind Blows', she retreats a little from any too explicit an identification. The pairing of Laurie and Laura in 'The Garden Party' is far more subtly done. Some of the memories conjured up in the back garden of 5 Acacia Road by the briefly reunited siblings are found in their rawest state in unbound notes dated simply October 1915, the very month in which Leslie died. Mansfield writes: 'We were almost like one child. I always see us walking about together, looking at things together with the same eyes.'[56] She quite explicitly claims a special relationship with her brother in a letter to her sister Vera, promising to 'tell you all I know of our dear Chummie', and adds: 'we understood each other so wonderfully – When we talked together we were like "one being".'[57] So, in losing Chummie, of course she was more upset than the 'facts' of family history might suggest; she felt as a twin might – she had lost part of herself.

But what of the young women Leslie met in England and elsewhere? We know only of 'Maureen' and 'Lydia' by name from his letters. It was not that he was insincere in his dealings with those that he met in Wellington, London and France, or that he was deliberately trying to mislead his parents. He had returned to Wellington after his last visit to England in 1911 sporting spats and a cane, a dandyism that must have worried his father. But the young women of his acquaintance would certainly have found him an attractive and engaging young man – and, understandably, quite a catch, given his father's wealth and status in New Zealand and his well-to-do circle of acquaintances in England. But in the society of which Leslie was a part and in deference to his father, he was playing a role and his sister knew it. Indeed, her need for a twin of some sort is discernible in a variety of relationships she wills into being – 'Wig' and 'Tig'; Mansfield and LM – or fantasises about, as in

'I should like to be dressed beautifully, beautifully down [to] the last fragment of my chemise, & I should like Colette Willy to be dressed just exactly like me.'[58] She knew too exactly what she was doing when she asked Ida to become 'Lesley' and had Jack become 'Bogey'.

Mansfield's war was not co-extensive with Murry's war; he certainly complained more than she did – D. H. Lawrence called it 'whining'.[59] And members of her family were directly and proudly engaged in the war as members of the Armed Forces. Lieutenant-Colonel J. C. C. Perkins, D.S.O., the husband of Mansfield's sister Charlotte ('Chaddie'), died in India in 1916 and Vera's husband, Major James Mackintosh Bell, O.B.E., served in France and Russia with the 73rd Royal Highlanders of Canada; a first cousin, Eric Waters, was a Second Lieutenant in the Signal Corps, New Zealand Expeditionary Force, in France. Harold Beauchamp featured full-page photographs of all his children and of both sons-in-law in uniform in *Reminiscences and Recollections*, but Murry is conspicuously absent. It is thus not surprising that Mansfield was defensive with the family members about *her* man not 'joining the Colours'. She insists that 'Jack was desperately upset that he could not get into anything – and I was too, for him.' In her desperation to give Murry status within the family, she suggests a degree of intimacy between Jack and her dead brother that probably appalled those who read it in 1916: 'He and Chummie were such great friends. They were great pa men together. They even had their baths together and went in for what Chummie called 'a very special kind of walrusing'.[60] It is almost as though she had borrowed a vignette out of one of D. H. Lawrence's homoerotic scenarios. Could she really have imagined this little anecdote would help her case?

The war haunted Mansfield long after it was over. She had dreamed of Rupert Brooke when he died in 1915, and of her erstwhile friend Gaudier-Brzeska, killed the same year; and she could not forget Frederick Goodyear, who loved her from afar and was killed in 1917. But always, always, she returned to Leslie, 'lying in the middle of a little wood [Ploegsteert Wood] in France'.[61] Even a performance of J. M. Barrie's play, *Mary Rose*, at the Haymarket Theatre in 1920, with its suggestion of another world where the dead still live (a preoccupation with Barrie, born of his own traumatic experience), brings her back to her brother's grave, to the pilgrimage she had never made, and she writes: 'If I could get back, the little grave should have what he wanted [. . .] But I shan't get back.' And then the poignantly cryptic final sentence: 'They suggest a slight wound – but not for me.'[62]

In *The Times* of Monday 9 October 1922, there was an 'In Memoriam' column for 1914–18. The third entry read: 'Beauchamp – In proud and loving memory of 2nd Lieut. Leslie Heron Beauchamp, 8th South / Lancs. who fell in France on the 7th Oct. 1915'. At the time, Mansfield was at the Select Hotel in Paris, where she had once stayed during the war and from where she would make her own final journey – to Fontainebleau and Gurdjieff's community. We cannot be sure that the memorial notice was published at Mansfield's behest, but it is a gesture she would certainly have approved. Her own hard-fought war with ill-health would soon be over.

Notes

1. Letter to Gilbert Murray (29 October 1914). British Library MS Gilbert Murray 25, folios 126–7.
2. Jeffrey Meyers, *Katherine Mansfield: A Biography* (New York: New Directions, 1980), p. 127.
3. 16–25 February 1915; 18–31 March 1915; and 5–19 May 1915.
4. John Middleton Murry, *Between Two Worlds: An Autobiography* (London: Jonathan Cape, 1935), p. 295.
5. 28 November 1915. Vincent O'Sullivan and Margaret Scott, eds, *The Collected Letters of Katherine Mansfield*, 5 vols (Oxford: Clarendon Press, 1984), Vol. 1, p. 201. Hereafter referred to as *Letters*, followed by volume and page number.
6. *Letters* 1, p. 251.
7. See www.pbs.org/greatwar/resources/casdeath_pop.html [accessed 9 December 2013].
8. Cited by Nicola Beauman in her preface to Cicely Hamilton, *William – An Englishman* (London: Persephone, 1999), p. x.
9. Murry, p. 297.
10. Murry, p. 299.
11. Murry, p. 299.
12. Murry, p. 493.
13. *Letters* 1, p. 140.
14. ATL-MS-Papers-2063–01.
15. Harold Beauchamp, *Reminiscences and Recollections* (New Plymouth, New Zealand: Thomas Avery, 1937), p. 93.
16. Margaret Scott, ed., *The Katherine Mansfield Notebooks*, 2 vols (Minneapolis: University of Minnesota Press, 2002), Vol. 1, p. 286. Hereafter referred to as *Notebooks*, followed by volume and page number.
17. *Notebooks* 1, p. 305.
18. *Notebooks* 2, p. 5, 16 January [1915].
19. *Notebooks* 1, p. 286.
20. *Notebooks* 2, p. 7.
21. *Notebooks* 2, p. 8.
22. Beatrice Lady Glenavy [Beatrice Campbell], *Today We Will Only Gossip* (London: Constable, 1984), p. 81.
23. *Notebooks* 2, pp. 10–11.
24. Gerri Kimber and Vincent O'Sullivan, eds, *The Collected Fiction of Katherine Mansfield*, 2 vols (Edinburgh: Edinburgh University Press, 2012), Vol. 1, p. 447. Hereafter referred to as *Fiction*, followed by volume and page number.

25. Beauchamp, p. 202.
26. Murry, p. 324.
27. *Letters* 1, pp. 141–2.
28. *Letters* 1, p. 144.
29. *Letters* 1, p. 167, n. 2.
30. Stephen Gray, *Beatrice Hastings: A Literary Life* (Johannesburg: Viking Penguin, 2004), p. 370.
31. *Fiction* 1, p. 460.
32. Antony Alpers, *The Stories of Katherine Mansfield* (Auckland: Oxford University Press, 1984), p. 555.
33. See J. Lawrence Mitchell, 'Katie and Chummie: Death in the Family', for a full discussion of the grounds for redating this letter; in Gerri Kimber and Janet Wilson, *Celebrating Katherine Mansfield: A Centenary Volume of Essays* (London: Palgrave Macmillan, 2011), pp. 32–3.
34. *Fiction* 2, p. 22.
35. *Fiction* 2, p. 24.
36. *Letters* 1, p. 142.
37. *Letters* 1, p. 159.
38. *Letters* 1, p. 164.
39. Murry, p. 350.
40. *The Times*, 26 August 1914.
41. The regiment was incorporated into the 75th Infantry Brigade of the 25th Division.
42. B. R. Mullaly, *The South Lancashire Regiment* (Bristol: White Swan, 1952), p. 201.
43. John Carswell, *Lives and Letters: A. R. Orage, Beatrice Hastings, Katherine Mansfield, John Middleton Murry, S. S. Koteliansky: 1906–1957* (London: Faber & Faber, 1978), p. 112.
44. Glenavy, p. 83.
45. Valerie Sanders, *The Brother–Sister Culture in Nineteenth-Century Literature* (Basingstoke: Palgrave Macmillan, 2002), p. 170.
46. C. A. Hankin, *Katherine Mansfield and Her Confessional Stories* (New York: St Martin's Press, 1983), p. 106.
47. Hankin, p. 106.
48. *Notebooks* 1, p. xxi.
49. Glenavy, p. 83.
50. *Letters* 1, p. 216, 18 December 1915.
51. George J. Zytaruk and James T. Boulton, eds, *The Letters of D. H. Lawrence*, Vol. 2, 1913–16 (Cambridge: Cambridge University Press), p. 481. Dated 20 December 1915.
52. Antony Alpers, *The Life of Katherine Mansfield* (London: Jonathan Cape, 1980), p. 91.
53. Alpers, *Life*, p. 182.
54. Vincent O'Sullivan, ed., *Poems of Katherine Mansfield* (Auckland: Oxford University Press, 1988), p. 90.
55. *Fiction* 1, p. 57.
56. *Notebooks* 2, p. 15.
57. *Letters* 1, p. 246.
58. *Letters* 1, pp. 212–13.
59. *Letters* 1, p. 221.
60. *Letters* 1, p. 246, 26 February 1916.
61. *Fiction* 2, p. 16.
62. *Notebooks* 2, p. 197.

Mansfield's 'Writing Game' and World War One

Isobel Maddison

In December 1915, three months after the death of her beloved younger brother, Leslie Beauchamp, as a result of the Great War,[1] Mansfield records in a letter to John Middleton Murry a 'vivid dream' she has experienced. She recounts that in this dream she and Leslie found themselves 'in Berlin without passports', 'having lunch in the waiting room of a railway station [. . .] with several german soldiers just back from the front' (216). Recalling the dream with the detailed eye of a cinematographer, Mansfield creates a poignant and dramatic scenario for the events that had surfaced in the depths of sleep. These reveal the troubled and polarised state of Anglo-German relations that one would expect at a time of war, as well as communicating the extreme anxiety experienced by so many on either side of this national divide. 'I see now', she writes, 'the proud [German] wives carrying the men's coats for them.' Then, continuing in the first person as though this is testimony to a real event, she adds, 'Suddenly in a dreadful pause I began to speak English'; 'In a flash I knew we were done for. Brother said "Make for the telephone box" but as we got in a soldier smashed his helmet through the glass door. Crash! I woke to a violent peal of thunder' (216).[2]

When Mansfield began her career as an author, publishing her 'Pension Sketches'[3] for the *New Age* four years earlier, she could not have known that these stories would become a literary preamble to her own personal loss and the terrifying realities of war communicated with such immediacy in her later dream. She may have known, however, that the grotesque caricatures of the German people she created in stories such as 'Germans at Meat',[4] 'The Sister of the Baroness'[5] and 'The Modern Soul'[6] would come to be regarded by some as British anti-invasion literature. This is particularly the case when the stories are read contextually and attention is paid to the ways in which they were shaped for publication, the subject of this paper. In fact, there has been much speculation about Mansfield's first published writings, especially because she came to regard them as 'young and bad'.[7] Furthermore, in 1914 she refused £500 to republish *In a German Pension*,[8] the collection that emerged from the sketches, because she did not wish 'to be increasing the odium against Germany'.[9]

Given this statement, it seems likely that, as anti-German sentiment proliferated with the outbreak of war and the creation by the British Government of the covert Bureau of Propaganda at Wellington House, London, Mansfield understood fully the significance of the brutish characterisations of the German people she had created.[10] Perhaps when originally conceived, these depictions seemed relatively innocuous since they appear to be written at a time when topicality overwhelmed Mansfield's fledgling aesthetic concerns. Antony Alpers, for example, argues that Mansfield used illustrations from the popular Munich-based magazine, *Jugend*, as one inspiration for her stories in the *New Age*, citing Mansfield's interest in the satirical slant of its cartoons and caricatures as an influence on her early German sketches.[11]

More recently, Jenny McDonnell suggests in *Katherine Mansfield and the Modernist Marketplace* (2010) that the satirical features of much of Mansfield's work for the *New Age* are evidence of the influence of A. R. Orage and Beatrice Hastings, the editors of the periodical throughout 1910 and 1911.[12] Certainly, editorial influences are likely to have shaped the work for marketability when British interest in Germany was rising and anti-invasion literature had reached its peak between 1906 and 1909. Elsewhere, I have demonstrated that the 'Pension Sketches' that later appeared in Mansfield's first collection of stories are indebted to the literary influence of her cousin, Elizabeth von Arnim,[13] who published several anti-invasion novels written from an English point of view prior to the outbreak of World War One.[14] Indeed, it seems probable that all these influences coalesce and find their home in Mansfield's first published work, while the 'Pension Sketches' are augmented by the wider contextual concerns about the possibility of war with Germany that were aired in the final decades of the nineteenth century and the first decade of the twentieth. Moreover, as Angela Smith points out, Mansfield's time in London (when she was working with Orage and for the *New Age*) was one where 'changes of mask are more evident' than 'at any other' stage in her life: a time when Mansfield's flair for mimicry was played out repeatedly.[15] In this context, then, it is possible to regard Mansfield's writing of the 'Pension Sketches' as another experimental and literary mask where Mansfield's original 'kick-off' in 'the writing game', as she calls it in 1918, is neither 'hate nor destruction' but 'an *extremely* deep sense of hopelessness, of everything doomed to disaster, almost wilfully, stupidly'.[16] In this sense, the 'Pension Sketches' become, in retrospect, symptomatic of Mansfield's oft-quoted '*cry against corruption*',[17] which, in 1910 and 1911, is at the root of her literary instinct. This intuition is honed by editorial forces in her first work and focused by the realities of personal experience and the rising tide of Anglo-German sentiment that reverberated in the context from which her first published writings emerged. Mansfield's literary apprenticeship in the *New Age* is, on this level, a particularly complex kind of 'writing game'.

This is not to suggest that the 'Pension Sketches' are, beneath their satirical surface, in any sense frivolous. Rather, Mansfield was trying writing styles 'on for size' (as it were) while simultaneously drawing on personal experience. We know, for instance, that the sketches are based on a particularly difficult time that Mansfield spent in the Bavarian spa town, Bad Wörishofen, where she was sent by her mother to reflect on her sexual 'transgressions'. Mansfield was pregnant with a child conceived out of wedlock, though this was 'legitimised' by a one-day marriage to George Bowden, who was not the child's father.[18] At the spa close to the *Pension Müller*, to where Mansfield had decamped in June 1909, she signed herself in as 'a writer' (*Schriftstellerin* in German) and called herself Käthe Beauchamp-Bowden, adding a German Christian name to her title and so effectively creating an Anglo-German mask.[19] At the *Pension Müller* Mansfield was subjected to the water-cure devised by Pastor Kneipp. In part, this meant being hosed down with icy water and eating a vegetarian diet, recalling the quasi-medicinal fashion for 'healthy living' that emerged in Germany before the Great War.[20] The intention was to 'cure' Mansfield of lesbianism by restoring her to psychological and physical health. It is believed she miscarried, however, if this is, as Kathleen Jones argues, the correct term for a child born at more than six months, albeit too early to be recorded in the German register of still births.[21]

It is hardly surprising that this was a miserable time for Mansfield and the situation must have been heightened by the national antagonisms that had surfaced in the first decade of the twentieth century, many of which were explored by Mansfield's contemporaries, who were writing popular anti-invasion fiction and similar forms of polemic.[22] Indeed, as Petra Rau has demonstrated, spy and anti-invasion fiction articulated and stoked anxieties about Britain's poor military preparedness for a war with Germany as its supreme continental rival.[23] In addition, anti-invasion fiction routinely offered thuggish physical models of the German people, even if these characterisations (in the works of

Saki, Elizabeth von Arnim and John Buchan, for instance) are far more complex than a cursory reading might suggest.[24] Nevertheless, when Mansfield returned to London in January 1910, with the drafts of the 'Pension Sketches' in her luggage, she did not have a publisher. It was only when her estranged husband, George Bowden, urged Mansfield to send the stories to A. R. Orage at the *New Age* that publication became a possibility.

When Mansfield met Orage he had recently reviewed her stories and recognised her evident talent.[25] At this stage, the *New Age* was certainly not a vehicle for disseminating the discourse of anti-invasion. Neither was it a jingoistic weekly preoccupied with the vilification of Germany. As Diane Milburn notes, the *New Age* was the first Socialist magazine alert to radical experiments in the arts, politics and the culture of the time.[26] Orage was interested in publishing German writers and translations, as well as publishing those English writers with experience of Germany. And though Mansfield was not, of course, English, her knowledge of Germany was fresh and probably also raw. She was no stranger to the German language either. As a pupil at Queen's College, London, between 1903 and 1906, she was taught German by Walter Rippmann.[27] She was taught history by J. A. Cramb, whose posthumously published letters, *Germany and England* (1914), would help connect General Bernhardi's name with Prussian military strategy.[28] She had read Nietzsche's *The Dawn of Day*[29] and Heine's *Ideas*,[30] so that her growing understanding of wider German thought had already been shaped by several influences.

Orage's interest in German ideas and philosophy was acute. In 1906 he had published a book, *Friedrich Nietzsche: The Dionysian Spirit of the Age*.[31] During the time Mansfield was working with him and Beatrice Hastings, he maintained a profound interest in German culture and continued to draw a distinction 'between Prussia (popularly associated with the dangers of militarism) and the rest of Germany'.[32] For Orage, as for others, Munich continued to be regarded as a centre of artistic excellence years after the unification of Germany in 1871, and the *New Age* became a vehicle for independent and competing discussions of German life, culture and politics, as well as much else, including cross-cultural articles on avant-garde art and literature.[33]

On one level, Orage exemplified the more nuanced English approach to German culture prior to the Great War that has also been traced by Peter Edgerly Firchow. He demonstrates, for instance, that though the period immediately before World War One was inevitably tense, the attitude to Germany as a whole was more complex than the limits of popular anti-invasion fiction might suggest. England, he observes, was struggling to come to terms with its changing perception of Germany. Even as some of its writers created monstrous German caricatures, there was simultaneous sadness about the slow 'death' of England's valued German 'cousin'. George Chesney, for example, claimed, in his seminal anti-invasion text, *The Battle of Dorking* (1871), 'To be at war with the countrymen of Schumann and Beethoven, of Goethe and Ranke' is 'an affliction to the very soul of England'.[34] In addition, Munich was regarded as a significant centre of culture and several English authors visited and recorded their impressions of the city and its environs, while other writers continued to include the region in their imaginative work. E. M. Forster in *Howards End* (1910),[35] for example, dispatches his character, Helen Schlegel, to Munich in 1909 to deal with personal circumstances that were similar to those experienced in reality by Mansfield in that same year.[36] As Firchow points out, D. H. Lawrence stayed in Munich in the summer of 1911 and expressed private enthusiasm for the city's culture and the beauty of the 'Bavarian Tyrol' (as Lawrence called it), while offering 'public fulminations against Germany in his essays' for the *Westminster Gazette*, two of which the paper refused to publish, even though it was hardly known for its friendly attitude to Germany.[37] Firchow also establishes connections with Munich and T. S. Eliot's 'The Love Song of J. Alfred Prufrock',[38] noting that Eliot visited Munich in the summer of 1911, and he argues for the influence of the city on Rupert Brooke, who visited in the winter of the same year.[39]

This is the context, then, in which Mansfield's 'Pension Sketches' first appeared in the *New Age*. And although it is clear that the outbreak of war had been imaginatively anticipated for some time, there is also a more complicated response at work during this period that emerges in the wider attitude to German culture, and especially Munich as its centre. This runs in parallel to the discourse of anti-invasion and is a tension borne out, in particular, in Mansfield's sketch 'Germans at Meat'. While, for instance, Herr Rat stares icily at the English narrator across the German dining table 'with an expression' that suggests 'a thousand pre-meditated invasions' (165), his equivalent passion for the unrivalled culture of Munich is largely treated as appropriate national pride:

> You have not seen Germany if you have not been to München. All the exhibitions, all the Art and Soul life of Germany are in München. There is the Wagner festival in August, and Mozart and a Japanese collection of pictures – and there is beer! (166)

In essence, Munich is presented (admittedly from a German point of view) as a centre of cosmopolitan and highbrow aesthetic production, accompanied by the everyday pleasures of consumption. And although in this story Mansfield inflates this idea of consumption beyond the production and enjoyment of German beer by enlisting the familiar trope of German greed (a staple of anti-invasion literature), she also tempers this with the inclusion of Wagner. The story is therefore briefly caught up in the contextual discussions about the international status of music at a time of approaching war whilst offering an alternative, aesthetic Germany set against the tide of incipient nationalism and the concerns of narrow propaganda.[40]

It is also important to note that the wider context of the *New Age*, in which the original version of 'Germans at Meat' appeared on 3 March 1910, avoids overt anti-German sentiment.[41] The sketch is enclosed by the broader 'political' writings typical of Orage's weekly, including Socialist commentaries on parliamentary debates and an argument about 'Feminism and the Franchise', the inclusion of the latter seeming to owe much to Beatrice Hastings.[42] It is, in fact, difficult to establish any intensifying, or cohesive, juxtapositions between Mansfield's negative conception of the German people in 'Germans at Meat' and the wider context in which the story first appeared. Furthermore, this edition includes a letter to the editor that contradicts Mansfield's earlier creation of a German household in her story 'Bavarian Babies', which appeared in the *New Age* on 24 February 1910.[43] The sole aim of this letter is to challenge Mansfield's depiction of a young girl beaten with a birch. The correspondent, signed simply as Vidi, deplores the 'wrong impression' of violence Mansfield has created in this sketch.[44]

Professing to have lived among the Bavarians 'for some years', the letter writer claims that the birch would not have been used on a girl 'in Bavaria', since a 'bundle of twigs tied with strong string' is intended, distastefully, only 'for the delectation of boys' (430) in this particular state. Drawing regional German distinctions that become increasingly familiar as the first decade of the twentieth century unfolds, this correspondent admits that while people from 'other German States' have been known to apply the birch to the bare back of a maidservant or a daughter, 'this does not apply to Bavaria' (430). And finally, enlisting familiar and entrenched oppositions, the letter ends with a rhetorical question that aims to reverse the national slight Mansfield has inflicted: 'May I ask', adds Vidi, 'in how many English homes does not the mother lay her children across her knee?' (430).

As we can see, in this particular issue of the *New Age*, 'Germans at Meat' sits rather oddly in its context because of its vigorous and satirical attack on the German people. It is not a 'misfit', however, if we consider it as anti-invasion fiction, displaying the journalistic style favoured in propaganda and commensurate with the *New Age* as a weekly.[45] The sketch nevertheless includes occasional nuance when Mansfield draws fine distinctions between the broadly drawn and caricatured German boarders staying in the pension and their appreciation of Munich and its art, of which they rightly boast. Accordingly, this is not a story where German culture is subjected to systematic ridicule, as it is in Mansfield's creation of the young Romantic 'poet from Munich' in her sketch 'The Sister of the Baroness', published in the *New Age* in August 1910. Here, a callow German youth is characterised chiefly by his 'suffering temperament' and the imagined 'Death spasms' and 'Odes to Solitude!' (191) that Mansfield attributes to him through the comic free indirect speech of her English narrator. And this is all before the young man's passionate tendencies are grossly and hilariously undercut by the 'severe nasal catarrh' (193) that threatens to accompany the clinching kiss that promises to seal the story. In 'The Modern Soul', too, the music of Wagner and Heinrich Heine's *Buch der Lieder* (1827) make brief appearances, though only because this is central to the characterisation of a young Viennese woman, Fraülein Sonia Godowska, who is depicted as a posturing, and somewhat shallow, high-art maiden. When she accuses the English of being 'Fish-blooded' (216), therefore, the comment is rather unconvincing. The Herr Professor in the sketch is also keen to establish an artistic hierarchy between German and English culture. He asserts, 'It is a great pity that the English nation is so unmusical' (217), though the fact that he plays a Bavarian dance on his trombone, while suggesting it should be regarded 'as a breathing exercise rather than an artistic achievement' (219), tends to undercut his judgment.

These shifts of attitude toward the German people in the 'Pension Sketches', as they emerge through references to music and art in 'Germans at Meat', 'The Sister of the Baroness' and 'The Modern Soul', are, I would argue, exemplars of Mansfield's fledgling 'writing game'. Augmented by humour and the creation of polarised national divisions, the predominant sense that arises from these stories is that everything is 'doomed to disaster, almost wilfully, stupidly', to recall Mansfield's letter of 1918. Furthermore, Mansfield's mimicry of the broad concerns of anti-invasion fiction is coupled with an awareness of the wider complications at work in the context, especially where these complexities focus on regional distinctions and the traditions of German culture. The work is also, of course, refined under the tutelage of professional editors and this is significant, as McDonnell argues. For instance, read in its original context, Mansfield's cruel satire in 'Germans at Meat' underscores the point that, prior to the First World War, the stance of the *New Age* in respect to Germany varied. It is also true that 'any full-blown anti-German sentiment was largely limited to J. M. Kennedy's column on 'Foreign Affairs'.[46] However, in the edition of the *New Age* published on 3 March 1910, it is Mansfield's 'Germans at Meat' that provides the topical anti-German counterpoint to its more measured pages. And certainly Mansfield's stories perform a similar function in the editions where 'Frau Fischer'[47] and 'The Modern Soul'[48] first appeared, while the issue in which 'The Sister of the Baroness' was published also includes a broad discussion of the dangers of jingoism in the weekly debate, 'Foreign Affairs'.[49] In the *New Age* of 10 March 1910, too, Mansfield's sketch, 'The Baron', is alone in its anti-German satire, where it is effectively accompanied by a vehement denunciation of the story 'Germans at Meat'. In a letter to the editor, M. Chesshyre of Dresden protests against Mansfield's 'indiscriminate generalisation' and her inconceivable portraits of the German people, so that, in essence, the *New Age* airs the discourse of invasion without endorsing it, prompting wider and independent discussions on a topical, and pressing, issue.[50]

It is nevertheless easy to see why Chesshyre levelled accusations at Mansfield about her sketch, 'Germans at Meat'. In the original version of the story, for instance, the biting critique of the German boarders is intensified by the use of the third person and this pushes the sketch into obvious anti-invasion territory. It is only when the piece appears in the 1911 collection, *In a German Pension*, that the perspective switches to the first person. And though this change was probably made to create greater coherence across those 'Pension Sketches' chosen for inclusion in the book, the alteration simultaneously dilutes (at least to a certain extent) the negative perception of the German people depicted, by narrowing it to a personal point of view. In the original 'Germans at Meat', for example, Herr Rat turns not 'to me'[51] as he brags about his ability to cook, but to 'the Englishwoman'.[52] The effect is that, from the outset in the version in the *New Age*, national considerations are highlighted before they are brought into stark collision, typified by Herr Rat's assertion: 'You have got no army at all – a few little boys with their veins full of nicotine poisoning.'[53] Because the narrator, Kathleen, is always mediated through a third-person perspective in the original ('she felt'[54] becomes 'I felt'[55] when the story is reprinted in the collection, for example), the immediacy of the first-person reactions to the dialogue are tempered, while the sense that the story could be oral history is undercut. Instead, the third-person point of view in the original universalises the experiences being communicated in 'Germans at Meat', and this sets up a more inclusive, and collusive, interpretative position for Mansfield's first readers. Moreover, the insertion in the original sketch of the line, 'Kathleen assured herself that it was the heated atmosphere which was making her flush,'[56] situates the Englishwoman in an extraordinarily sensitive context where her vulnerability to German probings is presented as almost unbearable. In the reframed version of 1911, however, this sentence is missing entirely, and the question from the German widow, 'Have you any family?', is answered simply with a trenchant 'No'.[57] The articulation of this simple negation suggests a stoical resistance on the part of the speaker that, in both versions, is confirmed by the narrator's subsequent retort, 'I assure you we are not afraid' – essentially of German invasion.[58]

While it is fair to say, therefore, that Mansfield's 'Pension Sketches' are engaged with the discourse of anti-invasion, there are also certain elements (of which 'Germans at Meat' is an exemplar) that qualify simplistic assumptions about them. These writings are not, for example, simply born of a personal dislike of the German people or from wider experience, and they do not really deserve the label 'juvenile' that Mansfield was later to attach to them, except in the sense that they were her first published writings.[59] Rather, the stories reflect a typical and complex process of distillation in which imagination, topicality, literary influence, context and editorial input combine. It would be particularly interesting to consider this idea in relation to an additional sketch, 'The Breidenbach Family in England', which appeared in the *New Age* on 17 August 1911, if we could be sure that Mansfield is its author; for now, though, it remains a doubtful attribution.[60] Nevertheless, as a sketch written at a time of burgeoning discussions of potential invasion, it challenges those who were writing one-dimensional and negative depictions of the German people from an English perspective. And if Mansfield is the author, it reverses the perceptions outlined in 'Germans at Meat', complicating her engagement with the discourse of anti-invasion further.

In this sketch, a German family is holidaying in an English village. They are also bemoaning the fact they have left Munich. Echoing Elizabeth von Arnim's novel, *The Princess Priscilla's Fortnight* (1905), in which a German Princess grows tired of her lavish life and escapes to the simplicity of an English cottage, in the story of the Breidenbach family, English custom is presented as entirely bemusing.[61] The family is, for instance, perplexed because English shops are so poorly stocked and closed for long periods over the weekend. The father, Herr Doctor, fears 'that the reputation of English judges' is 'declining' while wasps are 'too numerous in the country districts' (517). Having finished the last of the 'good Munich sausage' (516) they have brought with them, and horrified that there is not an egg to be found in the, heavily satirised, 'byootiful' English village that is 'oh, so much better than Germany!' (517), the story switches from gentle ridicule of the family along predictable lines to an acknowledgement of their fear at a time of encroaching war. Frau Breidenbach is, for instance, terrified of the English and prepared for anything to happen every time she steps 'from shelter' (517). Mindful of the potential national slight she may have inflicted on her sensitive English landlady by showing her a photograph of the 'dear Kaiserin', Frau Breidenbach suggests the family 'do not look to the right or the left' (517) in case offence is caused. And her concerns are presented as justified, since the omniscient narrator explains that, as the family walk along the road, 'rural England giggled audibly from behind its window-curtains' (517). It is no surprise, therefore, that after a farcical episode with a few wasps, a jar and a 'trap', the dialogue switches to ideas of enmity when Frau Breidenbach whispers to her family, 'Why even a child [. . .] must see' the English 'are dying for war' (519).

This story is, then, a far cry from the insistence on German barbarity, avarice and borderline insanity typical of the anti-invasion literature published in Britain prior to the Great War and during the first years of conflict. Even if Mansfield is not the author, this particular sketch provides a welcome balance to, and some relief from, the more extreme examples of this genre. It is insufficient, however, simply to acknowledge the discomfort we experience today when reading anti-invasion fiction, with its crude caricatures, polarised opinions and instrumental trajectory, and this includes those sketches written by Mansfield that were published in the *New Age*. We also need to understand the national paranoia that informed this genre, the fears that provoked its publication, the literary influences that informed the writing, the context from which these texts emerged and the ways in which these were shaped for dissemination. It is fair to say that Mansfield's first 'writing game' at the *New Age* exemplifies this complexity while reflecting a series of concerns that must surely have been increasingly difficult to ignore as the prospect of World War One came ever closer.

Notes

1. Antony Alpers, *The Life of Katherine Mansfield* (London: Jonathan Cape, 1980), p. 183. Alpers explains that Leslie joined a British regiment and left for France on 22 September 1915, having qualified as a bombing officer. On 6 October, while he was giving a demonstration of grenade-throwing at Ploegsteert Wood, a grenade exploded in his hand and he died, along with his sergeant.
2. Katherine Mansfield, 'To John Middleton Murry', 18 December 1915, in Vincent O'Sullivan and Margaret Scott, eds, *The Collected Letters of Katherine Mansfield,* 5 vols (Oxford: Clarendon Press, 1984–2008), Vol. 1, p. 216. Hereafter referred to as *Letters,* followed by volume and page number.

3. The 'Pension Sketches' were published over the course of eighteen months (beginning in February 1910 until the end of 1911). The title 'Pension Sketch' applies only to four of Mansfield's *New Age* contributions: 'The Baron', 'The Sister of the Baroness', 'Frau Fischer' and 'The Modern Soul'. Mansfield wrote in a similar vein in 'The Luft Bad', 'The Advanced Lady' and 'Germans at Meat', all of which appeared in the *New Age*.
4. Katherine Mansfield, 'Germans at Meat', in Gerri Kimber and Vincent O'Sullivan, eds, *The Edinburgh Edition of the Collected Works of Katherine Mansfield*, Vol. 1, *The Collected Fiction of Katherine Mansfield, 1898–1915* (Edinburgh: Edinburgh University Press, 2012), pp. 164–8. Hereafter referred to as *Collected Fiction* 1. All subsequent references are from this edition. 'Germans at Meat' first appeared in the *New Age*, 6:18, 3 March 1910, pp. 419–20.
5. Katherine Mansfield, 'The Sister of the Baroness', in the *Collected Fiction* 1, pp. 189–93. This story first appeared in the *New Age*, 7:14, 4 August 1910, pp. 323–4. All subsequent references are from the Edinburgh edition.
6. Katherine Mansfield, 'The Modern Soul', in *Collected Fiction* 1, pp. 214–21. This story first appeared in *New Age*, 9:8, 22 June 1911, pp. 183–6. All subsequent references are from *Collected Fiction* 1.
7. Alpers, p. 226.
8. Katherine Mansfield, *In a German Pension* (London: Stephen Swift, 1911).
9. Diane Milburn, *The Deutschlandbild of A. R. Orage and the New Age Circle* (Berlin: Peter Lang, 1996), p. 61.
10. Peter Buitenhuis, *The Great War of Words: Literature as Propaganda 1914–1918 and After* (London: Batsford, 1989). Buitenhuis records how the Government established a covert propaganda bureau in Wellington House, Buckingham Gate, London, under the direction of Charles Masterman in 1914.
11. Quoted in Angela Smith, *Katherine Mansfield: A Literary Life* (Basingstoke: Palgrave, 2000), p. 62.
12. Jenny McDonnell, *Katherine Mansfield and the Modernist Marketplace: At the Mercy of the Public* (Basingstoke: Palgrave, 2010), p. 44.
13. Katherine Mansfield was the daughter of Elizabeth von Arnim's first cousin, Harold Beauchamp.
14. See: 'The German Novels: *Elizabeth and her German Garden*, *The Solitary Summer* and *Christine*', and the chapter, 'Worms of the Same Family: Elizabeth von Arnim and Katherine Mansfield', in *Elizabeth von Arnim: Beyond the German Garden* (Farnham: Ashgate, 2013). Those novels by von Arnim that reflect the preoccupations of anti-invasion literature are, in particular, *Elizabeth and Her German Garden* (London: Macmillan, 1898), *The Solitary Summer* (London: McMillan, 1899) and *The Caravaners* (London: Smith Elder, 1909). All three novels have been reprinted by Virago.
15. Smith, p. 50.
16. Mansfield to Murry, 3 February 1918, *Letters* 2, p. 54.
17. *Letters* 2, p. 54.
18. Garnet Trowell was the father of Mansfield's child.
19. McDonnell, p. 15.
20. See: Chad Ross, *Naked Germany: Health, Race and Nation* (Oxford: Berg, 2005).
21. Kathleen Jones, *Katherine Mansfield: The Story-Teller* (Edinburgh: Edinburgh University Press, 2010), p. 113.
22. See, for example, Erskine Childers, *The Riddle of the Sands* (London: Smith, 1903), General Sir William Butler, *The Invasion of England: Told Twenty Years After. By an Old*

Soldier (London: Sampson Lows, 1882), H. G. Wells, *The War in the Air* (London: Bell, 1908) and William le Queux, 'The Invasion of 1910', *Daily Mail*, March 1906.

23. Petra Rau, *English Modernism, National Identity and the Germans, 1890–1950* (Farnham: Ashgate, 2009), p. 68.
24. For a discussion of Saki and Buchan see: 'Flirting with the Beastly Hun: Imperial Anxiety and Modern Militarism in the Popular Fiction of Buchan, Le Queux and Saki', in Petra Rau, *English Modernism, National Identity and the Germans, 1890–1950* (Farnham: Ashgate, 2009), pp. 65–87. See Saki, *When William Came: A Story of London under the Hohenzollerns* (London: John Lane, 1914) and John Buchan, *The Thirty-Nine Steps* (1915; repr. Oxford: Oxford University Press, 1993). Also see: Elizabeth von Arnim, *The Caravaners* (London: Smith Elder, 1909; repr. London: Virago, 1989).
25. It is widely known that, in her unconventional memoir, Beatrice Hastings claimed it was she who discovered Mansfield's literary talent when the first 'Pension Sketch' was submitted for consideration by the *New Age.* See: Beatrice Hastings, 'The Old "New Age", Orage – and Others', in Reginald Hastings, *Music of Those who Listen* (London: Blue Moon, 1934). Orage was a fellow guest at Gurdjieff's Institute for the Harmonious Development of Man in Fontainebleau near Paris when Mansfield died there.
26. Milburn, p. 30.
27. Milburn, p. 106.
28. Milburn, p. 106. See: J. A. Cramb, *Germany and England* (London: John Murray, 1914).
29. Friedrich Nietzsche, *The Dawn of Day* (London: Williams & Norgate, 1881).
30. Heinrich Heine, *Ideas 'Buch Le Grand' of the Reisebilder* (1826; repr. London: Macmillan, 1884).
31. Alfred Richard Orage, *Friedrich Nietzsche: The Dionysian Spirit of the Age* (London: T. N. Foulis, 1906).
32. McDonnell, p. 33.
33. For a full discussion, see: Bernard Bergonzi, 'Before 1914: Writers and the Threat of War', *Critical Quarterly*, 6 (1964), pp. 126–34.
34. Quoted in McDonnell, p. 34. See: George Chesney, 'The Battle of Dorking: Reminiscences of a Volunteer', *Blackwood's Magazine* (Edinburgh and London: Blackwood & Sons, 1871).
35. E. M. Forster, *Howards End* (London: Edward Arnold, 1910; repr. London: Penguin, 2012). E. M. Forster was a tutor to Elizabeth von Arnim's children at Nassenheide in Pomerania. He wrote *Where Angels Fear to Tread* (London: Blackwood & Sons, 1905; repr. London: Penguin, 2007) during his stay there.
36. Peter Edgerly Firchow, 'Sunlight in the Hofgarten: Eliot, Lawrence and Brook in pre-1914 Munich', in *Strange Meetings: Anglo-German Literary Encounters from 1910–1960* (Washington: Catholic Press, 2008), p. 25.
37. Firchow, p. 41. Also see: Peter Edgerly Firchow, *The Death of the German Cousin: Variations on a Literary Stereotype, 1890–1920* (Lewisburg: Bucknell, 1986). Firchow's principal aim is to demonstrate how social, political and military issues had a profound effect on how one nation viewed the other in literary and cultural terms.
38. T. S. Eliot, 'The Love Song of J. Alfred Prufrock', *Poetry: A Magazine of Verse*, June 1915, pp. 130–5.
39. Firchow, *Strange Meetings*, p. 46.
40. For a full discussion, see: Grace Brockington, *Internationalism and the Arts in Britain and Europe at the Fin de Siècle* (Bern: Peter Lang, 2009) and Glenn Watkins, *Proof*

through the Night: Music and the Great War (London: University of California Press, 2003). In essence, many believed that music was international, its influences and antecedents cross-cultural and its use as wartime propaganda entirely inappropriate. In London, others thought it unpatriotic to perform the work of German composers once war had broken out.

41. *New Age*, 6:18, 3 March 1910, pp. 419–20.
42. *New Age*, 6:18, 3 March 1910, pp. 415–16. Beatrice Hastings was well known as a radical exponent of women's rights.
43. See: Claire Tomalin, *Katherine Mansfield: A Secret Life* (London: Penguin, 1988). Tomalin gives a detailed account of the charge that Mansfield's story 'Bavarian Babies' was plagiarised from 'Sleepyhead', a Chekhov story that had been translated and published in English in 1903, pp. 261–72.
44. Vidi, 'Bavarian Babies: To the Editor of the New Age', *New Age*, 6:18, 3 March 1910, p. 430.
45. Buitenhuis argues, in his chapter 'Pamphlet War' in *The Great War of Words*, that many who wrote propaganda were skilled in bringing language to a high pitch of emotional effect. Examples are the authors Rudyard Kipling, Arthur Conan Doyle, Anthony Hope and Gilbert Parker, p. 21.
46. McDonnell, p. 33.
47. Katherine Mansfield, 'Frau Fischer', *New Age*, 7:16, 18 August 1910, pp. 366–8.
48. Katherine Mansfield, 'The Modern Soul', *New Age*, 8, 22 June 1911, pp. 183–6.
49. Katherine Mansfield, 'The Sister of the Baroness', *New Age*, 7:14, 4 August 1910, pp. 323–4.
50. Katherine Mansfield, 'The Baron', *New Age*, 6:19, 10 March 1910, p. 444. Chesshyre's letter is printed on page 454.
51. Mansfield, 'Germans' (Edinburgh University Press), p. 164.
52. Katherine Mansfield, 'Germans at Meat', *New Age*, 3 March 1910, p. 419.
53. Mansfield, 'Germans' (Edinburgh University Press), p. 167.
54. Mansfield, 'Germans', *New Age*, p. 419.
55. Mansfield, 'Germans' (Edinburgh University Press), p. 165.
56. Mansfield, 'Germans', *New Age*, p. 419.
57. Mansfield, 'Germans' (Edinburgh University Press), p. 166.
58. Mansfield, 'Germans' (Edinburgh University Press), p. 167.
59. Antony Alpers, *Katherine Mansfield* (London: Jonathan Cape, 1954), p. 288.
60. 'The Breidenbach Family in England', *Collected Fiction* 2, pp. 516–19. Alpers thought this story was a clever parody of the 'German Pension' sketches. B. J. Kirkpatrick thought it a doubtful attribution. Paraphrased from *Collected Fiction* 1, p. 516.
61. Elizabeth von Arnim, *The Princess Priscilla's Fortnight* (London: Smith & Elder, 1905). Von Arnim wrote this novel as a fairy tale for her children. The dramatic rights for the book were bought by the playwright, Herbert Trench, for a production at the Haymarket Theatre. J. M. Barrie helped von Arnim adapt the novel for the stage, and the production was a West End hit. The first night was on 29 June 1910, testament to the continuing preoccupation with Anglo-German relations during this period.

Ordinary Discordance: Katherine Mansfield and the First World War

Helen Rydstrand

After the First World War, Katherine Mansfield reacted strongly against literature that she felt had failed to respond to the war's profound implications for society and culture. A letter to her husband John Middleton Murry dated 16 November 1919 indicates the extent to which Mansfield felt that this collective trauma had changed their world. She writes:

> Speaking to *you* Id [sic] say we have died and live again. How can that be the same life? It doesn't mean that Life is the less precious [or] that the 'common things of light and day' are gone. They are not gone, they are intensified, they are illumined.[1]

This response is one that Mansfield shared with her contemporaries. Pericles Lewis identifies 'the sense of a radical discontinuity between the pre-war and the post-war worlds' as the 'greatest force contributing to the development of modernism after the war'.[2] It has often been noted that this intensification and illumination of the everyday by the cataclysm of war pervades some of Mansfield's best-known works, particularly those set in the New Zealand of her youth, such as 'Prelude'[3] or 'The Garden Party'.[4]

This essay, however, will concentrate not on how Mansfield's post-war writings integrate this profound sense of severance with the past, but on the moment of rupture itself: her immediate literary responses to the event that caused it. I am interested in the way that Mansfield explored, questioned and represented the lived experience of wartime as both a continuation of the rhythms of everyday life and a radical departure from them in two stories that deal directly with wartime experiences: 'An Indiscreet Journey',[5] written in 1915 shortly after her foray into the war zone in France to visit Francis Carco but unpublished until after her death; and 'Two Tuppenny Ones, Please', a brief, critically neglected satirical dialogue which was first published in the *New Age* in May 1917.[6] Both these stories aim for a new kind of mimesis that represents a strange tension between the ordinary and the extraordinary in wartime; 'An Indiscreet Journey' limns the intermingling of the horrific and the mundane at the front, while the blithe, detached subsumption of the tragedies of war into everyday life on the British home front in 'Two Tuppenny Ones, Please' forms the locus of the story's blunt social critique. This interest in the ordinary makes fruitful a focus on the rhythmic elements of these texts. As Henri Lefebvre writes in his late work, *Elements of Rhythmanalysis*:

> Rhythms unite with one another in the state of health, in normal (which is to say normed!) everydayness; when they are discordant, there is suffering, a pathological state (of which arrhythmia is generally, at the same time, symptom, cause and effect). The discordance of rhythms brings previously eurhythmic organisations towards fatal disorder.[7]

This passage provides a rhythmic theory of the ordinary in which harmony, or eurhythmia, functions as a measure of health and peace, in opposition to discordance, or arrhythmia. Attention to the interplay of the everyday and textual rhythms in Mansfield's texts illuminates her portrayal of the war itself and of society's response to it as arrhythmic. Furthermore, Lefebvre suggests that:

> Musical rhythm does not only sublimate the aesthetic and a rule of art: it has an **ethical** function. In its relation to the body, to time, to the work, it illustrates *real* (everyday) life. It *purifies* it in the acceptance of **catharsis**. Finally, and above all, it brings compensation for the miseries of everydayness, for its deficiencies and failures. Music integrates the functions, the **values** of Rhythm . . . .[8]

Lefebvre's alignment of musical, or artistic, rhythm with the real, with ordinary, embodied experience and with the classical, ethical function of art is reminiscent of modernist ideas about the function and central importance of rhythm as a philosophical concern as well as a formal one. This intellectual affinity makes Lefebvre's terminology invaluable for attempts to unravel and describe Mansfield's textual rhythms.

Rhythm and the ordinary emerge as key coordinates in the modernist renovation of the scope of mimesis, and in Mansfield's work in particular. Analysis of the rhythms in 'An Indiscreet Journey' and 'Two Tuppenny Ones, Please' illuminates Mansfield's immediate literary engagement with the war through its vexed relation to the ordinary. Mansfield's interest in this relation is not unusual; Liesl Olson observes that many 'modernists fixate on this tension between the war and everyday life; the "before and after" of the war emerges as a major modernist subject'.[9] Olson is interested in the questions raised about the ordinary by war: 'How, these modernists ask, does ordinary experience continue? What happens to routine and habit when a violent disruption like world war intrudes?'[10] In this essay, however, I will investigate the way that the ordinary, figured through rhythm, functions as a rhetorical strategy that supports Mansfield's ethical interrogation of the war. Olson argues that 'Woolf depicts the war by depicting the everyday [. . .] *in spite of* the war, so that the war's devastations are pervasively felt,' a strategy with which this pair of Mansfield's stories has much in common.[11] The two stories considered in this essay both disrupt the classically masculine tradition of war literature, first and foremost by eliding the scene of battle. Although the First World War features prominently in each story, and in the case of 'An Indiscreet Journey' the proximity of the battlefield is palpable, the violence itself is not described.

This essay works from the premise that not only is it productive to look for rhythm in Mansfield's wartime stories, but that it is also felicitous, given the broader conversation concerning this amorphous term in the intellectual context of her day. Michael Golston's book, *Rhythm and Race in Modernist Poetry and Science* (2007), has drawn compelling links between the centrality of rhythm as an object of study in an astonishing range of disciplines between 1890 and 1940 (including psychology, biology, pedagogy, gymnastics and politics) and the modernist debate about poetic rhythm of the same period – initiated, Golston says, by Ezra Pound's idea of 'absolute rhythm' in 'A Few Don'ts', his Imagist manifesto of 1913.[12] The influence of this intellectual context on modernist prose is yet to be comprehensively explored, although here, too, there are compelling links. For example, echoes of the period's scientific interest in rhythms can also be found in the contribution of the Australian novelist and poet, Frederic Manning, to the 1921 debate on prose poetry in *The Chapbook*. Manning asserts that 'the rhythm of prose depends entirely upon breathing, [so] it reflects perfectly the physical distress of one labouring under any passion, or touched either by sorrow or joy. It may be completely mimetic.'[13] This linkage of rhythm, prose and mimesis is an important one, especially in light of the problem that plagued artists of this generation: the question of how to understand and represent a 'new reality' caused by the Great War.[14]

This assertion of prose's mimetic capacity should be considered contiguous with the pervasive contemporary idea that all of human experience is underpinned by one universal rhythm, of which the many kinds of rhythm being studied and employed in literature are simply echoes. Thus, connections may be drawn between the period's academic and artistic interests in rhythms and the vitalist thinking made popular by the philosophy of Henri Bergson: in particular, his notion of *élan vital.* This connection may be observed in Virginia Woolf's early essay, 'Street Music' (1905), in which she speaks of a 'vast pulsation' with which music (and, she says, literature, both poetry *and* prose) allows us to connect. This suggestion surely anticipates the expression, in her 1939–40 memoir, 'A Sketch of the Past', of her conception of the unity underlying human existence: 'that behind the cotton wool [of daily life] is hidden a pattern'.[15] Similarly, in 'Aims and Ideals', the 1911 manifesto of his Bergsonian little magazine *Rhythm*, John Middleton Murry declares that the journal will 'provide art [. . .] which shall be vigorous, determined, which shall have its roots below the surface, and be the rhythmical echo of the life with which it is in touch'. In this piece, Murry also emphasises the necessity of 'art that strikes deeper, that touches a profounder reality'.[16] Rhythm is therefore a pivotal source of the 'real' for modernist writers, and its role in prose, as in poetry, is one of both technical and thematic centrality because of its mimetic possibilities.

Meanwhile, many contemporary writers, including Woolf and Eliot, were noting the absorption of what were traditionally considered prose techniques into modern poetry.[17] In a 1917 review of Siegfried Sassoon's war poems, Woolf praises Sassoon's 'power as a realist', specifying that it is 'realism of the right, of the poetic kind'.[18] Integral to Woolf's sense of the realism of Sassoon's poetic evocation of the war is his inclusion of ordinary and familiar details, which allow for the expression of the moment as a whole. Nevertheless, for Woolf, prose is the mode most suited to mimesis; she writes in another review, published in 1918, that 'reality is best conveyed by prose'.[19] This sentiment seems to be behind Mansfield's continued commitment to prose, too, even though, as she writes in her journal after the wartime death of her younger brother, Leslie Beauchamp, at moments of intense emotion she feels 'always trembling on the brink of poetry'. Nevertheless, she inclines towards writing her 'long elegy' to him 'in a kind of special prose'.[20] Mansfield also expressed her conviction of the significance of the ordinary earlier in her career, seen in this passage from a letter to her friend S. S. Koteliansky dated 17 May 1915:

> Do you, too feel an infinite delight and value in *detail* – not for the sake of detail but for the life *in* the life of it. I can never express myself [. . .] But do you ever feel as though the Lord threw you into eternity – into the very exact centre of eternity, and even as you plunged you felt every ripple that flowed out from your plunging – every single ripple floating away and touching and drawing into its circle every slightest thing it touched.[21]

In spite of her frustration at the difficulty of expressing her ideas, Mansfield's language here makes clear her philosophical affinities with Woolf's 'vast pulsation' and 'hidden [. . .] pattern', as well as with Murry's Bergsonian 'profounder reality'. Moreover, this passage demonstrates a link in Mansfield's thinking between this rhythmic, vitalist conception of existence and the prosaic minutiae of ordinary experience, and thus the importance of the ordinary in her writing.

Like Woolf, Mansfield emphasises the pervasive effect of the war on all aspects of life. Unlike Woolf, Mansfield's primary literary response to the war takes the form of short fiction, which a number of critics have noted for the immediacy of its response to the war:

> The short story's strength is its affinity to the experience of the mere moment, which goes hand in hand with a special closeness to its moment of publication and reception. Written and published much faster than novels or memoirs, short stories are close to the pulse of their audience and can provide insight into *current* attempts at making sense of the war and coping with its consequences.[22]

Mansfield's modernist short stories stand out from the vast majority of war stories being published in the popular presses, which, according to Emma Liggins, Andrew Maunder and Ruth Robbins, were generally traditional in form and often propagandist in content, upholding notions of masculine British heroism, German barbarism and even divine favour.[23] An example is 'The Bowmen' by Arthur Machen, published in September 1914, which portrayed British soldiers being rescued by the ghosts of mediaeval warriors and was believed by many readers to be a true story.[24] By contrast, 'Sapper' (the pen-name of H. C. McNeile, so named because of his affiliation with the Royal Engineers[25]) was a prolific and abidingly popular writer of gritty tales of heroism and adventure in combat, who 'viewed army training as a useful way of educating men to be men'.[26] Mansfield's formally and thematically experimental wartime stories undermine these more sympathetic perspectives on the war.

Many alternate and dissenting treatments of the war in short-story form, such as the collection by Richard Aldington, *Roads to Glory* (1930), or Radclyffe Hall's *Miss Ogilvy Finds Herself* (1934), were not published until many years after the war.[27] 'An Indiscreet Journey' is, then, as Gerri Kimber has noted, a particularly early example of modernist literature that questions the mainstream principles on which the war was fought.[28] It was written at a time when Rupert Brooke's romantic war poems were still central to the public's military imagination, and before the trench poems of Siegfried Sassoon, Wilfred Owen and others had made their more enduring marks.[29] Lewis argues that 'English modernism was invented during the First World War (not, I believe, after it) by writers who had little direct involvement in the war.'[30] Women writers such as Mansfield are curiously absent from his account of that invention. Yet it is Mansfield's modernist technique, in particular her rhythmic employment of various types of repetition, that helps to develop a tension between routines of ordinary experience and the extraordinary event of war. To illustrate this, I focus first on Mansfield's structural rhythms and second on the proliferation of rhythmic devices in each story.

Mansfield's representation of the collision of the ordinary and the extraordinary during wartime is enabled by her employment of the short-story genre itself, in particular the 'plotless' form that Sydney Janet Kaplan, among others, identifies as one of her principal contributions to the genre.[31] Barbara Korte and Ann-Marie Einhaus have suggested that Mansfield's generation of writers

> were apparently aware of a particular potential of the short story for the representation of the war. Its emphasis on moments and fragments of experience, and its art of ambiguous expression seemed ideal not only for capturing modern life in general, but also the first fully industrialised war that exploded extant norms of perception, interpretation and representation.[32]

Christine Reynier has compellingly described Woolf's short fiction as 'literary fragments', following Jean-Luc Nancy and Philippe Lacoue-Labarthe's idea of the fragment as both 'an autonomous form and part of a whole', a formulation which helps to describe the operation of the fragmentary qualities of the two stories under study here.[33] It is in part through her use of these fragmentary, or plotless, forms that Mansfield manages to create a sense of both continuity and radical rupture with the past.

'An Indiscreet Journey' is based on a trip that Mansfield took only seven months into the four-year war, and was written at a time when most writing about the war was inspired by patriotic feeling, and idealistic notions of duty and heroism. According to Samuel Hynes, this positive early attitude to the war even extended to the idea that 'war would purify and cleanse' England of an excessive Edwardian hedonism that had consumed its simpler rural past.[34] These attitudes are challenged by Mansfield's eyewitness account of the atmosphere in the war zone. 'An Indiscreet Journey' approaches the problem of representing this unprecedented reality through the ordinary and its disruption, thus presenting a vision of a reality at once continuous with, and radically different to, the world that had been. This is another iteration of the 'curious disjunction' that Angela Smith identifies in the story's imagery and narrative voice.[35] 'An Indiscreet Journey' describes a short span of time and an incomplete journey, and is divided into three episodic sections, which have in common the shape of their narrative arc. In each section, the expectation of a particular event is established (being reunited with the little corporal in the first and second sections, and trying a plum-based liqueur called *mirabelle* in the last) before the narration is truncated abruptly when the event arrives, ending without resolution. The repetition of this underlying narrative structure, in which the final consequences of the event remain unknown, enacts the combination of monotony and anxious anticipation that characterises war itself.

By the time Mansfield published 'Two Tuppenny Ones, Please' in May 1917, the public and artistic perception of the war had shifted. Mansfield was part of an increasingly vocal anti-war milieu, and this story belongs to the same moment as *The Old Huntsman*, Sassoon's collection of visceral anti-war poems, which was published the same month.[36] By the end of July 1917, his famous public statement of protest (on which he collaborated with Mansfield's husband, John Middleton Murry, and her friend, Bertrand Russell, following consultation with their friends Ottoline and Philip Morrell; Russell and the Morrells were noted pacifists) had been published in major newspapers and read in the House of Commons. As well as registering his objection to what he saw as a deception being practised against the men fighting the war, Sassoon hoped 'that it may help to destroy the callous complacence with which the majority of those at home regard the continuance of agonies which they do not share, and which they have not sufficient imagination to realise'.[37]

'Two Tuppenny Ones, Please' shares this aim, using a satirical dialogue of Juvenalian ferocity to castigate those in Mansfield's society, in particular the upper classes, who failed to respond with adequate seriousness to the tragedy of the war. In this story, an even briefer slice of time is presented, in which the rhythm is one that alternates between clear and muffled speech. The piece consists of just over three pages of dialogue between a 'lady' and her 'friend', with occasional interjections from the 'conductor' of the bus that the two women are taking home to an exclusive part of London. It is presented in dramatic form, without narration, and as though overheard by another passenger; the lady speaks at length, while her friend's responses are indistinct, and represented only by ellipses. By mimicking the eavesdropper's experience of the conversation, the ellipses enforce a pause that enhances the satirical force of the story by positioning it as a real conversation. W. H. New has observed that Mansfield 'used space to affect rhythm' within her stories, and this is an important function of the ellipses in 'Two Tuppenny Ones, Please'.[38] The lady's speech visually overwhelms in quantity the ellipses of her friend's replies, such that the rhythm created by this dialogue may be seen as unbalanced, thus establishing an arrhythmic sense which evinces the discordance between the lady's reaction to the war, and the response demanded by its realities.

Repetition is the fundamental prerequisite of rhythm: as Lefebvre writes, 'No rhythm without repetition in time and space, without *reprises*, without returns, in short without **measure**.' Repetition is also the central feature of the ordinary; the 'everyday establishes itself' through 'its repetitive organisation'.[39] Olson argues that the ordinary is the central focus of modernism, and highlights its presence in modernist literature in the patterns of language: 'the ordinary can be a mode of organizing life and representing it; it is a *style*, best represented by the routine, and aesthetic forms such as the list, or linguistic repetition, both of which attempt to embody the ordinary, to perform it'.[40] Thus, Mansfield's use of rhythmic linguistic technique to explore and represent the ordinary may be considered one of her fundamental affinities with the modernist movement. In both 'An Indiscreet Journey' and 'Two Tuppenny Ones, Please', Mansfield uses the rhythms created by the repetition of linguistic, structural and tropological features both to establish and to disrupt the everyday, and thus to depict what she saw as the truth about the war.

In 'An Indiscreet Journey', the repeated return to the familiar scene of the café establishes what Lefebvre would call a eurhythmic normality, into which the war intrudes and disrupts. The narrator visits three cafés, one in each section of the story. The descriptions of the first two bear striking similarities. The 'buffet' in 'X.Y.Z.' that the narrator stops in for lunch on her journey is described as:

> A green room with a stove jutting out and tables on each side. On the counter, beautiful with coloured bottles, a woman leans, her breasts in her folded arms. Through an open door I can see a kitchen, and the cook in a white coat breaking eggs into a bowl and tossing the shells into a corner.[41]

This configuration of details is reprised in the café of the second section in which the narrator waits to dine with her lover, referred to only as 'the little corporal':

> Into the middle of the room a black stove jutted. At one side of it there was a table with a row of bottles on it, behind which Madame sat and took the money and made entries in a red book. Opposite her desk a door led into the kitchen. The walls were covered with a creamy paper patterned all over with green and swollen trees – hundreds and hundreds of trees reared their mushroom heads to the ceiling.[42]

In both cases, Mansfield highlights the jutting stove, the green on the walls, the door leading to the kitchen, Madame behind a row of bottles, a waiting-boy (too young for military service) and, finally, the ubiquitous and disruptive presence of soldiers. Rhythm is a consideration at multiple levels of the text; as well as the reappearance of the everyday social space of the café itself and the reproduction of its internal features, in the first café war is analogised as a disruptive vibration of the air itself. 'War and noise' are placed in dialectical opposition to the commonplace phrase 'peace and quiet', and the violent, disturbing quality of war is represented by a group of soldiers so large and loud that the narrator exclaims 'Heavens! what a noise. The sunny air seemed all broken up and trembling with it.'[43]

In the second section, the narrator sits alone in the café while she waits for the little corporal:

> The clock ticked to a soothing lilt, *C'est ça, C'est ça.* In the kitchen the waiting-boy was washing up. I heard the ghostly chatter of the dishes. And years passed. Perhaps the war is long since over – there is no village outside at all – the streets are quiet under the grass. I have an idea this is the sort of thing one will do on the very last day of all – sit in an empty café and listen to a clock until – .[44]

This passage dramatises Henri Bergson's notion of pure duration through a rhythmic representation of the affective experience of the ordinary. Though the time that the narrator spends waiting in the café is measured by the regular ticking of the clock, the time seems to drag out in a way that is universally familiar. This scene therefore configures the experience of ordinariness rhythmically, through the sound of the ticking clock (and by reference to the routine chore of dish-washing), yet is imbued simultaneously with a sense of looming apocalypse; the dishes make a 'ghostly chatter', and the narrator imagines a future in which the everyday life of the village has been erased, and the end of the world has come.

This otherwise ordinary scene is disrupted most overtly not by the mere presence of soldiers, as the first few who enter fit seamlessly into the rhythm of the café (they know Madame and pass the time playing cards and teasing the waiting-boy), but by an injured, shell-shocked soldier, a victim of mustard gas, who has just had bandages removed from his eyes. This soldier stands as an embodiment of the destructive, disturbing and pervasive presence of the war, his mental and physical pathology manifested through linguistic repetition:

> In his white face his eyes showed, pink as a rabbit's. They brimmed and spilled, brimmed and spilled. [. . .] His comrades watched him a bit,

> watched his eyes fill again, again brim over. The water ran down his face, off his chin on to the table. He rubbed the place with his coat-sleeve, and then, as though forgetful, went on rubbing, rubbing with his hand across the table, staring in front of him. And then he started shaking his head to the movement of his hand. He gave a loud strange groan and dragged out the cloth again. '*Huit, neuf, dix,*' said the card-players.[45]

The wounded soldier's weeping, suggestive of both physical and emotional trauma, is portrayed as a repetitive action, and through repetition; the reiteration of the words 'brimmed' and 'spilled', combined with the anadiplosis centred around 'fill again, again brim', establishes a ongoing rhythmic pattern. This sense of the permanent disturbance of this soldier's rhythm (his everyday life) is supported by Mansfield's multiplication of synonymous descriptors of his repetitive neurotic movements: rubbing and mopping and shaking and rocking. As the human manifestation of the damage caused by war – in this case the after-effects of gas poisoning – this wounded soldier, both disturbed and disturbing, functions arrhythmically in the scene, interrupting the ordinary activities of eating, drinking, flirting, working and talking in which the café's other occupants are engaged. Yet the other soldiers in the café soon return to their prior occupations, signalling that the ordinary, the surface of that 'vast pulsation' of life, ultimately prevails. The third section differs from the preceding pair in that the café itself is sketched with less detail, though a Madame is again present and, crucially, the female, civilian narrator has become implicated in the disturbance created by the war, when the group of soldiers that she is with is berated by Madame for coming to her café after their curfew, risking serious punishment for everyone. This final, inconclusive scene gestures, perhaps, to society's shared responsibility for this destruction, which is also the theme of 'Two Tuppenny Ones, Please'.

The satirical effect of 'Two Tuppenny Ones, Please' is also achieved in part through linguistic repetition, both as an efficient method of sketching a stereotypical character, and as a portrayal of the particular banality of this failure. The lady's class is recognisable by her diction as much as by the content of her speech; words and phrases like 'dear' and 'you know' are used repeatedly, as are colloquial words that punningly refer to the actualities of war, such as 'extraordinary', 'frightfully', 'dreadful' and 'afraid'.[46] The discordance created by this juxtaposition of the comfortable lady's lifestyle with the horrific reality of the war pervades the text, demonstrated at the level of diction and connotation: 'I 'phone Cynthia,' she says, if she wants to borrow a car to go to the theatre, while in the line below she mentions the chauffeur being 'called up'.[47] The title of the story is taken from the lady's first interaction with the conductor:

> CONDUCTOR: Fares, please. Pass your fares along.
> LADY: How much is it? Tuppence, isn't it? Two tuppenny ones, please. Don't bother – I've got some coppers, somewhere or other.
> FRIEND: ... !
> LADY: No, it's all right. I've got some – if only I can find them.
> CONDUCTOR: *Parse* your fares, please.[48]

The lady goes on to dispute the fare. As well as imitating the accent of the working-class man and thereby signalling attendant class divisions, Mansfield's antanaclasis on pass/parse explicitly demands analysis, hinting that the fare may represent more than the cost of the journey. Rather, the lady's reluctance to pay the fare that is due may be an analogy for her resistance, and that of the class for whom she stands, to paying the respect and compassion that are due to those who are suffering on the field of battle. This quibble is part of a pattern of double meaning that echoes throughout the text. The lady also repeatedly admits to ignorance about the details of the war, particularly as they are affecting those around her. She mentions that the chauffeur of her friend, Cynthia, has been conscripted, and is probably 'Killed by now, I think. I can't quite remember.'[49] Neither can she quite recall what military rank her friend, Teddie, now holds. She eventually guesses it may be Chief of Staff, yet suggests that he goes '"over the top" every day' regardless of his senior position, although it is surely she who is going 'over the top' either in her estimation of his rank or in her claim that 'everybody goes over the top nowadays.' Nor does she remember the role that his wife holds at the War Office: 'She's something to do with notifying the deaths, or finding the missing.' Whatever it is, 'it is too depressing for words,' so she changes the topic to gossip and fashion.[50]

The lady refers to the real tragedies of life during wartime as though to incidents of personal inconvenience. Cynthia's dead chauffeur has been replaced by a crippled man whose driving she does not like, one of her maids has quit her job to work in a munitions factory (she tells her 'not to come back and disturb the other servants'), and she is unable to play bridge on Tuesday because 'I trot out the wounded every Tuesday you know. I let cook take them to the Zoo, or some place like that – don't you know.'[51] These repetitions of comments revealing the lady's 'callous complacence' and lack of 'sufficient imagination' regarding the suffering occurring in Europe downgrade war to the level of the ordinary, where its details are not quite memorable, and its tragedies merely inconvenient and annoying.[52] Olson observes that

> the 'shock' of modern wartime is sometimes represented as strangely repetitious, even boring, both for those far removed from the fighting and for soldiers at the front. [. . .] In some instances, the ordinary consumes and absorbs a wartime fear of what will happen next.[53]

'Two Tuppenny Ones, Please' both engages with, and critiques, this response to the war, and Mansfield's satire leaves no doubt as to how despicable she finds this trivialising discourse.

In her essay, 'Women in the Forbidden Zone: War, Women, and Death', Margaret Higonnet wonders 'What can a woman writer have to say about war?'[54] Mansfield trespassed in the forbidden, masculine zone of war both geographically and in her writing, and her responses to it and the social issues that surround it are characteristically both nuanced and unsparing. While Mansfield expressed her profound sense that this event had created an irrevocable rupture with the past, she nevertheless retained a belief in the persistence of the ordinary. This persistence of the ordinary appears, in Mansfield's wartime stories, as appalling and yet expressive of the natural rhythm of life. In 'An Indiscreet Journey' and 'Two Tuppenny Ones, Please', Mansfield uses structural, tropological and linguistic rhythms to enact the simultaneous continuance of the ordinary and its violent disruption during the war. In so doing, she employs a novel method of mimesis that is able to respond to the representational challenges generated by the First World War, as well as to contemporary notions of the rhythmic nature of life itself. Analysis of these formal rhythms helps to evince Mansfield's progressive ethical engagement with the First World War, and her literary investigation of the relationship between the 'common things of light and day' and a 'vast pulsation' that underpins the universe.

Notes

1. Vincent O'Sullivan and Margaret Scott, eds, *The Collected Letters of Katherine Mansfield*, 5 vols (Oxford: Clarendon Press, 1984–2008), Vol. 3, p. 97. Hereafter referred to as *Letters*, followed by volume and page number.
2. Pericles Lewis, 'Inventing Literary Modernism at the Outbreak of the Great War', in Michael J. K. Walsh, ed., *London, Modernism, and 1914* (Cambridge: Cambridge University Press, 2010), p. 150.
3. 'Prelude', in Gerri Kimber and Vincent O'Sullivan, eds, *The Collected Works of Katherine Mansfield*, 4 vols (Edinburgh: Edinburgh University Press, 2012–15), Vol. 2, pp. 56–93. Hereafter referred to as *Collected*, followed by volume and page number.
4. 'The Garden Party', in *Collected* 2, pp. 401–14. For examples, see Christine Darrohn, '"Blown to Bits!": Katherine Mansfield's "The Garden-Party" and the Great War', *Modern Fiction Studies*, 44 (1998), pp. 513–39; and Gerri Kimber, *A Literary Modernist: Katherine Mansfield and the Art of the Short Story* (London: Kakapo, 2008), p. 66.
5. 'An Indiscreet Journey', in *Collected* 1, pp. 439–51.

6. 'Two Tuppenny Ones, Please', in *Collected* 2, pp. 22–4.
7. Henri Lefebvre, *Rhythmanalysis: Space, Time and Everyday Life* (New York: Continuum, 2004), p. 16.
8. Lefebvre, p. 66. Emphasis, bold and ellipsis original.
9. Liesl Olson, *Modernism and the Ordinary* (New York: Oxford University Press, 2009), p. 28.
10. Olson, p. 28.
11. Olson, p. 28.
12. Michael Golston, *Rhythm and Race in Modernist Poetry and Science* (New York: Columbia University Press, 2007), p. 3.
13. Frederic Manning, 'Poetry in Prose', *The Chapbook*, 22 (1921), p. 15. This special issue also contains two now famous essays on prose poetry by Richard Aldington and T. S. Eliot.
14. Samuel Hynes, *A War Imagined: The First World War and English Culture* (London: Pimlico, 1992), p. 11.
15. Virginia Woolf, 'Street Music', in Andrew McNeillie, ed., *The Essays of Virginia Woolf*, 6 vols (London: Hogarth Press, 1986–2011), Vol. 1, p. 31. Hereafter referred to as *Essays of Virginia Woolf*, followed by the volume and page number. Virginia Woolf, 'A Sketch of the Past', in Jeanne Schulkind, ed., *Moments of Being* (San Diego: Harcourt, 1985), p. 72.
16. John Middleton Murry, 'Aims and Ideals', *Rhythm*, 1 (1911), p. 36.
17. T. S. Eliot, 'Prose and Verse', *The Chapbook*, 22 (1921), p. 9; Virginia Woolf, 'Mr Symons's Essays', in *The Essays of Virginia Woolf* 2, p. 70.
18. *Essays of Virginia Woolf* 2, p. 120.
19. *Essays of Virginia Woolf* 2, p. 218.
20. Margaret Scott, ed., *The Katherine Mansfield Notebooks: Complete Edition*, 2 vols (Minneapolis: University of Minnesota Press, 2002), Vol. 2, pp. 32–3. Underscore original.
21. *Letters* 1, p. 192.
22. Barbara Korte and Ann-Marie Einhaus, 'Short-Term Memories: The First World War in British Short Stories, 1914–39', *Literature & History*, 18 (2009), p. 55. See also Emma Liggins *et al.*, *The British Short Story* (Basingstoke: Palgrave Macmillan, 2010), p. 134.
23. Korte and Einhaus, p. 55.
24. Liggins *et al.*, pp. 134–5.
25. Liggins *et al.*, p. 136.
26. Liggins *et al.*, p. 140.
27. For a fuller account of these collections, see Liggins *et al.*, pp. 141, 51.
28. Kimber, *A Literary Modernist*, p. 65.
29. Hynes, pp. 11–13.
30. Lewis, p. 148.
31. Sydney Janet Kaplan, *Katherine Mansfield and the Origins of Modernist Fiction* (Ithaca, NY, and London: Cornell University Press, 1991), p. 3.
32. Korte and Einhaus, p. 55.
33. Christine Reynier, *Virginia Woolf's Ethics of the Short Story* (Basingstoke: Palgrave Macmillan, 2009), p. 56.
34. Hynes, pp. 11–13.
35. Angela Smith, 'Katherine Mansfield at the Front', *First World War Studies*, 2 (2011), p. 68.

36. Hynes, p. 189.
37. Quoted in Hynes, pp. 174–5.
38. W. H. New, *Reading Mansfield and Metaphors of Form* (Montreal: McGill–Queen's University Press, 1999), p. 55.
39. Lefebvre, pp. 6–7. Emphasis and bold original.
40. Olson, p. 6. Emphasis original.
41. *Collected* 1, p. 441.
42. *Collected* 1, p. 446.
43. *Collected* 1, p. 441.
44. *Collected* 1, p. 446.
45. *Collected* 1, pp. 447–8.
46. *Collected* 2, pp. 22–4.
47. *Collected* 2, p. 22.
48. *Collected* 2, p. 22. My emphasis.
49. *Collected* 2, p. 22.
50. *Collected 2*, pp. 22–3.
51. *Collected 2*, p. 24.
52. Sassoon, quoted in Hynes, pp. 174–5.
53. Olson, p. 9.
54. Margaret R. Higonnet, 'Women in the Forbidden Zone: War, Women, and Death', in Elisabeth Bronfen and Sarah Goodwin, eds, *Death and Representation* (Baltimore: Johns Hopkins University Press, 1993), p. 192.

Katherine Mansfield's Home Front: Submerging the Martial Metaphors of 'The Aloe'

Alex Moffett

In November 1919, Katherine Mansfield's critical review of Virginia Woolf's novel *Night and Day*[1] was published under the title 'A Ship Comes Into the Harbour' in her husband John Middleton Murry's journal, the *Athenaeum*.[2] Her private sentiments on the novel, expressed in letters to Murry in November of the same year, were equally negative. Well known to Mansfield scholars, these letters articulate a slightly different critique from that of the review. While her review concentrates on questions of form, specifically the very conventional novelistic structure Woolf had chosen for the novel, Mansfield's private reaction focuses upon another matter entirely: Woolf's evocation of an Edwardian setting that, to Mansfield, was tantamount to an evasion of the subject of the war altogether:

> My private opinion is that it's a lie in the soul. The war never has been: that is what its message is. I don't want (G. forbid!) mobilization and the violation of Belgium, but the novel can't just leave the war out.[3]

A defender of Woolf's novel might raise a legitimate objection to this charge. When living through a historical event as momentous as the First World War, is a past setting necessarily tantamount to an elision? And does Mansfield not leave herself open to precisely the same criticism? Mansfield never published a novel, but her longest story, 'Prelude' (1917),[4] a distillation of an earlier draft entitled 'The Aloe', is similarly set in a historical past that predates the war. At first glance, 'Prelude' seems, like *Night and Day*, absolutely to 'leave the war out'; however, examining the textual history of 'Prelude' reveals a quite different story. Unlike the work into which it would evolve, the original draft of 'The Aloe', primarily composed in Paris in early 1915, has a number of scenes in which echoes can be heard of the conflict that was raging less than a hundred miles away when Mansfield first wrote them. In this essay, I identify and analyse these moments in 'The Aloe', and link them both to Mansfield's experiences of the First World War in early 1915, and to her other writing of the period. Through the process of editing 'Prelude', I argue that the war moves from a metaphorical yet tangible presence in the text, to a seeming and signifying absence. The absence of these moments in 'Prelude', therefore, represents not so much an elimination of the war as a submergence of it. By examining Mansfield's initial attempts to write her experiences of the war in early 1915, I will demonstrate how her representational strategies changed after the tragic death of her beloved brother, Leslie, and how those changes affected the final form of 'Prelude'.

Mansfield's experience of the war differed not only from that of other women writers, but also from that of most other women more generally. On the one hand, she did not serve in the capacity of a field nurse, in the manner of, for instance, Vera Brittain. However, neither was she entirely at home in England during the four years of the conflict. Mansfield spent many months in France, both in Paris and in Bandol, on the Mediterranean; at first, she was mourning the death of her brother and then her worsening health impelled her to seek a more salutary climate. In 1915, she spent a daring five days in the war zone (although not at the front itself) in Gray, on a clandestine visit to see Francis Carco.[5] This extensive travel and diverse set of experiences gave Mansfield a perspective on the war unlike that of any other writer. She was able to witness, if not the actual fighting itself, then certainly the consequences of that warfare. For instance, in the story 'An Indiscreet Journey', the fictionalised account of her illicit rendezvous with Carco, she describes a soldier in whose 'white face his eyes showed, pink as a rabbit's. They brimmed and spilled, brimmed and spilled.'[6] As Vincent O'Sullivan notes in his annotation of the story, this is one of the first written descriptions of a victim of a chlorine gas attack.[7] More generally, Mansfield witnessed much of the apparatus of war: soldiers travelling on trains, bereaved women, and air raids on Paris, all of which she recorded in her letters and journals. However, this act of witnessing coexisted with a palpable sense of distance from the scenes she was describing. As Christiane Mortelier argues, Mansfield's writings about France and the French people are characterised by a 'detached vision', one in which 'France was presented in diminutive pictures of insect-like human activity from up high looking down.'[8] This sense of distance also applies to her relationship with the war. With the possible exception of the Carco affair, the purposes underlying Mansfield's French journeys were always unrelated to the fighting that was going on to the east; her travels were both conceptually and geographically tangential to the war itself. Consequently, Mansfield was both witness and outsider, a chronicler who was far removed from the experiences she related.

The moment when the war did touch Mansfield was on 11 October 1915, when she received notification that her younger brother Leslie had been killed in a hand-grenade accident while serving at the front in northern France. The death of Leslie devastated his sister, but it would also mark an important point in her literary career, one at which she rededicated herself to a project she had already commenced before his death: chronicling their New Zealand childhood. It also inaugurated for her a different set of representational strategies for dealing with the First World War. When the conflict appears in her later fiction, it most frequently asserts its presence through absence. For instance, in 'The Fly', a chance comment momentarily plunges a character into a traumatic memory of a son who was killed in the war some years before.[9] These absences can comprise not just absent individuals, but also the war. For example, Christine Darrohn argues that the dead body of Scott in 'The Garden Party', a story that is set prior to the First World War and which in no way mentions it, is a version of the body of Leslie: a displacement that allows Mansfield to explore the intersections of class and gender in the context of the war.[10]

Prior to October 1915, the war is explicitly referred to in two of Mansfield's stories – 'An Indiscreet Journey' and 'Spring Pictures' – as well as in her letters and journals.[11] These references differ from her later stories' invocations of war in two ways. Firstly, they always assert the war's presence by representing the tangible appearance of bodies and things. The war is not absent in these texts, the wounded soldiers of 'An Indiscreet Journey' and the model Zeppelins of 'Spring Pictures' (a story that I will discuss in more detail later in this essay) are physically present. Secondly, unlike her in later stories, the tonality of these representations is suffused with romance. The first half of 1915 was a very romantic period for Mansfield. It was in February that she embarked on her trip to Gray to be with Francis Carco. She had two sojourns in Paris in March and in May. These stays were necessarily frugal and blemished by Mansfield's ongoing health problems, but in other ways they were idyllic, despite the presence of the war. Staying at Carco's flat in Paris, in a building on the Quai aux Fleurs on the Ile de la Cité, she spent her days as a literary *flâneuse*. She wrote and read Stendhal and watched people in Parisian cafés and public gardens. She composed loving and affectionate letters to Murry, with whom she had recently been reconciled. These letters frequently report beautiful warm weather. 'An Indiscreet Journey' and 'Spring Pictures' were both written during this period, as was the first section of 'The Aloe'. Concerning the latter, Mansfield directly attributed its style to the season and environment: 'Its queer stuff. Its the spring makes me write like this [. . .] Of course it is not what you would call serious – but then I cant be just at this time of year & Ive always felt a spring novel would be lovely to write.'[12] She even likens the act of commencing 'The Aloe' to a romantic encounter; earlier in the same letter, she reports to Murry that yesterday she 'fell into the open arms of my first novel'.[13]

This romantic environment seeps into Mansfield's writing about war during this period. This is not to say that she glorified the fighting itself or its causes; Mansfield deplored the war and the vulgar nationalism that was fuelling it. However, experiencing the war was also something of an adventure: a dangerous and exhilarating backdrop both to her romantic rendezvous with Carco and to her literary retreats to Paris. Sights such as marching soldiers or the floodlights that deterred air raids over Paris were part of the tableaux she was thrilled to observe. Such scenes became intertwined with more romantic images in her writing from this period, thereby generating close juxtapositions of two radically divergent elements. One example of this entanglement can be seen in the long journal entry that would form the basis for 'An Indiscreet Journey'. Mansfield recounts the scene of their first dinner together in Gray, shortly after she and Carco have shared their first kiss:

> Then he left me for a moment. I brushed my hair and washed and was ready when he came back to go out to dinner. The wounded were creeping down the hill. They were all bandaged up. One man looked as though he had two red carnations over his ears; one man as though his hand was covered in black sealing wax. F. talked and talked and talked.[14]

Mansfield did not intend, of course, for this account to have an audience of anyone but herself, and consequently this paragraph reveals much about her mindset as she retrospectively collected her own observations. A thrilling moment of romantic connection is followed by a grim encounter with the realities of the war, as Mansfield sees wounded soldiers returning from the front-line. The dividing point between these two moments is a jarringly abrupt transition: an image of the author in an intimate moment preparing for dinner, followed immediately and without any kind of segue by the image of the staggering wounded men. The simile that loosely joins these two strains together is that of the soldier's bandaged ears, which to Mansfield seem like bloody flowers in his hair.

Mansfield's account of the Zeppelin raids on Paris during March 1915, as recorded in letters to Murry and others, evinces a similar radical dualism. While she is quite conscious of the danger these raids are causing to herself and the citizens of Paris, the predominant tone in her descriptions is that of exhilarated wonder. Her lengthy account of an air raid in her 21 March letter is an example of this response:

> there was a sharp quick sound of running and then the trumpets from all sides flaring *garde à vous!* [. . .] In a minute every light went out except one point on the bridges. The night was bright with stars [. . .] I never thought of Zeppelins until I saw the rush of heads and bodies turning upwards as the Ultimate Fish (see *The Critic in Judgment*) passed by, flying high, with fins of silky grey. It is absurd to say that romance is dead when things like this happen . . . .[15]

The romanticism of the situation is constituted by several different elements. The city of Paris has been plunged into an unfamiliar darkness, revealing a beautiful starry night. The sight of scores of Parisians leaning out of their windows and looking upwards fills Mansfield with a sense of wonder. She comments on the dreamlike quality of this sight in a letter to Carco written on the same day: 'C'était comme un rêve. J'ai pensé que toutes ces personnes ont, subite, l'idée de voler.'[16] And then there is the Zeppelin itself, an image so sublime to Mansfield that it has made her think of a passage from Byron.[17] In Mansfield's reckoning, it is monstrous and yet natural, something akin to an aerial sea monster. And, as this passage from the same letter reveals, it is also oddly enticing:

> And the noise it made – almost soothing, you know, steady and clear *doo-da-doo-da* – like a horn. I longed to go out and follow it, but instead I waited, and still the trumpets blared – and finally when it was over I made some more tea and felt that a great danger was past and longed to throw my arms around someone.[18]

The Zeppelin becomes Satanic in the specifically Romantic sense of the word: attractive and alluring, yet also dangerous and deceptive. The effect of its passing is the longing for physical contact, and possibly also literary production; it is only a few days later that Mansfield will fall 'into the open arms' of 'The Aloe'.

After another breathless description of air-raid sirens (this time a false alarm) and the responses of the Parisian citizens, Mansfield is somewhat more clear-eyed about the effects of the raids: 'These raids after all are *not* funny. They are extremely terrifying and one feels such a horror of the whole idea of the thing.'[19] However, this moment of stark consideration of the dynamic of aerial warfare is then immediately followed by another abrupt transition to romance: an account of a party held by her friend Beatrice Hastings, and of dancing with 'a very lovely young woman – married & *curious* – blonde passionate . . .'.[20] Like her embrace of 'The Aloe', which will take place three days after this party, her impassioned dance with the anonymous woman seems to be a response to her desire for physical contact after the first Zeppelin raid, and her description of it in her letter comes across as a psychic defence against the hard realities of warfare she had considered just sentences before. Mansfield's turn towards the language of romance takes on yet another manifestation in a letter from the same period to Samuel Koteliansky, a letter whose tone sounds rather like something from a fairy story: 'The nights are full of stars and little moons and big Zeppelins – very exciting.'[21] Here, the airships become just another component of a dreamlike Paris nightscape.

A brief indication of the influence that the atmosphere of France in early 1915 had upon Mansfield is in 'Spring Pictures'. Probably written at some point during her second sojourn in Paris, it remained unpublished until it was included in the posthumous collection *Something Childish and Other Stories* (1924).[22] As in her letters and journals, her invocation of the war in this story is entangled with wondrous tonality and imagery. 'Spring Pictures' is a plotless, imagistic story in three parts, narrated in the present tense. In an unidentified city that resembles Paris, the rain falls in 'immense warm drops like melted stars' (534), and an old woman is selling flowers against the backdrop of a gaudy commercial street, in which 'every shop shows a tattered frill of soiled lace and dirty ribbon to charm and entice you' (534). Amongst the erotic pictures and children's clothing that are displayed in the stalls is a very palpable reminder of the war: 'There are tables set out with toy cannons and soldiers and Zeppelins and photograph frames complete with ogling beauties' (534). This is the only place in her fiction where the Zeppelins she witnessed in the Paris air raid are explicitly mentioned. The childlike tone of her letter to Koteliansky becomes hypostasised in the story so that the Zeppelins are rendered as literal toys: ostensibly harmless playthings, but an indication of the very real horror occurring. Like the real Zeppelins of her remembrance, these toys are enticing yet deceptive. All the objects in the stalls are dirtier and tawdrier than they seem upon first inspection; underlying the romantic objects is a cheap commercial reality. The flowers sold by the old lady are the perfect symbols of this dualism; they are seemingly beautiful, but 'the lilies, bunched together in a frill of green, look more like faded cauliflowers' (534). The juxtaposition of the romantic, attractive objects and their fundamental griminess functions on yet another level; this indictment of cheap commercialism is ensconced in an impressionistic and dreamlike narrative. These various juxtapositions indicate that Mansfield's experiences of the war were influencing her early attempts to represent that war in her fiction.

The association of two divergent elements lends itself to the construction of figurative language. Metaphor and metonymy emerge from a dualistic comparison or substitution. The play between the two terms in figurative language generates a spectrum of meaning. Mansfield's texts of early 1915 demonstrate that she was conceiving of the war in a dualistic way – wondrous and yet dangerous – that provides a fertile ground for recasting in metaphor. It is little wonder, then, that she would turn to metaphors of warfare in her initial composition of 'The Aloe'.

The textual history and evolution of 'The Aloe' is well known, if a little fuzzy in its particulars.[23] After commencing her 'novel' on 24 March 1915, Mansfield continued to work on it over the next couple of months, mostly in Paris. By the end of her second Paris trip in mid-May, she had completed about fifty pages of the manuscript.[24] She then set it down for several months, returning to it in early 1916. The death of Leslie the previous October had spurred her to reapply herself to her writing and especially to bring 'The Aloe', which recounted a fictionalised version of their childhood, to fruition. This second period of work seems to have concluded by May of 1916, when, in a letter to Beatrice Campbell, Mansfield expresses pride in what she has accomplished so far: 'Ive reread my novel today, too and now I cant believe I wrote it.'[25] At this point, Mansfield once again set aside the manuscript for many months but, by the end of that year, she had met Virginia Woolf, and in the spring of 1917, Woolf had asked her if she might provide a story to be published by her new Hogarth Press. Mansfield edited 'The Aloe' considerably in the summer of 1917, cutting many scenes and recasting others. The Hogarth Press printed and published the revised and shortened work, now retitled 'Prelude', in the autumn of 1917.

The transformation of 'The Aloe' into 'Prelude' certainly produced a leaner text but, as many Mansfield scholars have observed, the final version had other significant differences as well. Sydney Janet Kaplan points out that the editing process adjusts the narration by de-emphasising an omniscient narrator and focalising the narrative through the consciousness of specific characters.[26] This shift, argues Kaplan, 'result[s] in a more complex rendering of several female points of view', and thereby allows the text to explore more fully the theme of 'awakening into female sexuality'.[27] Jenny McDonnell suggests that in achieving this recalibrated narrative voice, Mansfield was influenced by her own interests in and experiments with dramatic form – especially dialogue – in the period from 1916 to 1917.[28] Concentrating more on thematic content than narrative structure, Pamela Dunbar argues that the editing process was an act of self-censorship for Mansfield, one which resulted in her excision of some of the more radical material included in the original manuscript of 'The Aloe'.[29] But there is another dimension of 'The Aloe' that was also jettisoned in the editing process that produced 'Prelude': the presence of the First World War. There are numerous reminders of the war in the original 'Aloe' manuscript, and most of them are in the first part of the manuscript, written while Mansfield was in Paris in May 1915. However, by the time 'Prelude' was printed two years later, these references had largely been eliminated, leaving the war as an ominous undercurrent rather than a persistent metaphorical reference point.

The clearest way in which this submersion of the war takes place is in the elimination of language, figural or otherwise, that would remind her readers of the conflict. At the most granular level, Mansfield adjusted her word choice. For instance, the sentence 'They were trooped off to bed by the Grandmother' (52) in 'The Aloe' is changed to the less martially suggestive 'They were taken off to bed by the grandmother' (53) at the beginning of the fourth section of 'Prelude'. Mansfield also amended and eliminated some of the dialogue of her characters. When Kezia and Lottie arrive at the new house in the final version of 'Prelude', their weary mother enquires as to their presence: '"Are those the children?" But Linda did not really care; she did not even open her eyes to see' (48).[30] In the original 'Aloe' manuscript, Linda's query is followed by a darker, if mostly unserious, speculation: '"Are those the children" – Mrs. Burnell did not even open her eyes – her voice was tired and trembling – Have either of them ~~killed on the dray~~ maimed for life?"' (49). Here we see a nascent version of Linda, whose difficult pregnancies have left her with a resentful, even fearful attitude towards her children and to childbirth more generally. That attitude is expressed in a darkly flippant enquiry that perhaps conceals a genuinely violent impulse. Mansfield ameliorates the sentiment in her first edit, striking through the words 'killed on the [dray]' in her notebook and replacing them with 'maimed for life'. However, this impulse would still have resonated uncomfortably with a readership that was all too used to hearing of loved ones being killed or maimed for life. And the Mansfield who edited the 'Aloe' manuscript in 1917 would have been keenly aware of this feeling in a way that the younger version of herself who wrote those words would not have been.[31] Consequently, the words are eliminated, if not perhaps the psychological urge, for she jokes in the final version of 'Prelude' about Kezia being tossed by a bull (90).

'The Aloe' has a second fantasist about disastrous and unexpected death: the other Fairfield sister, Doady Trout, who keeps imagining 'some shocking catastrophe' occurring to members of her family.[32] While Doady uses scenes and characters from *David Copperfield* as a way of fleshing out these scenarios (127), an episode from one of them contains a more uncomfortably realistic situation:

> Suddenly the gate opened. A ~~rough~~ working man, a perfect stranger to her, pushed up the path, and standing in front of her, he pulled off his cap, his rough face full of pity. 'I've bad news for you, Mam' .... 'Dead?' cried Dora, clasping her hands. 'Both dead?' (129)

These scenes are strongly redolent of those which occurred throughout Britain in the war years, as families received bad news of the demises of soldiers in France. Written in Mansfield's 1916 'Aloe' notebooks, this episode – and Doady's character – are eliminated altogether in 'Prelude'.

Mansfield also eliminated some of the harsher and more martial imagery from the original 'Aloe' manuscript. One such instance occurs as Kezia looks up at the stars from the cart in which she is being taken to her new home. In 'The Aloe', as in 'Prelude', she asks if 'stars ever blow about' (40), an enquiry somewhat reminiscent of Mansfield's own wondrous astronomical observations during the Paris air raids. And as in those raids, a *memento mori* suddenly looms: 'Came a thin scatter of lights and the shape of a tin church, rising out of a ring of tombstones' (41). In 'Prelude', the church and tombstones are eliminated. Mansfield also removed an even more suggestive image from earlier in 'The Aloe', one that is once again associated with Linda Burnell's difficult pregnancies. The birth of Kezia is described as taking place against a backdrop of an aural and meteorological tumult that draws on the sights and sounds of warfare:

> She had come forth squealing out of a reluctant mother in the teeth of a 'Southerly Buster'. The Grandmother, shaking her before the window, had seen the sea rise in green mountains and sweep the esplanade. The little house was like a shell to its loud booming. Down in the gully the wild trees lashed together and big gulls wheeling and crying skimmed past the misty window. (35)

In its emphasis on the storm's sublimity, the diction of this passage recalls Mansfield's writing about the Paris air raids. The sounds of the storms and the cries of the gulls are accompanied by visual upheaval: the lashing of the trees and the rise of the sea in 'green mountains'. A 'southerly buster' is a real weather phenomenon in Australia and New Zealand, but it is also hazily suggestive of military slang for weaponry; for instance, the pilots who shot down observation balloons during the war were known as 'balloon busters'. And most telling of all is the doubly coded metaphor that Mansfield chooses to describe the house. The 'shell' denotes a seashell amplifying the noise of the waves, but potential readers in 1915 would be more likely to think of an altogether different sort of booming shell.

There are two excised episodes in 'The Aloe' whose events possess resonances of the First World War. The first is the lengthier account of Kezia and Lottie's brief stay with the Samuel Josephs family. Kezia's disdain for the Samuel Josephs is palpable in 'Prelude', but in the original 'Aloe' manuscript that attitude is heightened to the point of aggressive antagonism. Firstly, the omniscient narrator describes the Samuel Josephs family as if they were vermin: 'The Samuel Josephs were not a family. They were a swarm [. . .] Impossible to count them: impossible to distinguish between them' (27). The description dehumanises the family, rendering them not as individuals, but as a seething, countless, collective enemy. Their only individual characteristic is their propensity for combat: 'And every single one of them started a pitched battle as soon as possible after birth with every single other' (27). Appropriately enough, the matriarch of the family is transfigured into the very model of an ignorant and uncaring military officer:

> When Mrs. Samuel Josephs was not turning up their clothes or down their clothes [. . .] and beating them with a hair brush, she called this pitched battle 'airing their lungs'. She seemed to take a pride in it and to bask in it from far away like a fat general watching through field glasses his troops in violent action. (27)

After an afternoon of being the brunt of mockery, Kezia has an idea about how to get back at the Samuel Josephs children: an idea that 'frightened her so that her knees trembled but [. . .] made her so happy she nearly screamed aloud with joy' (31, 33). She proceeds to trick the Samuel Josephs into eating a noxious flower:

> The Samuel Josephs suspected nothing. They liked the game. A game where something had to be destroyed always fetched them. Savagely they broke off the big white blooms and stood in a row before Kezia . . . .
>
> She flung up her hands with joy as the Samuel Josephs bit, chewed, made dreadful faces, spat, screamed, and rushed to Burnell's garden tap. But that was no good – only a trickle came out. Away they sped, yelling.
>
> 'Ma! Ma! Kezia's poisoned us.'
>
> 'Ma! Ma! Me tongue's burning off.'
>
> 'Ma! Ooh, Ma!'
>
> 'Whatever *is* the matter?' asked Lottie, mildly, still twisting the frayed, oozing stem. 'Kin I bite my lily off like this, Kezia?'

> 'No, silly.' Kezia caught her hand. 'It burns your tongue like anything.' (33)

Playing on the Samuel Josephs' 'savage' desire for destruction, Kezia engages in a botanical form of chemical warfare, one that is more dangerous than the playful overtone might suggest. As Mansfield (and maybe Kezia) knows, the arum lily is a toxic plant that is potentially deadly if consumed.[33] It is native to the Southern Hemisphere and would likely be unfamiliar to a potential European readership. But that readership would have been very familiar with accounts of gas attacks on the front in France, and the description of the Samuel Josephs' reaction – the 'burning' and the screaming – would have struck a sinister chord. The arum lily, with its toxicity and aggressive fecundity, functions as an antithesis to the titular aloe flower in this draft.

The second excised section that possesses echoes of the First World War pertains to Stanley Burnell, whose scenes in the first section of 'The Aloe' are peppered with references to militarism and warfare. The history of Linda's meeting Stanley, which was the last section Mansfield wrote before leaving Paris and setting 'The Aloe' aside in May 1915, has many such martial reminders. This episode incorporates an account of Mr Fairfield, Linda's father, who, in an echo of early First World War optimism, has 'one saying with which he met all difficulties. "Depend upon it, it will all come right after the Maori war"' (71). He accompanies Linda to the social event where she will meet Stanley, an event that, in Mansfield's rendering, possesses distinctly militaristic undertones. Individuals wear clothing suggestive of military uniform: Mr Fairfield 'wore a frock coat' while the pianist complements his evening clothes with 'brown button boots' (75, 77). The evening begins with a 'painful' concert, performed by a chorus in which the men are possessed of an appearance and demeanour more suitable to soldiering than singing: 'The gentlemen sang with far greater vigour and a kind of defiant cheerfulness which was almost terrifying. They looked very furious, too. Their cuffs shot over their hands, or their trousers were far too long . . .' (75). One of their performed songs – 'She Wore a Wreath of Roses' – is about seeing a bereaved widow.[34] Mr Fairfield playfully informs Linda that Stanley will 'sandbag you with one of old Ma Warren's rock cakes' (77), a choice of verb that not only anticipates Stanley's future hectoring, but also alludes to the never-ending rows of sandbags in the front-line trenches. And the choice of quadrilles is also telling: the pianist 'sat down at the piano, and crashed into the "Lancers"' (77), a nineteenth-century dance based on the movements of lance-bearing soldiers. This scene is of course a flashback, and these martial undertones serve to prefigure

Stanley's temperament, which, in another passage Mansfield removed from 'The Aloe', is presented as being like that of a colonial conqueror:

> They must wave when [Stanley] waved, give him good-bye for good-bye and lavish upon him unlimited sympathy, as though they saw on the horizon's brim the untamed land to which he curved his chest so proudly – the line of leaping savages ready to fall upon his valiant sword. (63)

Here, Mansfield makes explicit a point that 'Prelude' will leave implicit: that Stanley's patriarchal brand of familial governance and capitalistic enthusiasm is intrinsically bound up with the hypermasculine ideologies that lead to colonialism and militarism.

What the invocations of the First World War in 'The Aloe' have in common with one another is that they exist primarily on a metaphorical or referential level. A word here possesses a double meaning; a description there evokes an image from the front. Only the Samuel Josephs episode – with its images of combative children and its invocations of a swarming, collective enemy – works towards functioning on a deeper, more allegorical level. By removing these references, Mansfield submerges the war, rather than eliminating it from the story altogether. There are two important consequences of this submersion. Firstly, removing the references to the war facilitates Mansfield's quest to achieve a different sort of narrative technique. The war references in 'The Aloe' exist in a parallel continuum to the primary narrative; they possess a straightforward, referential schema in which metaphor binds the two elements together. In contrast, 'Prelude' has a depth that 'The Aloe' never quite achieves. With its representations of gender dynamics and unconscious impulses, and its simultaneous exploration of different stages in women's life narratives, 'Prelude' possesses the deep structure of psychology. While 'The Aloe' is a fairly two-dimensional text, 'Prelude' has strata of meaning. It stands as one of the great works of literary modernism.

The second consequence pertains to Mansfield's concern about the effect the war should have on a responsible artist. In a letter to Murry shortly after her previous expression of frustration about Woolf's *Night and Day* and its avoidance of the war, Mansfield explains how, in the wake of the war, a new literature might achieve a seemingly paradoxical assertion of presence through absence:

> No, I mean 'deserts of vast eternity'. But the difference is (perhaps I'm wrong) I couldn't tell anybody *bang out* about those deserts: they are my secret. I might write about a boy eating strawberries or a woman combing her hair on a windy morning, and that is the only way I can ever mention them. But they *must* be there. Nothing less will do.[35]

This is a widely quoted and analysed passage, one that proposes, in Angela Smith's words, that '[t]he war transforms, through tragic knowledge, familiar reality'.[36] As she clarifies to Murry in the second paragraph what precisely she meant in the first, Mansfield implicitly provides the logic for excising the war references from 'Prelude'. If knowledge of death can be seen through the things of everyday life, if 'the deserts of vast eternity' can be represented even while they are not explicitly mentioned, then there is no need for the referentiality that was present in 'The Aloe'; indeed, it might have weakened the final story. Marvell's deserts are very much present in 'Prelude': in the scene where Pat the handyman kills a duck, in Linda's silent desperation and, at the deepest level of all, in the story's celebration of the lost Beauchamp childhood. Without any reference to the First World War, 'Prelude' and Mansfield's subsequent New Zealand stories contain a grim teleology: they intend to commemorate the creation of a life that would, in reality, be tragically cut short.

Acknowledgements

The author wishes to thank Martha Kuhlman for her invaluable editorial assistance and David Mickelsen for the use of his shed in the Maine woods, which proved to be a restful venue for conceiving and drafting this essay.

Notes

1. Virginia Woolf, *Night and Day* (London: Penguin, 1992).
2. Reprinted in John Middleton Murry, ed., *Katherine Mansfield, Novels and Novelists* (New York: Knopf, 1930).
3. Vincent O'Sullivan and Margaret Scott, eds, *The Collected Letters of Katherine Mansfield*, 5 vols (Oxford: Clarendon Press, 1984), Vol. 3, p. 168. Hereafter referred to as *Letters*, followed by volume and page number.
4. *The Collected Stories of Katherine Mansfield* (London: Wordsworth, 2006), p. 5. Unless otherwise noted, all references to Mansfield's stories are from this edition.
5. In *The Great War and Women's Consciousness* (Iowa City: University of Iowa Press, 1990), Claire Tylee suggests that visiting the war zone might have been a central motive, rather than being incidental to her visit to Carco (p. 84).
6. *Stories*, p. 529.
7. Vincent O'Sullivan, ed., *Katherine Mansfield's Selected Stories* (New York: W. W. Norton, 2006), p. 71.
8. Christiane Mortelier, 'The French Connection: Francis Carco', in Roger Robinson, ed., *Katherine Mansfield: In From the Margin* (Baton Rouge: Louisiana State University Press, 1994), p. 138.
9. *Stories*, p. 344.
10. *Stories*, p. 197. Christine Darrohn, '"Blown to Bits!": Katherine Mansfield's "The Garden-Party" and the Great War', *Modern Fiction Studies*, 44 (Fall 1998), pp. 515–21.

In *Death, Men and Modernism: Trauma and Narrative in British Fiction From Hardy to Woolf* (New York: Routledge, 2003), Ariela Freedman also reads 'The Garden Party' as a text in which the war has an implicit presence, pp. 81–102.

11. *Stories*, pp. 520, 534.
12. *Letters* 1, p. 168. As Sydney Janet Kaplan observes in *Katherine Mansfield and the Origins of Modernist Fiction* (Ithaca, NY: Cornell University Press, 1991), the milieu of wartime Paris had an influence on the creation of 'The Aloe', pp. 107–8.
13. *Letters* 1, p. 167. Sydney Janet Kaplan notes of this metaphor that, for Mansfield, '[o]pen arms had long been associated with female sexuality', p. 108.
14. Margaret Scott, ed., *The Katherine Mansfield Notebooks*, 2 vols (Minneapolis: University of Minnesota Press, 2002), Vol 1, Notebook 4, qMS-1251, p. 11.
15. *Letters* 1, p. 159.
16. 'It was like a dream. I thought that everyone, quite suddenly, was going to fly.' Translated by O'Sullivan, *Letters* 1, p. 161.
17. As O'Sullivan says in his annotation of the letter, Mansfield seems to be mistaking the title of her husband's poem, *The Critic in Judgment*, with that of the Byron poem, *The Vision of Judgment*; *Letters* 1, p. 160.
18. *Letters* 1, p. 160.
19. *Letters* 1, p. 164.
20. *Letters* 1, p. 164.
21. *Letters* 1, p. 163.
22. Roger Norburn, *A Katherine Mansfield Chronology* (Basingstoke: Palgrave MacMillan, 2008), p. 33. Katherine Mansfield, *Something Childish and Other Stories* (London: Constable, 1924).
23. Vincent O'Sullivan's introduction to the Carcanet New Press edition of the 'Aloe' manuscript (Manchester: Carcanet New Press, 1983) provides a fuller account of this history, as does the seventh chapter ('From *The Aloe* to "Prelude"') of Kaplan's *Katherine Mansfield and the Origins of Modernist Fiction.*
24. O'Sullivan, *The Aloe*, p. 12.
25. *Letters* 1, p. 261.
26. Kaplan, p. 113.
27. Kaplan, pp. 113, 114.
28. Jenny McDonnell, *Katherine Mansfield and the Modernist Marketplace: At the Mercy of the Public* (Palgrave Macmillan: New York, 2010), p. 96. McDonnell argues that the dialogic form's absence of a narrator gave Mansfield a paradigm for recasting the narrative voice of 'The Aloe'.
29. Pamela Dunbar, *Radical Mansfield: Double Discourse in Katherine Mansfield's Short Stories* (New York: St Martin's, 1997), p. 143. One example of Mansfield's self-censorship, according to Dunbar, is the expunging of a scene in which Beryl Fairfield accuses her sister Linda of being incapable of insincerity ever since the death of their father.
30. All quotations from both 'Prelude' and 'The Aloe' are from Vincent O'Sullivan's edition of *The Aloe*, which helpfully juxtaposes the final version of 'Prelude' on the facing page of the text.
31. Christine Darrohn discusses the way that Mansfield compulsively imagines her brother's dead body in the months following his death, pp. 517–18.
32. Sydney Janet Kaplan suggests that the emphasis on male death in Doady's fantasies implies a hostile attitude towards heteronormative sexual modes, p. 115.
33. The lily is probably *Zantedeschia aethiopica*, a non-native plant which is endemic in New Zealand (Sue Edmonds, 'Arums', www.lifestyleblock.co.nz/lifestyle-file/

running-the-farm/weeds/item/825-arums.html [accessed 29 August 2013]). It is a 'common garden plant toxic to stock and humans with fatalities in both recorded' ('Weeds Australia: Arum Lily', www.weeds.org.au/cgi-bin/weedident.cgi?tpl=plant.tpl&card=H10 [accessed 29 August 2013]).

34. The third verse is as follows:

    And once again I see that brow no bridal wreath is there,
    The widow's somber cap conceals her once luxuriant hair;
    She weeps in silent solitude, and there is no one near
    To press her hands within his own and wipe away the tear;
    I see her broken hearted! Yet me thinks I see her now,
    In the pride of youth and beauty, with a garland on her brow.
    ('The Lied, Art Song, and Choral Texts Archive', www.recmusic.org/lieder/get_text.html?TextId=21857 [accessed 29 August 2013])

35. *Letters* 3, p. 197.
36. Angela Smith, *Katherine Mansfield and Virginia Woolf: A Public of Two* (Oxford: Clarendon Press, 1999), p. 147.

War Thoughts and Home: Katherine Mansfield's Model of a Hardened Heart in a Broken World

Richard Cappuccio

Katherine Mansfield's circle of friends would have recognised Mary Thriplow in Aldous Huxley's *Those Barren Leaves.* Thriplow writes running dialogues with her dead brother in a 'secret diary devoted to his memory', including tales of growing up in 'Weltringham'.[1] Huxley asks, 'Wasn't she deliberately scratching her heart to make it bleed, and then writing stories with the red fluid?' (82). Mansfield's journals during the period following the death of her brother Leslie ('Chummie') Beauchamp are conversational and emotionally introspective, but her fiction written during this period is more complicated than confessional writing. After her visit to Francis Carco in February 1915, Mansfield had started writing 'The Aloe', and she continued to work on it through to its 1917 publication as 'Prelude'.[2] 'The Aloe' is a narrative with images and motifs of the Great War that help define the modern age as one of despair and loss of direction. It stands as a powerful modernist statement of the tragedy of those whose deaths were left without closure as a result of the war. Allyson Booth in *Postcards from the Trenches* argues

> that even at moments when the spaces of war seem most remote, the perceptual habits appropriate to war emerge plainly; that the buildings of modernism may delineate spaces within which one is forced to confront both war's casualties and one's distance from those casualties; that the dislocations of war often figure centrally in modernist form, even when war itself seems peripheral to modernist content.[3]

Set in New Zealand in 1893, 'The Aloe' is a commentary on the fate awaiting the unborn child of the Burnell family and, as such, it is the prelude to the tragedy that awaits the real Beauchamp family.

In 1915 Mansfield had travelled into the war zone and lied her way through military checkpoints for her brief rendezvous with Francis

Carco. Leslie, who had recently arrived in England 'to join a British regiment', helped finance her travel to France that February.[4] The following month, the affair with Carco was over but, after her experience of travelling through military lines, she stayed alone in Carco's Paris flat to write. Not just alienation from her native country, but also dislocation from the borders of the Empire created an opportunity to focus on her work. That combination of displacement and concentration was fruitful. In March 1915 she wrote to John Middleton Murry, 'I had a great day yesterday. The Muses descended in a ring like the angels on the Botticelli Nativity roof – or so it seemed to "humble" little Tig and I fell into the open arms of my first novel.'[5] The result was 'The Aloe', and Mansfield's manuscript reflects the experience of the Great War: the destruction of boundaries, aggression, lingering absence and tragic foreboding.

In Booth's analysis of the motifs that emerge in modernist literature during and after the Great War, she writes about the common theme of the erasure of home:

> The diaries, memoirs, and novels of many veterans suggest [. . .] one of the most devastating consequences of fighting the war was combatants' discovery that the concept of 'home' no longer existed as a geographical site. Instead, 'home' merely registered a set of collapsing imaginative expectations.[6]

This erasure of home propels the opening of 'The Aloe'. Not only are Kezia and Lottie left behind at the abandoned home, but also they are left with a surrogate family that is foreign to their experience. The boorish Samuel Josephs are shocking to Kezia. Mansfield had previously explored the crude behaviour of the 'Other' in her German pension sketches.[7] British reports spoke of the penetration of Belgium's borders by the German army as rape, 'part of the larger violation against civilized standards of behavior'.[8] The difference between the Burnells and the Samuel Josephs is the difference between civilisation and barbarism. The Samuel Josephs are dirty and crude. They lack the boundaries of the Burnell children. When the discussion turns to water closets, Miriam brags, 'We've got two at ours. One for men and one for ladies. The one for men hasn't got a seat' (10). To Kezia this is unthinkable, and she expresses her scepticism: 'I *don't* believe you.' Miriam responds with a rapid-fire: 'It's-true-it's-true-it's-true!' (10). The cultural divide is accented when Miriam taunts Kezia with a vulgar dance that includes 'showing her flannelette drawers' (10). These transgressions would not be tolerated in the Burnell household.

By 1916 elements of the war had been integrated into the everyday lives of children. For example, a set of ABC blocks from the era features a letter of the alphabet on a paper label and an image that relates to an aspect of the war: D for Dreadnought, H for Howitzer, T for Trench.[9] Similarly, Mansfield has readied her children in 'The Aloe' for battle. Lottie and Kezia are dressed with a nautical theme, 'reefer coats with brass anchor buttons and little round caps with battle-ship ribbons' (4). When they are left behind, Mansfield uses military language: they get 'ready for the fray'. Battle will soon occur with the Samuel Josephs, an enemy who 'jumped out at you from under the tables, through the stair rails, behind the doors, behind the coats in the passage' (6–7). This enemy 'swarm' is a formidable opponent; new recruits appear in 'white sailor suit[s]' and 'every single one of them started a pitched battle as soon as possible after birth'. Mrs Samuel Josephs views these fights as a natural 'airing [of] their lungs' (7). Mansfield goes so far as to add that Mrs Samuel Josephs seems 'to take pride in it and to bask in it from far away like a fat general watching through field glasses his troops in violent action' (7–8). Even the household servant girl summons the children to bed 'banging on a tin tray with a potato masher' (9), a term that by 1915 was synonymous with a German stick grenade.

Miriam articulates the eagerness with which the Samuel Josephs wish to invade the Burnell homeland: 'Let's go an' play hide-an'-seek all over Burnell's. Their back door is still open [. . .] Come on! Come on!' (9). Kezia halts that advance, but ultimately she has no safe retreat. The house that once represented a safe and stable border is abandoned and ghostly, and she walks through a building that is haunted by the missing. There are no adults present; in fact, there are only eerie remnants of the house's previous inhabitants. By the sink there is a stained 'piece of flannel'; all that remains of the servant girl's presence is a 'hair-tidy' in the fireplace mixed in with the remains of rubbish; there are other small evidences of life in her own room: 'a stray button stuck in a crack of the floor and in another crack some beads and a long needle' (14). These fragments evoke the same effect that Booth points out as the civilian 'experience of disembodied death [that] arose from the fact that huge numbers of soldiers simply disappeared on the battlefields of World War I'.[10] She points to a passage in *All Quiet on the Western Front*, in which three of the characters discuss a victim of an explosion who has 'been blown out of his clothes'.[11] The narrator observes,

> I search around, and so it is. Here hang bits of uniform, and somewhere else is plastered a bloody mess that was once a human limb. Over there lies a body with nothing but a piece of the underpants on one leg and the collar of the tunic around its neck. (210)

In 'The Aloe', the fragments that Kezia observes are less shocking than the body in Remarque's text. The two scenes, however, share the struggle to find coherence among arbitrary remains. Kezia pauses at the sight of a 'lump of gritty yellow soap in one corner of the window-sill' (13). Mansfield's contemporaries would have likely associated this with Sunlight Soap, a product that was later advertised as particularly tied to the war effort. The advertisements claimed that it played an important role for the Tommys in the trenches:

> We'll win the fight, our men are right;
> The cleanest fighters ever seen!
> We've shot and shell, Pure soap as well,
> To keep these cleanest fighters clean.[12]

Other Sunlight Soap advertising reminds readers that the 'beautiful oils and tallow from which Sunlight Soap is made come from overseas – from Australia [and] the Islands of the Pacific'.[13] The sentiment is clear: in the honourable path to victory, the Empire must use its purest resources from across the globe. In contrast to the hygienic Tommys, the Samuel Josephs 'with [their] blackheads' (7) are constructed as the opposite of purity and cleanliness; Zaidee Josephs casually recounts the time her brother Stan 'was sick – all over the table' (12), and Mansfield makes a particular point of the children's 'ink black finger nails' (7). The Burnells reward their children for cleanliness: 'I get a penny', Kezia tells Alice Samuel Josephs, 'for having my hair washed' (11). In contrast, Mr Samuel Josephs promotes a barbaric zeal; he pays his children a half-penny for every hundred snails they gather and kill. Alice reports that they 'put them in a bucket with salt and they all go bubbly like spittle' (11). The Samuel Josephs are clearly terrifying; they relish leaving their victims unrecognisable.

The children have one thing in common: they are ready for battle. Kezia is markedly skilled in the subtle art of war. Her strategy is introduced as a 'new game' with an unconventional weapon and the enemy is poisoned when convinced to eat the head of 'a narum lily' (12). Kezia lays down the ground rules. She tells everyone that the one 'who swallows first – wins', and the Samuel Josephs children are soon in retreat: '"Ma! Ma! Kezia's poisoned us." | "Ma! Ma! Me tongue's burning off." | "Ma! Ooh, Ma!"' (13). Although pleased with her victory, Kezia succeeds only in defending an abandoned home.

When she takes her final walk through the house, it is oppressive in its quiet. As Booth observes, the 'only honest representation of absence is silence'.[14] In the room in which Kezia was born she thinks about internalised sounds: her own 'squealing out of a reluctant mother in the teeth of a "Southerly Buster"' (15). From the night of her birth, she reflects further on the sounds of the sea 'sweep[ing] the esplanade' (15). Of course, Kezia would not herself remember those sounds, so she must be referencing the echoes of the memories of those, now missing, that witnessed it. The dwelling itself is silent and still: 'The little house was like a shell to its loud booming' (15). Here the simile works on several levels: there is the image of an eggshell that harbours life, or a seashell that connects the listener to the comfort of the sea. However, there is also the silence of the unused military ordnance before its deafening report. That stillness shifts to the crying of the gulls in the distance, and that uneasiness comes closer when Mansfield notes:

> the windows shook, a creaking came from the walls and floors, a piece of loose iron on the roof banged forlornly – Kezia did not notice these things severally, but she was suddenly quite, quite still with wide open eyes and knees pressed together – terribly frightened. (15–16)

For Kezia the quiet of the empty house is even more fearful than the visible enemy, and Mansfield emphasises this idea with a litany about the spectre of the dark. What once was home is replaced with fear:

> *It* had a face. *It* smiled, but *It* had no eyes. *It* was yellow. When she was put to bed with two drops of aconite in a medicine glass *It* breathed very loudly and firmly and *It* had been known on certain fearful occasions to turn round and round. *It* hung in the air. [. . .] *It* was at the top of the stairs; *It* was at the bottom of the stairs, waiting in a little dark passage, guarding the back door. (16)

Kezia is, in essence, battle-worn. This interior monologue communicates a wide range of fears from the image of a hollow-eyed skull to the sounds of breathing; from the ability of fear to hang in a cloud like a gas attack, to its power to move up and down the stairs and stalk its prey. Kezia is waiting in the trenches, her enemy vigilant nearby.

The appearance of the store-man, Fred, breaks the tension, but the final images are far from comforting. Mrs Samuel Josephs may give the Burnell girls a shawl for the journey, but even she has become a phantom who 'won't come out'. Mrs Samuel Josephs sends a warning to Kezia about her unconventional tactics: 'Never do it again' (17). Lottie and Kezia have survived the fray, but their future is uncertain. They ride into a grotesque landscape with 'houses much smaller' than they look by day, and 'the trees and the gardens far bigger and wilder' (21).

The most terrifying image of bloodshed occurs later in the manuscript when Pat slaughters a duck for the evening meal. That carnage is carefully foreshadowed in the language of the story. For example, as soon as Mrs Samuel Josephs enters the narrative, she comforts Lottie by saying, 'There-there, ducky!' (6). Soon after, she instructs Lottie to 'Go and sit by Zaidee, ducky' (8). Later, even Rags Trout is described with bird imagery: he was 'very small, and so thin that when he was undressed his shoulder blades stuck out like two little wings' (89). While initially readers might interpret Mrs Samuel Josephs' words as terms of endearment, or the description of Rags as one that simply accentuates his slight build, Mansfield's diction builds to the fateful slaughter that traumatises Kezia and jars the reader. With the diction that links animals to children, Mansfield implies their vulnerability and the randomness of fate.

In December 1915 in her notebook, she considers how destiny brought Leslie to his end with the words '*Et in Arcadia Ego*'.[15] When Mansfield returns to work on 'The Aloe' a year after she started writing and several months after Leslie's death, she has Doady Trout voice a mother's recognition of fate: 'Each time before her children were born she had thought that the tragedy would be fulfilled then' (106). Her premonitions are so strong she senses that 'something very tragic was going to happen to her soon. She had felt it coming on for years. What it was she could not exactly say, but she was fated somehow' (106). This foreboding might involve her wish that she had given birth to girls instead of her two boys, both potential soldiers.

In this pairing, the older child, Pip, sees himself as ready for combat; he imagines opponents who are weaker than he is. As a result, Pip likes playing with girls because he can 'fox them so', while foes like timid Lottie are 'so easily frightened' (91). He childishly boasts about hardening himself to pain with a claim that when he skins almonds he sticks his hand 'in a saucepan of boiling water' (91). Pip even trains his dog, Snooker, for combat by concocting mixtures of 'carbolic tooth powder and a bit of sulphur and perhaps a pinch of starch to stiffen up [. . . his] coat'. This formula includes a secret ingredient that 'Rags privately' thinks is 'gunpowder'. It could result in blinding and there is 'always the chance – just the chance – of it exploding' (90). Pip prepares his reluctant pet 'to look a bit more fierce' (94) by tying his ears, training them to 'lie kind of back and [. . .] prick up' (93). When Pat decapitates the duck, Pip shouts with excitement.

In contrast, Rags is sensitive. The delicate younger boy is ominously 'small, and [. . .] thin' (89). When he witnesses the death of the duck, his 'cheeks [are] as white as paper'. Even though he puts out a 'finger' as if he means 'to touch' the duck's head, he draws it 'back again, [. . .] shivering all over' (98). Clearly, Rags is not cut out for bloodletting. Instead, he adores dolls: 'The great treat it was to him to stretch out his arms and be given a doll to hold!' (91). Antony Alpers suggests that Mansfield's cousins, Barrie and Eric Waters, were 'the originals of Pip and Rags'.[16] More important than their inspiration, however, is their uncertain fate; this is the generation of boys who would grow up and find themselves on the battlefields in the Great War, where the chance of things 'exploding' would not be playful and thrilling but immediate and final (90).

Pat, in turn, caters to a childish fantasy of war. His slaughter of the duck is framed in political and military terms: he tells the children, '"Come with me now, [. . .] and I'll show you how the Kings of Ireland chop off the head of a duck"' (94). Pat takes on the identity of a national ruler, and he accepts the sacrifice of his military: '"There they are [. . .] There's the little Irish Navy, and look at the old Admiral there with the green neck and grand little flagstaff on his tail"' (96). As this King inflicts casualties on his own forces, the scene eerily mirrors Chummie's death, not at the hand of the declared enemy but in the midst of his brothers-in-arms.

At this point, Mansfield scholars may well be reminded of Beatrice Campbell's memories of visiting Acacia Road:

> There was a photograph of her brother 'Chummy' in uniform on her desk [. . .] I took up the photograph to look at it and asked if she had heard from him since his leave. I noticed that she was looking at me in a queer, wild, hard way; then she said, "Blown to bits!"[17]

The duck similarly is reduced 'to bits'; its head flies 'off the stump – and [. . .] the blood' spurts 'over the white feathers' (98). The image of decapitation is even more upsetting when Pat puts 'down the white body' and it begins 'to waddle with only a long spurt of blood where the head had been'. As if words alone could alter the shock of death, Kezia chants, 'Put head back, put head back [. . .] Head back, head back' (99).

While Kezia is traumatised, Stanley Burnell offers a sanguine view later that day: the duck was fated for the table. When the meal is served, the 'white duck' no longer looks 'as if it had ever had a head when Alice placed it in front of Stanley Burnell' (100). The duck is so delicious, Stanley pontificates, 'Father would say [. . .] this is one of those birds whose mother must have played to it in infancy upon the German flute, and the sweet strains of the dulcet instrument acted with such an effect upon the infant mind' (113). In quoting his father, Stanley reinforces a paternal view of sacrifice which pays homage to maternal care, but denies the realities of the slaughter that shocked Kezia.

Stanley Burnell's chatter is self-absorbed, but it is not as monstrous as the remarks of Mrs Busk in 'Stay-Laces' (1915).[18] Alpers is critical of that work: it 'seems to have more of eavesdropping in it than creative imagination'. Nevertheless, he also concedes that 'at least it records an early protest' against the 'war's destruction'.[19] Mrs Busk, frustrated by not finding out the details of another traveller's conversation, tells her voiceless companion, Mrs Bone,

> 'I thought the war had done away with the idea that there was anything you couldn't speak about. I mean the things one reads in the papers, and the wounded that one even sees in the streets have made such a difference'.[20]

Mrs Busk, whose Dickensian name is synonymous with an unsolicited public performance, loudly continues with words that are enough to make anyone within earshot wince: 'I *love* the wounded, don't you?'[21] Mrs Busk repeats the sentiment with even greater false conviction: 'Oh, I simply love them.' Adding increments of insincerity, she says: 'And their sweet blue and red uniforms are so cheerful and awfully effective, aren't they? I can't think who thought of that bright red tie against that bright blue. It's such a note, isn't it?'[22] If, as Alpers suspects, this sketch is a result of eavesdropping, the sentiments are shocking in their exaggerated shallowness.

On the other hand, the characterisation of Mrs Busk may reflect Mansfield's amplified anger at the insensitivity of those around her about the suffering she had witnessed. For instance, Beatrice Campbell recounts going with Mansfield to meet the ambulance trains at the time when the war had escalated with the sinking of the *Lusitania* and the use of poison gas.[23] Mansfield had also seen William Orton go off to fight and survive the Dardanelles, but 'in May [. . .] Rupert Brooke, and in June, Henri Gaudier-Brzeska [were] killed in battle'.[24] Mansfield's notebooks from Paris in May 1915 indicate how heavily the destruction of the war weighed on her. She not only records a dream about Brooke, but she also details her anxiety about the hardening effect the war had on children: 'In the big sandheaps down by the river children had hollowed out tunnels and caverns. They sat in them stolid and content [. . .] Now and then a man lay stretched on his face, his head in his arms.'[25] Despite the mention of white clouds, the glistening sun and ambling on the quays, there is an eerie transformation from children in trenches to an adult lying face down. This jarring mixture of images of stolid children among the casualties of war might reflect Mansfield's fears for Leslie, who had recently arrived in England for his military training.

Beatrice Campbell bears witness to Mansfield's relationship with her youngest sibling: 'She had always spoken happily about him and of their love for each other, for he seemed to be the one member of her family with whom she was absolutely in tune.'[26] The history of Mansfield's reunion with Leslie, his death, and her decision to write more about New Zealand is well documented. Alpers relates that after Chummie arrived in England, in February 1915, he wrote to his parents with 'slightly protective' news of his sister:

> She is more than ever in love with J. M. Murry which is a thing to be thankful for and with a new contract with one of the monthlies for a series of war sketches, they have prospects of a little money coming in, though these times are exceptionally trying for their itinerant sort of writings. They are going over to Paris at the end of this week to collect materials for the new job.[27]

It is difficult to tell if Mansfield's desire to write 'a series of war sketches' is part of the false narrative she appears to have planted for Chummie to send home. By March she had written about Kezia and the Samuel Josephs. By October, Mansfield had put the manuscript aside for the more immediate need to record her anguish over her brother's death. With hindsight, one sees a tragic prophecy when, as part of Leslie's training, 'he had been given instruction in the handling [. . .] of the delicate hand-grenade'.[28] One letter to his parents ominously documents the danger he was facing: 'These bombs are frightfully deadly and very tricky to handle.'[29]

Mansfield's grief in the aftermath of her loss inspires a dialogue that explores the nature of fate as she confronts mortality and the promises of the past. In her journal, she focuses on the emotion and imagery she had used in her meditations after the death of Rupert Brooke, once again juxtaposing images of nature with images of the fallen. She writes: 'From the old fruit-tree at the bottom of the garden [. . .] falls a little round pear, hard as a stone. Did you hear that, Katie? Can you find it?'[30] Here, nature, like the garden of Tarana in 'The Aloe', is within tentative borders and under the control of man. In the voice that Mansfield creates for Leslie to ask questions, she imagines a fruitful time when the two siblings would move 'their hands [. . .] over the thin moist grass' and collect 'the enormous number of pears [... that] used to be on that old tree'.[31]

While the speakers in the dialogue offer comfort to each other, the images of fruitful abundance are not without spoil. This is not an idealised, Arcadian vision but one that hints of decay; the plentiful fruit pelts the characters and 'the ants' soon get 'to them'.[32] This garden is disfigured; the fruit has mysterious teeth marks in it. Even an unforgettable 'pink garden seat' is tempered with the memory that 'it always wobbled a bit & there was [sic] usually the marks of a snail on it'.[33]

This is a garden in which death exists. In these visions, discerning who is speaking presents its own challenge because as one of the speakers states, 'We were almost like one child [. . .] looking at things together with the same eyes.' Leslie's voice is filtered through Mansfield's, too, though the dialogue imagines that Leslie shows the greater understanding of death as 'he puts his arm around her [and] suddenly kisses her', before he says goodbye three times.[34]

Mansfield's private writing articulates her torment as she continues to address Leslie: 'Awake awake! my little boy.'[35] The shock of Leslie's death is followed by Mansfield's admission that 'I am not afraid of death [. . .] I will come as quickly as I can to you.'[36] But despair does not have the finality of a thrice-spoken goodbye; she can really only promise what she can control: 'I will write for you.'[37] She slips into the first person plural when she speaks of her duty as a writer: to find inspiration from the 'lovely time when we were both alive'.[38]

The entry that follows reads like the beginning of a short story: 'The wind died down at sunset. Half a ring of moon hangs in the hollow air.'[39] While she is reminded of Leslie's absence and 'feeling the sun and the wind from the sea', her setting is one in which the sun has set and there is no visible sea. Instead she is drawn into a distant landscape where she first hears a lament and then focuses on visual images:

> I can hear a woman crooning a song. Perhaps she is crouched before the stove in the corridor, for it is the kind of song that a woman sings before a fire – brooding, warm, sleepy and safe. I see a little house with flower patches under the windows and the soft mass of a haystack at the back. The fowls have all gone to roost – they are wooly blurs on the perches. The pony is in the stable and with a cloth on. The dog lies in his kennel, his head on his forepaws. The cat sits up beside the woman, her tail tucked in and the man, still young and careless comes clinking up the dark road. Suddenly a spot of light shows in the window and in the pansy bed below & he walks quicker, whistling.
>
> But where are these comely people? These young strong people with hard healthy bodies and curling hair. They are not saints or philosophers. They are decent human beings – but where <u>are</u> they?[40]

The balance that Mansfield achieves in this diary entry hovers between a controlled landscape, flowerbeds and domesticated animals, and an accentuated presence of the missing. It expands upon her dream of Rupert Brooke, in which she focuses on the memory of sound and the presence of shadows: her backdrop there is empty, 'white square houses – quite hollow [. . .] with the windows gaping open'. She walks with an 'invisible, imaginary companion' and she writes of the game she plays: 'I like to walk and to talk with the dead who smile and are silent.'[41] By the time Mansfield has refashioned this mood in 'The Aloe', Linda speaks freely to her dead father and Beryl to her imaginary suitor. They are more connected to absent figures than to the present occupants of the new house. Instead of an empty house, Tarana is cluttered with insignificant possessions which reflect the characters' struggle with their hollow feelings.

Just as Linda and Beryl reveal most about themselves when they are outwardly silent, Mansfield privately calls upon someone who is not otherwise present in her entries about Chummie. With a Biblical invocation, she fashions an unusual prayer: 'Give me a hard heart, oh Lord, Lord harden thou my heart.'[42] The idea of a hardened heart draws attention to the power of God to do what Mansfield requires: she needs courage to enable her to follow through with her promise to write for Leslie. In December 1915, when she eventually recalls the *memento mori* '*Et in Arcadia Ego*',[43] the words anticipate her struggle in finding the proper medium to address the death of her brother. Her untapped memories of her homeland may offer experience to draw on, but she must simultaneously explore the tragic fate that existed even before Leslie was born.

Mansfield's struggle to find this balance is memorialised when she returns to 'The Aloe' in February 1916. Again in her diary she addresses Chummie:

> I found The Aloe this morning. [. . .] The Aloe is right. The Aloe is lovely. It simply fascinates me, and I know that it is what you would wish me to write. And now I know what the last chapter is. It is your birth – your coming in the autumn, you in Grandmothers [sic] arms under the tree, your solemnity, your wonderful beauty, your hands, your head, your helplessness – lying on the earth, & above all your tremendous solemnity. That chapter will end the book.[44]

This, however, is not how Mansfield ends the story; she had little patience for sentimentality. Instead 'The Aloe' is a tale of ominous foreboding, a tale of paternal *hubris*, and a tale of the foreshadowed tragedy of Linda's pregnancy. Leslie's ethereal presence is most clearly stated when Stanley Burnell looks to the empty chair at the head of the table and thinks 'That's where my boy ought to sit.' At the same moment Stanley thinks he is 'a perfect fool' to feel so 'happy' (81), and indeed he is the fool since he cannot intuit maternal fears. Linda's dread of another birth belies Stanley Burnell's Arcadian fantasy since Linda has been threatened by this pregnancy from the story's opening. When she talks with her mother about the rare occurrence of the blooming of the aloe near the new home, she articulates the uncertainties of fate to Mrs

Fairfield: 'You know as well as I do that my heart is seriously affected, and Doctor Dean has told you that I may die at any moment. I've had three great lumps of children already.'[45] The future is heavy with tragic possibility, and she admits that she hates Stanley: 'It had never been so plain to her as it was at this moment' (120) when the aloe is about to flower, an occurrence that one may experience only once in one's life. Linda, however, understands its significance in relationship to her pregnancy; both she and Doady Trout know that in giving birth they are defenceless against fate. In the case of Linda's child, this is the son who will be off to a war, the circumstances of which are both distant and unimaginable.

Fate collapses time in the same way that Mansfield does in the episodic structure of 'The Aloe'. The tragic ending is set. In the final lines Beryl rushes downstairs, and Kezia plays with her aunt's cream jar. She puts the lid on her toy cat's ear: the animal, like a soldier fallen in battle, topples 'backwards and bumped and bounced on the floor' (135). Even though readers are told the lid 'did not break', Kezia views the situation with an attitude akin to a modernist's resignation: 'For Kezia, it had broken the moment it flew through the air; and she picked it up, hot all over, put it on the dressing table and walked away, far too quickly and airily' (135). She accepts that this is a world that can only be seen as broken.

Mansfield's criticism of Virginia Woolf's *Night and Day*[46] indicates the seriousness with which she viewed her own writing and, in a letter to Murry, Mansfield is far more honest about Woolf's novel than in her published review:

> I don't like it [. . .] My private opinion is that it is a lie in the soul. The war never has been, that is what its message is. [. . .] [T]he novel cant [*sic*] just leave the war out. [. . .] [W]e have to take it into account and find new expressions new moulds for our new thoughts & feelings. [. . .] We have to face our war.[47]

This disparagement of Woolf would have little weight unless Mansfield had already assessed her own writing more clearly than Huxley eventually would. Her writing was not simply bloody ink on the page. Mansfield's suffering hardened her to create a new model in which children become the vehicle to explore fate in a broken world.

Notes

1. Aldous Huxley, *Those Barren Leaves* (London: Chatto & Windus, 1928), p. 82.
2. Katherine Mansfield, *The Aloe* (New York: Knopf, 1930). All references are to this edition and inserted in the body of the essay. Quotations were checked against Vincent O'Sullivan, ed., *The Aloe with Prelude* (Manchester: Carcanet, 1983). I have

cited multiple references to the same page after the first quotation in a paragraph. Katherine Mansfield, *Prelude* (Richmond: Hogarth Press, 1918).

3. Allyson Booth, *Postcards from the Trenches* (New York: Oxford University Press, 1996), p. 4.
4. Antony Alpers, *The Life of Katherine Mansfield* (New York: Viking, 1980), p. 175.
5. Vincent O'Sullivan and Margaret Scott, eds, *The Collected Letters of Katherine Mansfield*, 5 vols (Oxford: Clarendon Press, 1984–2008), Vol. 1, p. 167. Hereafter referred to as *Letters*, followed by volume and page number.
6. Booth, p. 31.
7. Katherine Mansfield, *In a German Pension* (London: Stephen Swift, 1911).
8. Booth, p. 71.
9. World War I Papers and Memorabilia Chiefly Regarding Thomas R. Pleucker, 1914–30, in the Joseph M. Bruccoli Great War Collection, Accession #10875-r, Special Collections Dep., University of Virginia Library, Charlottesville, VA.
10. Booth, p. 29.
11. Erich Maria Remarque, *All Quiet on the Western Front* (Boston: Little Brown, 1929), p. 210.
12. 'Sunlight Soap', *Great War Forum* (11 March 2013); http://1914–1918.invisionzone.com/forums/index.php?showtopic=192065 [accessed 13 August 2013] (post 10).
13. 'Sunlight Soap', *Great War Forum* (post 11).
14. Booth, p. 49.
15. Margaret Scott, ed., *The Katherine Mansfield Notebooks*, 2 vols (Minneapolis: University of Minnesota Press, 2002), Vol. 1, p. 17. Hereafter referred to as *Notebooks*, followed by volume and page number.
16. Alpers, p. 11.
17. Beatrice, Lady Glenavy [Beatrice Campbell], *Today We Will Only Gossip* (London: Constable, 1964), pp. 82–3.
18. Antony Alpers, ed., *The Stories of Katherine Mansfield* (Oxford: Oxford University Press, 1984), pp. 195–8. Hereafter referred to as *Stories* followed by page number.
19. *Stories*, p. 555.
20. *Stories*, p. 196.
21. *Stories*, p. 196.
22. *Stories*, p. 196.
23. *Stories*, p. 196.
24. Alpers, *The Life of Katherine Mansfield*, p. 180.
25. *Notebooks* 2, p. 13.
26. Glenavy, p. 82.
27. Alpers, p. 175.
28. Alpers, p. 181.
29. Quoted in Alpers, p. 181.
30. *Notebooks* 2, p. 14.
31. *Notebooks* 2, p. 14.
32. *Notebooks* 2, p. 14.
33. *Notebooks* 2, p. 15.
34. *Notebooks* 2, p. 15.
35. *Notebooks* 2, p. 15.
36. *Notebooks* 2, p. 15.
37. *Notebooks* 2, p. 16.
38. *Notebooks* 2, p. 16.

39. *Notebooks* 2, p. 16.
40. *Notebooks* 2, p. 16.
41. *Notebooks* 2, p. 13.
42. *Notebooks* 2, p. 17.
43. *Notebooks* 2, p. 17.
44. *Notebooks* 2, p. 60.
45. Rather than Murry's transcription of 'Doctor Dear', I've substituted 'Doctor Dean' from O'Sullivan, p. 141.
46. Katherine Mansfield, 'A Ship Comes Into the Harbour', in John Middleton Murry, ed., *Novels and Novelists* (London: Constable, 1930), pp. 107–11.
47. *Letters* 3, p. 82.

Mythology and/of the Great War in Katherine Mansfield's 'The Daughters of the Late Colonel'

Erika Baldt

In Katherine Mansfield's 1922 story 'The Fly', a father, mourning the loss of his son in the Great War six years earlier, tortures a fly until it dies, because he 'wasn't feeling as he wanted to feel'.[1] The story bears similarities to Shakespeare's *Titus Andronicus*, in which the eponymous general, after the murder of his sons and the rape of his daughter, enacts similar revenge on a harmless insect, because 'Grief has so wrought on him / He takes false shadows for true substances.'[2] Shakespeare's tale of a Roman general facing the consequences of his wartime choices is paralleled in Mansfield's story, which Claire Buck argues is a representation of 'the national task of mourning' in which 'the apparent simplicity of grief is refused'.[3] Indeed, the father in Mansfield's story, known as 'the Boss' throughout the text, challenges the reader's efforts to sympathise with the character, as his 'grinding feeling of wretchedness' (361) is in part a function of the pride and control that tempers his ability to express emotion even when 'He wanted, he intended, he had arranged to weep . . .' (359).

Reading Mansfield's story with the allusion to Shakespeare's play, which is itself based on Greek and Roman antecedents, suggests that a correlation can be found between the Great War and both classical and contemporary mythology. Even if, according to Vincent Sherry, a common interpretation is that the Great War 'stands as a watershed episode: it draws a line through time, dividing the nineteenth from the twentieth centuries', I would argue that for Mansfield this line through time serves not solely to separate but also to connect.[4] It is a means for drawing parallels between women's experiences of conflict through the ages to the contemporary moment in which daughters, as well as sons, succumb to the Great War's destruction.

The idea that the First World War is a great divide, separating present from past, old from new, ancient from modern is not entirely accurate. For though, in many ways, as Susan Kingsley Kent notes, the war 'defied traditional terms and habits of thought',[5] it also marked a continuation of the developments that had been building for decades, 'a kind of imaginative continuity', as Trudi Tate puts it.[6] In fact, Gertrude Stein claims that the changes wrought by war are always already in place by the time the fighting begins:

> The spirit of everybody is changed, of a whole people is changed, but mostly nobody knows it and a war forces them to recognise it because during a war the appearance of everything changes very much quicker, but really the entire change has been accomplished and the war is only something which forces everybody to recognise it.[7]

That 'line through time', then, is not as direct as popular consciousness would suggest.

Discrepancies like these, revolving around the conflicting interpretations of shared experience, have led some critics to regard the resulting discourse as the mythology of the First World War. Samuel Hynes in *A War Imagined* argues, for instance, that 'this sense of radical discontinuity of present from past is an essential element in what eventually took form as the Myth of the War'.[8] It was not the only one, however. A dichotomy was created between those who fought and those who did not. For Hynes, the line is drawn between youth and age ('the old betray the young'),[9] while for Claire Buck the divide separates soldiers from the women they fought to protect: 'Not only was it presumed that the soldiers' first-hand experience of the horrors of trench warfare protected them from the naïve jingoism of the civilian, but women all too soon came to represent the culpable war enthusiasm of the home front.'[10] In this mythology, the 'line' becomes further blurred between victim and aggressor, protector and protected. As Hynes notes, 'The Myth is not the War entire: it is a tale that confirms a set of attitudes, an idea of what the war was and what it meant.'[11] In essence, the war's importance was based on a confirmation of beliefs derived from fact but that soon, like Athena springing fully formed from Zeus's head, took on a life of their own.

According to Claire Tylee, however, 'one matter has remained unchanged since the time of the Ancient Greeks: the access of women to the crucial sphere of culturally significant experience'.[12] Tylee's link to the Ancient Greeks provides another distinct layer to the mythology of the First World War: its conscious association with Greek and Roman mythology as a means of both propaganda and subversion. Tylee argues that 'the mythical conceptualization of soldiers and warfare which implied a passive, bystander role for women, dominated the popular consciousness'; she cites Frederic Leighton's painting *Perseus and Andromeda* as 'a variation of the theme of St. George and the Dragon' that was itself a metaphor for England's role in the Great War, as well as May Cannan's description of her own war experience as 'The Iliad'.[13]

At the same time that ancient mythology was being used to support and justify the war effort, it was also being used to undermine it, as in T. S. Eliot's 'Sweeney among the Nightingales'[14] and Ezra Pound's 'Homage to Sextus Propertius',[15] in which Pound 'translated' a Roman poet's verses. According to Sherry,

> In his *Elegiae*, Propertius presents himself as a poet desiring to write of love when conventional expectation pressures him to proclaim a martial-minded verse. A poet of this moment is supposed to celebrate the imperial aims and military campaigns of the Augustan dynasty. [. . .] Propertius provides Pound a model for echoing the times against the times. This is a pattern the modern poet adapts to the syntax and vocabulary of his own political present.[16]

Using ancient texts to filter and reflect on the Great War was a common occurrence,[17] and it is a strategy, I would argue, employed by Mansfield in her 1921 story 'The Daughters of the Late Colonel'.[18]

While the Boss in 'The Fly' and Titus Andronicus mourn for their sons and themselves, women's experience of conflict, as Tylee suggests, has historically been marginalised. As the Boss dismissively claims, 'we know a bit more than the ladies' (358). Yet the female voices that are absent in 'The Fly' are explored in 'The Daughters of the Late Colonel' through similar connections with *Titus Andronicus* and the older myths on which it is based. Although Josephine and Constantia's experiences in Mansfield's story seem worlds apart from those of the young men whose time at the front left them psychologically scarred, the suffering induced by the demands of their military father makes it possible to read their situation in similar terms. Or, as Trudi Tate puts it, 'Civilians exposed to violence and terror, whether public and shared [. . .] or individual and private [. . .] can suffer from serious traumatic symptoms. Direct experience of pain, loss of autonomy, and fear of mutilation or death can produce mental disturbance'.[19] Josephine and Constantia experience a 'loss of autonomy' at the hands of a more powerful military official in a way that mirrors both the contemporary and the classical mythology of the Great War.

Antony Alpers claimed in a letter to T. O. Beachcroft that Mansfield 'had absolutely no Classics in her education'; yet there is plenty of evidence that she was familiar with classical mythology.[20] For instance, she would have been acquainted with the interpretations of the Trojan War through Shakespeare and Chaucer[21] and, knowing both James Joyce's *Ulysses*[22] and T. S. Eliot's poetry,[23] Mansfield was more than aware of contemporary re-imaginings of classical texts. We know she had read Theocritus and even, as Beachcroft notes, adapted his XVth Idyll as a contemporary sketch of the coronation of George V for *The New Age.* 'The Festival of the Coronation (With apologies to Theocritus)' is a comic skit describing the attempt of two women to catch a glimpse of the coronation procession.[24] Quickly tiring of the effort, however, they return home, with one of the pair concluding, 'It seems to me that on occasions like this the best thing to do is to remain quietly in the house and wait for the evening papers.'[25] Before Pound's 'Homage to Sextus Propertius', Mansfield turns to an ancient model to undermine the values of the current moment. It is possible, then, to read 'The Daughters of the Late Colonel' (a story that does not directly reference the Great War) as a contribution to, and reinterpretation of, the 'idea[s] of what the war was and what it meant'.[26] In this interpretation, Constantia and Josephine are faced with their own 'line through time' drawn by their father's death, and, I would argue, this event 'unfolds and opens', as Mansfield described the story's construction, to speak to the myth of the war itself.[27]

Mythological Intertextuality

Before addressing specific myths of the Great War, it is important to identify the ancient tales that can help illuminate some of the themes in 'The Daughters of the Late Colonel'. Along with *Titus Andronicus*, two additional texts are interwoven around the symbol of the nightingale, which, I suggest, is a central motif in Mansfield's story. Josephine, the elder daughter, is called throughout the story by the nickname 'Jug', which, Alpers claims, was a pet name for Mansfield's cousin, Sylvia Payne, on whom the character was thought to be based.[28] However, the term itself is loaded with association. According to the *Oxford English Dictionary*, one of the definitions of 'jug' is 'an imitative representation of one of the notes of the nightingale, and some other birds, usually repeated as jug, jug'.[29] This link is made more explicit at the end of Mansfield's story when Josephine attempts to understand the full significance of her father's absence:

> Some little sparrows, young sparrows they sounded, chirped on the window-ledge. *Yeep – eyeep – yeep.* But Josephine felt they were not sparrows,

> not on the window-ledge. It was inside her, that queer little crying noise. *Yeep – eyeep – yeep*. Ah, what was it crying, so weak and forlorn? (247–8)

Here, Josephine identifies herself with the birds, while her own 'forlorn' cry connects the story to the myth of Philomela and Procne, two sisters of Ancient Greece who are transformed into a nightingale and a swallow after wreaking a horrific revenge on Procne's husband, Tereus, for his rape and mutilation of Philomela. The two women kill the couple's son, Itys, and serve his flesh to the unsuspecting Tereus, and these devastating events account for the nightingale's mournful song, and connect the tale to Aeschylus' *Agamemnon*.[30] The eponymous Greek king returns from the Trojan War after more than a decade, haunted by memories of cannibalism amongst his ancestors, and by Agamemnon's own sacrifice of his daughter, Iphigenia, for success in battle. Agamemnon is accompanied by the Trojan princess, Cassandra, herself likened to Philomela: 'you wail in a wild tune, like some brown nightingale, that with singing never sated laments, alas, heart-sore, for Itys, Itys all her sorrow-filled days' (42). Both of these stories became source material for *Titus Andronicus*, in which Lavinia, Titus' daughter, is violated in a manner that intentionally imitates Tereus' abuse of Philomela. The treatment of women in these myths – specifically daughters of military figures – finds echoes in 'The Daughters of the Late Colonel' as Mansfield weaves these classical tales into her depiction of Josephine and Constantia's experiences with their own military father in a way that reflects the contemporary mythology of the Great War.

Myth: Women are Not Combatants

The original title of 'The Daughters of the Late Colonel' was 'The Non-Compounders', a reference, as Gerardo Rodríguez-Salas notes, to students at Mansfield's boarding school 'who attended classes but were not officially registered, which suits the two protagonists [Josephine and Constantia], at the same time members and marginal figures in the patriarchal social system'.[31] The phrase, 'Non-Compounders', suggests a lack of belonging, of being outside of the action. It also echoes the term non-combatants, those who do not engage in conflict. Whether it was the Trojan War or the Great War, women were expected to submit to the will of others, not to attack. For example, Aeschylus' Cassandra foretells her own and Agamemnon's death at the hands of his wife, Clytemnestra, and though she longs for a miraculous transformation like 'the fate of the musical nightingale', she accepts that she 'must be parted by the steel's sharp edge' instead of fighting or fleeing for her life (42). This female passivity was encouraged even into the twentieth century. For instance, according to Tylee, the Great War 'emphasized an essential difference between men and women. Women were not combatants.'[32] While the title of Mansfield's story was eventually changed, the feeling that Constantia and Josephine are non-combatants is strong throughout it. Their lives, according to Josephine, have been determined by 'looking after father, and at the same time keeping out of father's way' (248), while their days are punctuated by the 'thump' of his stick or 'that loud, strange bellow when father thought they were not hurrying enough' (246). Instead of protesting, they develop strategies that allow them to divorce themselves from the reality of their situation.

Josephine, for example, is prone to fits of giggles at inopportune moments, a reaction, according to David Trotter, to the Colonel's control. Trotter argues that the sisters 'cannot throw off the shadow of the most powerful feeling either of them has ever known: the fits of giggling which once sustained them, when they were much younger, against their father's tyranny, and which now recur with a vengeance'.[33] Josephine's response to the Colonel's 'tyranny' is to expel her feelings in a nervous outburst, while Constantia's is to turn inwards. She recalls a time when she would lie 'on the floor with her arms outstretched, as though she was crucified' (248), a form of meditation that provides an escape from 'this other life, running out, bringing things home in bags, getting things on approval, discussing them with Jug, and taking them back to get more things on approval, and arranging father's trays and trying not to annoy father' (248). The behaviour of both women suggests a resistance to their father's excessive demands, but rather than contradict his unfair expectations, or even attempt to engage with him in any meaningful way, the sisters choose the route of acquiescence, of 'trying not to annoy father'.

At the same time, it is not that the two women are fragile, however. An actual breakdown is rare, as when Josephine cannot bring herself to go through her father's personal possessions after his funeral. Constantia, in particular, embraces the change:

> 'But why not be weak for once, Jug?' argued Constantia, whispering quite fiercely. 'If it is weak.' And her pale stare flew from the locked writing-table – so safe – to the huge glittering wardrobe, and she began to breathe in a queer, panting way. 'Why shouldn't we be weak for once in our lives, Jug? It's quite excusable. Let's be weak – be weak, Jug. It's much nicer to be weak than to be strong.' (238)

Though an observer may not consider their seemingly comfortable middle-class existence to be one of hardship, Constantia's claim that this weakness is occurring only 'once in [their] lives' suggests that dealing with their father's demands has required a steely resolve. And, in fact, here Mansfield seems to be ironically exploring one of the myths Tylee mentions: namely, that 'the war re-asserted gender distinctions that women had been contesting: women were frail and had to be defended by strong protectors, who were prepared to kill or die on their behalf'.[34] Clearly, Constantia's insistence on giving in to weakness echoes the Great War's propaganda that women were incapable of protecting themselves, while simultaneously highlighting that the experience of non-combatants was marked by dangers largely unrecognised by society.

Myth: The Old Betray the Young

Constantia and Josephine's years with the Colonel set them apart from others. The experience of the trauma that emerges from the paternal demands placed on them is arguably akin to that of the Great War's 'lost generation'.[35] This is a term first coined by Gertrude Stein, but also powerfully described in Erich Maria Remarque's *All Quiet on the Western Front*, in which the narrator, Paul Baumer, describes the limbo experienced by those thrust into the war:

> the generation that grew up before us, though it has passed these years with us here, already had a home and a calling; now it will return to its old occupations, [. . .] the war will be forgotten – and the generation that has grown up after us will be strange [. . .] and push us aside. We will be superfluous even to ourselves, we will grow older, a few will adapt themselves, [. . .] others will merely submit, and most will be bewildered; – the years will pass [. . .] and in the end we shall fall into ruin.[36]

Although Baumer is here referring to himself and his comrades who fought in the trenches, the adjectives 'superfluous' and 'bewildered' are just as appropriate as descriptions of Constantia and Josephine. Moreover, the idea that the men and women of this generation have been treated unfairly connects to one of the strongest beliefs to contribute to the Myth of the War. Indeed, as Hynes argues, a key idea of this Myth is that 'the old betray the young'.[37] He describes the culprits as '*The Old Men* [. . .] all those conservative elders who were established in their professions before the war, and who saw the war as a continuation of their pre-war values'.[38] Their victims were boys like Mansfield's own brother, Chummie, whose death inspired John Middleton Murry to describe him as being 'sans peur & sans reproche [sic]'.[39] The betrayal was not, however, limited to one gender. As we have seen, in Mansfield's story women are also broken by a similar representative of 'the old men'.

Constantia and Josephine's fraught relationship with their father colours their interactions with others. They have no true peers, only servants or relatives. Any interpersonal contact ranges between the patently 'awkward' (like their brief meeting with the vicar, Mr Farolles [234]) and the stressful. Awkwardness, in particular, turns swiftly to anxiety, especially with those (like their father's caregiver and housekeeper, Nurse Andrews) who maintains the Colonel's rigid authority. Although they invite Nurse Andrews to stay on as a guest for a week after their father's death, her presence only adds to the strain: 'it was a bother. It meant they had to have regular sit-down meals at the proper times' (232). Continuing to adhere to a fixed schedule in this way perpetuates the routine imposed by their father. In addition, Nurse Andrews becomes an extension of Colonel Pinner: 'her eyes wandered, spying at everything behind her eye-glasses' (233). Similarly, the sisters fear further observation when discussing their housekeeper, Kate: 'it was always to the drawing-room they retired when they wanted to talk over Kate' (244). Described as an 'enchanted princess' (233), Kate is nevertheless the young manager of the Colonel's home, and she is firmly associated with Constantia's and Josephine's father, and with the fear he has previously induced. Like the other members of the 'lost generation' described in *All Quiet on the Western Front*, Josephine and Constantia continue to submit to those more powerful than themselves, and their employees simply return to their 'old occupations' as if nothing has changed.

At the same time, however, the sisters, like Baumer and his comrades, cannot relate to 'the generation that has grown up after [them]'. Though both dote on their nephew, Cyril, whose visits are so infrequent he poses no real threat to their domestic equilibrium, their communication is stilted and unsatisfying:

> 'Is your dear father still so fond of meringues?' Asked Auntie Con gently. She winced faintly as she broke through the shell of hers.
>
> Well, I don't quite know, Auntie Con,' said Cyril breezily.
>
> At that they both looked up.
>
> 'Don't know?' almost snapped Josephine. 'Don't know a thing like that about your own father, Cyril?' (241)

Though seemingly inconsequential (neither Cyril nor Colonel Pinner can understand the women's sudden interest in the subject [243]), the meringues symbolise the contrast, not between the old and the young, but between presence and absence. Colonel Pinner and Cyril have each made a place in the world, the Colonel in the military and Cyril in business, and there is no room for such triviality in their lives. Constantia and Josephine, on the other hand, and even their brother Benny, Cyril's father (who is spending his later years 'on the verandah' in Ceylon [240]), have retreated from the world, and their interests are confined to their own limited domestic sphere. The sisters either focus on seemingly superficial matters, like the meringues, or fail to communicate complete thoughts, an indication, according to Janka Kaščáková, 'that a great part of the sisters' lives is not worth talking about'.[40] Constantia and Josephine can thus be seen to represent 'an emptiness *between* generations', as Hynes describes the war generation.[41]

This 'emptiness' is reflected in more than one sense in the sisters' lives. The Colonel's oppressive demands have deprived Constantia and Josephine of more than the ability to hold a meaningful conversation; he has also deprived them of a voice. 'Silence' and 'Silence again' (231) characterise the women's existence, to the point that they are not merely unheard but almost invisible. After the Colonel's death, Josephine declares 'nobody sees us' (230); it is as if the women themselves are casualties of war. The depth of their suffering becomes even clearer when placed alongside the myths previously mentioned. In classical texts, for instance, daughters have been expendable resources to the war effort. They have also been the recipients of a great deal of collateral damage. The basis for the murder plot that Cassandra foretells in *Agamemnon* is, for example, the sacrifice of the King's daughter, Iphigenia, deemed a necessity to secure strong winds for the sails of his warships (22). She, like Josephine and Constantia, cannot protest, but 'smote each one of the sacrificers with glance of eye that sought their pity, and seemed like as in a painting, fain to speak' (22). In *Titus Andronicus*, the general's daughter, Lavinia, is raped. She has her tongue removed, and her hands are cut off so she cannot reveal her attackers. Lavinia's uncle, Marcus, describes her plight:

> Sorrow concealèd, like an oven stopped,
> Doth burn the heart to cinders where it is.
> Fair Philomel, why she but lost her tongue
> And in a tedious sampler sewed her mind.
> But, lovely niece, that mean is cut from thee.
> A craftier Tereus, cousin, hast thou met. (II. 4. 36–41)

Whereas the mythological Philomel used her hands to reveal Tereus' attack by weaving the details into a tapestry, Lavinia has no such means at her disposal. Not only does the reference to Philomel, the nightingale, connect Lavinia to Josephine, but her 'sorrow concealèd' bears similarities to the Colonel's daughters. Even if, for example, there is no evidence that Josephine and Constantia suffered physical abuse at the hands of their father, they have been betrayed by the Colonel's lifelong insistence that his needs be placed above their own. His demands for conformity have robbed the sisters of the emotional and practical tools for independence. Like Lavinia and Iphigenia, they have no means of articulating their distress so that Mansfield's story ends with both women slipping into silence and inaction:

> Constantia said faintly, 'I can't say what I was going to say, Jug, because I've forgotten what it was . . . that I was going to say.'
> Josephine was silent for a moment. She stared at a big cloud where the sun had been. Then she replied shortly, 'I've forgotten too.' (249)

The final message is that, instead of taking advantage of their new-found freedom, the sisters have little option but to retreat further from the world. As Mansfield explained in a letter to William Gerhardi,

> All was meant, of course, to lead up to that last paragraph, when my two flowerless ones turned with that timid gesture, to the sun. 'Perhaps *now.*' And after that, it seemed to me, they died as truly as Father was dead.[42]

Much like the soldiers in *All Quiet on the Western Front* who, because of decisions made by their elders, 'sit as if in [their] graves waiting only to be closed in', Josephine and Constantia wait for a change that will never come, and Mansfield condemns the daughters of the late Colonel to a living death that is a reflection of the fates of so many young people whose futures were destroyed by the 'old men' that sent them to the Great War.[43]

Myth: Women are Culpable

The last 'Myth of the War' to which 'The Daughters of the Late Colonel' speaks is that noted by Claire Buck: 'women all too soon came to represent the culpable war enthusiasm of the home front'.[44] Either as frail beings in need of defending or as enthusiastic promoters of the war effort, Buck argues that women came to be seen as responsible for the tragedies of battle. T. S. Eliot's 1920 poem, 'Sweeney Among the Nightingales', contributes to this myth. The speaker describes two women who are 'suspect, thought to be in league' against the unwary Sweeney, the poem's ostensible protagonist (60). According to Vincent Sherry, 'Sweeney is the soldier, returned to London from the Front', with '[t]he "zebra stripes along his jaw" reflect[ing] the creases cut into his neck by the stiff collar of the dress uniform worn by military personnel in the Great War'.[45] The treacherous environment in which Sweeney now finds himself, however, is more like Ancient Greece than contemporary London, as Eliot, like many of his contemporaries, refers back to classical texts to make sense of the impact of the Great War. For instance, the poem's epigraph and final stanza reference Aeschylus' *Agamemnon*:

> The nightingales are singing near
> The Convent of the Sacred Heart,
> And sang within the bloody wood
> When Agamemnon cried aloud
> And let their liquid siftings fall
> To stain the stiff dishonoured shroud. (60)

The link to Agamemnon suggests that Sweeney, though he may have come through the war physically unscathed, cannot escape the women (Cassandra, Clytemnestra) whose perfidy has been threatening men since ancient times. And, as Sherry notes, the French word for nightingale is also slang for prostitute,[46] so that the sense of shame that often accompanies encounters like those between 'Apeneck Sweeney' and the 'person' (whose gender is not revealed until several lines later) who 'tries to sit on Sweeney's knees' (59) is evident in the poem. There are echoes, too, of *Titus Andronicus* in that Lavinia, once violated, becomes her father's disgrace, and Titus is considered justified in killing her for the indignity she brought to his life and reputation (V. 3. 35–57). The nightingales here, and similarly in Mansfield's text, are harbingers of shame, their mere presence enough to 'dishonour' a noble soldier.

Indeed, in Mansfield's story, though it is clear that neither Constantia nor Josephine has ever brought attention to herself, the idea that their behaviour could still dishonour their father is foremost in their minds. The women speculate that their father's death and burial are somehow their fault, and we are told that in his last moments their father:

> lay there, purple, a dark, angry purple in the face, and never even looked at them when they came in. Then, as they were standing there, wondering what to do, he had suddenly opened one eye. Oh, what a difference it would have made, what a difference to their memory of him, how much easier to tell people about it, if he had only opened both! But no – one eye only. It glared at them a moment and then . . . went out. (234)

Here, Mansfield not only suggests a terrifying mythological Cyclops in focusing on Colonel Pinner's single eye, but also echoes the sentiment of Marcus in *Titus Andronicus* that the sight of the violated and mutilated Lavinia will 'blind a father's eye' (II. 4. 53). The sisters interpret the Colonel's 'angry' colouring and one-eyed glare as evidence of a fault in themselves, and the resulting shame is clear from their unwillingness 'to tell people about it' and from their conviction that 'the eye wasn't at all [. . .] peaceful' (234). The guilt only mounts after the women bury their father:

> Josephine had had a moment of absolute terror at the cemetery, while the coffin was lowered, to think that she and Constantia had done this thing without asking his permission. What would father say when he found out? For he was bound to find out sooner or later. He always did. 'Buried. You two girls had me *buried*!' [. . .] The other people seemed to treat it all as a matter of course. They were strangers; they couldn't be expected to understand that father was the very last person for such a thing to happen to. No, the entire blame for it all would fall on her and Constantia. (235–6)

While it seems Josephine's 'terror' is unfounded and the daughters cannot possibly be blamed for attending to their father's last rites, her emotions correspond to the idea that women in wartime often become scapegoats, taking 'the entire blame' for events far beyond their control.

Conclusion

It is unclear whether Mansfield was consciously reinterpreting classical myths in order to understand the myths of the Great War as they emerged before, during, and after the conflict. None the less, the resonance that arises from an intertextual acknowledgement of these myths in 'The Daughters of the Late Colonel' sheds light on the issues with which British society has grappled even after the Armistice, while Mansfield's story reflects the universal grief and mourning that accompany all wars. While it may have been true that women were not combatants, they were profoundly affected by the hostilities. Indeed, many suffered the same betrayal by their elders as those men considered the 'lost generation'. Mansfield's story suggests that though many laid the blame for the hardships of war at women's feet, such an idea is as absurd as burying a dead man without his permission. Mansfield's intention was not to inspire social change with this story, however. As Alpers suggests, 'Kass Beauchamp was never an incipient feminist [. . .] and of all her numerous *dame seule* stories and fragments, not one would have bestirred an Edwardian reader to "sit down and write a cheque"' in support of women's causes.[47] Instead, Mansfield's aim was to record that suffering is suffering, whether in the past or in the present. Writing in her journal in 1922 about *Cosmic Anatomy*, a study of theosophy in which she became immersed towards at the end of her life, Mansfield situates 'The Daughters of the Late Colonel' in a wider context:

> To get even a glimpse of the relation of things, to follow that relation & find it remains true through the ages enlarges my little mind as nothing else does. [. . .] its [sic] that reactions to certain causes & effects always have been the same. It wasn't for nothing Constantia chose the moon & water.[48]

For Mansfield, there is comfort in knowing that while times have inevitably changed throughout history, emotions or 'reactions' to events have not. Simple objects are evidence of deeper beliefs that link the universe together, and her story is part of that grander scheme. So while Mansfield claimed in a letter to Murry on 16 November 1919 that 'I cant [*sic*] imagine how after the war these men can pick up the old threads as tho' it never had been',[49] her work nevertheless suggests that an interest in a collective impulse 'through the ages' can exist simultaneously with the transformation she expects from fiction after the Great War. Binding the 'old threads' of mythology to the Great War's 'line through time', Mansfield's story weaves past and present into a timeless continuity.

Notes

1. Katherine Mansfield, 'The Fly', in Angela Smith, ed., *Selected Stories* (Oxford: Oxford University Press, 2002), p. 360. Further references will be placed parenthetically in the text.
2. William Shakespeare, *Titus Andronicus*, in Stephen Greenblatt *et al.*, eds, *The Norton Shakespeare*, 2nd edn (New York: Norton, 2008), III. 2. 78–9. Further references will be placed parenthetically in the text.
3. Claire Buck, 'British Women's Writing of the Great War', in Vincent Sherry, ed., *The Cambridge Companion to the Literature of the First World War* (Cambridge: Cambridge University Press, 2005), pp. 85–112 (p. 105).
4. Vincent Sherry, 'The Great War and Literary Modernism in England', in Vincent Sherry, ed., *The Cambridge Companion to the Literature of the First World War* (Cambridge: Cambridge University Press, 2005), pp. 113–37 (p. 113).
5. Susan Kingsley Kent, *Gender and Power in Britain, 1640–1990* (London: Routledge, 1999), p. 280.
6. Trudi Tate, *Modernism, History and the First World War* (Manchester: Manchester University Press, 1998), p. 4.
7. Gertrude Stein, *Picasso* (New York: Dover, 1984), p. 30.
8. Samuel Hynes, *A War Imagined: The First World War and English Culture* (New York: Athenaeum, 1991), p. xi.
9. Hynes, p. xii.
10. Buck, p. 87.
11. Hynes, p. xi.
12. Claire M. Tylee, *The Great War and Women's Consciousness: Images of Militarism and Womanhood in Women's Writings, 1914–64* (Iowa City: University of Iowa Press, 1990), p. 8.

13. Tylee, pp. 71, 72, 82.
14. T. S. Eliot, 'Sweeney Among the Nightingales', in *Collected Poems: 1909–1962* (London: Faber & Faber, 1963), pp. 59–60. Further references to the poem will be placed parenthetically in the text.
15. Ezra Pound, 'Homage to Sextus Propertius', in *Poems 1918–1921* (New York: Boni & Liveright, 1921), pp. 11–34 (archive.org [accessed 10 November 2013]).
16. Sherry, p. 120.
17. See also Tylee's discussion of H. D.'s *Bid Me to Live: A Madrigal* (1960), pp. 231–44, and Rowena Fowler's exploration of Virginia Woolf's interest in Greece and its mythology in 'Moments and Metamorphoses: Virginia Woolf's Greece', *Comparative Literature*, 51.3 (Summer 1999), pp. 217–42.
18. Katherine Mansfield, 'The Daughters of the Late Colonel', in Angela Smith, ed., *Selected Stories* (Oxford: Oxford University Press, 2002), pp. 230–49. Further references to the story will be placed parenthetically in the text.
19. Tate, p. 15.
20. T. O. Beachcroft, 'Katherine Mansfield's Encounter with Theocritus', *English, 23.115* (Spring 1974), pp. 13–19 (p. 15) (english.oxfordjournals.org [accessed 16 July 2013]).
21. See Mansfield's journal entry of 4 February 1916 on Shakespeare's *Troilus and Cressida* in Margaret Scott, ed., *The Katherine Mansfield Notebooks*, 2 vols (Minneapolis: University of Minnesota Press, 2002), Vol. 1, p. 296 (hereafter referred to as *Notebooks*, followed by volume and page number), and her letter of 21 May 1921 to John Middleton Murry about Chaucer's 'Troilus & Cressida [sic]' in Vincent O'Sullivan and Margaret Scott, eds, *The Collected Letters of Katherine Mansfield*, 5 vols (Oxford: Clarendon Press, 1984–2008), Vol. 4, p. 233. Hereafter referred to as *Letters* followed by volume and page number.
22. James Joyce, *Ulysses*, ed. Hans Walter Gabler (New York: Vintage, 1986).
23. For a comparison of Mansfield with both Eliot and Joyce, see Sydney Janet Kaplan, '"A Gigantic Mother": Katherine Mansfield's London', in Susan Merrill Squier, ed., *Women Writers and the City* (Knoxville: University of Tennessee Press, 1984), pp. 161–75.
24. Beachcroft, p. 15.
25. Katherine Mansfield, 'The Festival of the Coronation (With apologies to Theocritus)', *New Age*, 29 June 1911, p. 196.
26. Hynes, p. xi.
27. Letter to Richard Murry, 1 January 1921, in *Letters* 4, p. 156.
28. See Antony Alpers, *The Life of Katherine Mansfield* (Oxford: Oxford University Press, 1980), p. 29; and also Ida Baker, *Katherine Mansfield: The Memories of LM* (London: Virago, 1985), p. 153, in which the author refers to 'The Daughters of the Late Colonel' as 'that gentle caricature of her cousin Sylvia Payne and me'.
29. 'Jug'. *Oxford English Dictionary* (www.oed.com.ez-srv.bcc.edu:2048/view/Entry/101931?isAdvanced=false&result=3&rskey=iA2oQ4& [accessed 5 August 2013]).
30. Aeschylus, *Agamemnon*, trans. A. W. Verrall, in Moses Hadas, ed., *Greek Drama* (New York: Bantam, 1965), pp. 17–55. Further references will be parenthetical.
31. Gerardo Rodríguez-Salas, '"The Daughters of the Late Colonel": Feminine Temporality in Katherine Mansfield's Short Fiction', in Gema Soledad Castillo García *et al.*, *The Short Story in English: Crossing Boundaries* (Alcalá de Henares: Servicio de Publicaciones de la Universidad de Alcalá, 2006), pp. 786–98 (pp. 790–1) (www.academia.edu/3353912/_The_Daughters_of_the_Late_Colonel_

Feminine_Temporality_in_Katherine_Mansfields_Short_Fiction [accessed 23 July 2013]).
32. Tylee, p. 253.
33. David Trotter, 'Modernism Reloaded: The Fiction of Katherine Mansfield', *Affirmations: of the Modern*, 1.1 (2013), pp. 21–43 (p. 41) (http://affirmations.arts.unsw.edu.au [accessed 1 August 2013]).
34. Tylee, p. 254.
35. See Ernest Hemingway, *A Moveable Feast* (New York: Simon & Schuster, 1996), p. 29: '"That's what you are. That's what you all are," Miss [Gertrude] Stein said. "All of you young people who served in the war. You are a lost generation."'
36. Erich Maria Remarque, *All Quiet on the Western Front*, trans. A. W. Wheen (Boston: Little, Brown, 1929), p. 290.
37. Hynes, p. xii.
38. Hynes, p. 384. Italics original.
39. Letter from John Middleton Murry to Katherine Mansfield, 19 January 1920, in C. A. Hankin, ed., *The Letters of John Middleton Murry to Katherine Mansfield* (New York: Franklin Watts, 1983), p. 254.
40. Janka Kaščáková, 'Speaking Silence in "The Daughters of the Late Colonel"', *Anachronist*, 15 (2010), pp. 93–103 (p. 99) in *Literary Reference Center* [accessed 23 July 2013].
41. Hynes, p. 385.
42. Letter to William Gerhardi, 23 June 1921, in *Letters* 4, p. 249.
43. Remarque, p. 109.
44. Buck, p. 87.
45. Sherry, p. 124.
46. Sherry, p. 125.
47. Alpers, p. 328.
48. *Notebooks* 2, p. 313.
49. *Letters* 3, p. 97.

CREATIVE WRITING

POETRY

Miss Mansfield selects a word

Her words grew in a garden
choked with commonplace implications.
But she picked up on colour, strength and clarity.

Words thought to be too ordinary
or useless disclosed how intricately
their stems were bound in an undergrowth of meaning.

In the end each word was selected
to take its chance in new-found situations.
It had adopted native company and simply had to get on

with its own erratic reckonings.
If the word wilted and packed it in
somehow fresh growth always struck out once again.

KEVIN IRELAND

Fosterage

For Michael McLaverty

'Description is revelation!' Royal
Avenue, Belfast, 1962,
A Saturday afternoon, glad to meet
Me, newly cubbed in language, he gripped
My elbow. 'Listen. Go your own way.
Do your own work. Remember
Katherine Mansfield – *I will tell*
How the laundry basket squeaked . . . that note of exile.'
But to hell with overstating it:
'Don't have the veins bulging in your Biro.'
And then, 'Poor Hopkins!' I have the *Journals*
He gave me, underlined, his buckled self
Obeisant to their pain. He discerned
The lineaments of patience everywhere
And fostered me and sent me out, with words
Imposing on my tongue like obols.

SEAMUS HEANEY

Seamus Heaney and Katherine Mansfield

The death of Seamus Heaney on 30 August 2013 left thousands of his readers with a sense of personal loss. Although his poetry is deeply rooted in the history and culture of Ireland, it appeals to people all over the world; whether it is about his childhood or the time of the Troubles in Northern Ireland, it says important things about our common human experience. One of his early poems, which sheds some light on Heaney's writing philosophy, may be of special interest to Mansfield scholars. It is 'Fosterage', part 5 of the longer poem 'Singing School', from the 1975 volume *North.*[1] In *North,* Heaney found a way of speaking about the conflict in Northern Ireland and defined his artistic method using the words of Wallace Stevens: 'Description is revelation.' Description, Jerzy Jarniewicz observes, has become Heaney's 'trademark' – in description his words materialise and become 'a source of sensuous experience'.[2] The name and the words of Katherine Mansfield are evoked in the poem for a good reason.[3] In her fiction, too, language 'materialises', leading to sensuous experience, and offering 'enlightenment and awareness'; in her stories 'one event may offer us, in miniature, something which holds true of an entire life, or perhaps of life itself'.[4] In the work of both artists, description, to use the words of Stevens, is 'intenser than any actual life could be'.[5]

Mirosława Kubasiewicz
University of Zielona Góra, Poland

Notes

1. Seamus Heaney, *North* (London: Faber & Faber, 1975), p. 71.
2. Jerzy Jarniewicz, *Heaney. Wiersze pod dotyk* (Kraków: Znak, 2011), pp. 18–19 (trans. M. K.).
3. The quotation comes from Katherine Mansfield's notebook entry:

> Oh, I want for one moment to make our undiscovered country leap into the eyes of the old world. It must be mysterious, as though floating – it must take the breath. It must be 'one of those islands' . . . I shall tell everything, even of how the laundry basket squeaked at '75 – but all must be told with a sense of mystery, a radiance, an after glow [. . .] (Margaret Scott, ed., *The Katherine Mansfield Notebooks*, 2 vols (Canterbury, New Zealand, and Wellington: Lincoln University Press and Daphne Brasell Associates, 1997), Vol. 2, p. 32)

4. Vincent O'Sullivan, 'The Magnetic Chain: Notes and Approaches to K.M.', in Jan Pilditch, ed., *The Critical Response to Katherine Mansfield* (Westport: Greenwood, 1996), pp. 129–55.
5. Wallace Stevens, *Collected Poems* (New York: Vintage, 1990), p. 344.

SHORT STORY
After the Pictures

Emily Perkins

The night before the casting call, Amber's hosts, Bee and John, held a party in their garden. Children thundered up the long hallway, through the open French doors at the back of the house, around the puriri tree with the swing hanging from it, down the side of the house by the fence and back through the front door to repeat the circuit. The effect was of constant, noisy motion. Their parents, locals from the school, older friends, some random adults John taught piano, clustered in groups drinking and passing food around, discussing work and politics, local gossip, kids. Amber drifted outside, and hovered at the edge of a conversation by a camellia tree. Two women she didn't know stepped apart to make a space for her, but she didn't follow what they were talking about, and she smiled and drained her glass, waggled it, moved on. For a while she knelt beside a five-year-old girl who sat on the swing, counting early stars. The children were called in for ice creams and the girl burst out of the swing like a rocket, shouting, 'I'm here!' Amber pulled herself up by the thick white rope, grass stains on her white dress.

She came and went from a few conversations and stood by the piano for an impromptu concert. Later, music came on, and she danced, across the room from John's cousin Sam. They'd met last Christmas, when Tobias had still been alive. They hadn't spoken then, but as she danced and her gaze floated over the room she could feel that he was staring. The music changed and she poured another drink, took it into the garden. The lights from a side room, where the children now watched a film, flashed purplish on to the fence. Sam was in a dark corner of the garden, not knowing anyone either, drinking a beer. Now by some silent mutual agreement they wandered down the side of the house towards the purple lights. Amber had been drinking to stay awake, because she was sleeping in the living room and couldn't go to bed until everyone had left. Now the wine-buzz crested and made her drowsy. 'Sam,' she said. Leaning against the weatherboards round the side of the house. A bottle of beer dangled casually from his fingers, that arm he kept by his side, noncommittal. He tasted of beer. The kissing was woozy, dreamlike. She forced herself to notice how his mouth was different from Tobias's. It was six strange months since she had kissed anyone. But the kisses weren't that different, and she pulled away, confused.

He held the back of her neck. 'I've seen your pictures,' he said, close to her ear. 'Hot stuff, weren't you?'

Amber tried to step aside, but he had her pinned to the wall, a downpipe beside them. Her body sobered, and trickled with a cold, sick feeling. 'What pictures? Where?'

'Online. Sexy girl.'

'Oh.' There was the sound of John calling for Sam. *Get the white spirit.* 'We'd better help,' Amber said, needing him to stop leaning in on her, needing to breathe. 'I think you've got the wrong person.'

Sam smiled, his eyes nearly shut, and slowly shook his head. What would a person do, in this situation, if there really were no pictures? She should laugh, laugh or be offended, but was afraid that any protest would sound reedy, thin. John called again, and Sam let it go.

Amber walked the rest of the way down the side of the house, between the wall and the fence, and sat on the polished concrete front step. When Tobias died, a protective shell had cracked and peeled away. The house, which was his, had to be sold to cover the mortgage; he had no life insurance. He was old enough to be better organised, but the trappings of life hadn't much changed for either of them in decades. Amber had been working in a clothing shop when they met. Tobias was what other actors called successful. His agent had taken her on as a favour, but after the death he'd retired, and none of the younger agents returned her emails or calls. Over the eighteen months of the relationship she had started as Tobias's 'plus one' and graduated to being named on invitations, which had dwindled then stopped. Her mother offered a sanctuary, where she spent muffled days playing with the cat on the carpet. When the doctor told her she was sorry but no more lorazepam, she returned to the city, and Bee's sofa, and the search for work. And now, with the feeling of a final piece being pulled away, it seemed those photos, which she had done so long ago, in her teens, before the internet existed, had found their way online.

Behind her, the front door opened and someone nearly fell over her – 'Sorry, sorry!' she said, dusting herself off, ducking down the hall, knocking a framed photo on an angle, righting it, closing the door quietly into one of the children's rooms, and waiting until she could hear that everyone had gone. She was about to venture to the living room when John came in, the three-year-old sleeping in his arms. He was jovial, drunk. 'My cousin likes you.' He'd given Sam her number.

In the bathroom, light shone through the bottle of mouthwash and sparkled, fracturing green in the droplets on the shower door. Amber washed her face with Bee's flannel. Everything of hers was in storage. His things had gone back to his mother and sister. They hadn't lived together long and she didn't feel right about taking the offered shirts and records, though in retrospect that was stupid. Sometimes at night she helped herself fall asleep by mentally going through her belongings. There was a soft blanket that she missed.

Amber sat on the living room floor, washed with silvery moonlight, a glow from the open laptop casting up at her. The thought of searching for herself made her whole body clench. For images like those she had done such a good job of forgetting, she wouldn't know where to start. Under her name, there was a page of thumbnail photographs: her own head shot for castings and several other Amber Longs. But in those days she was Amba. She tried that, and clicked forward a few pages – nothing. Sam must have been on some specialist site. No one who mattered would find it. He wouldn't say anything to John.

The smell of wine hung in the air and she could smell Sam on her too. Tomorrow she must wake early. She must not press the snooze button for those nine delicious minutes, multiplying by magic numbers into nearly an hour bobbing in and out of sleep. These were the best, most intoxicating moments of bed, distantly aware of your own abandoned existence, and it took an effort of will to resist, but she would. The open call started at seven – if she was to be there, showered, made up, unflustered, by six thirty when the queue would start forming, she had to get up at five.

And when the marimba sound donk-a-donked into the room she was so good, swiping it away with her thumb, sitting up, head hanging, on the edge of Bee's couch, breathing heavily. She'd even set it for four-fifty to give herself those extra moments in case anything went wrong with her hair, or the train was late . . . and knowing this was probably unnecessarily prudent she lowered herself again on to the cushions for just a moment, the sheet rucked cool and soft beneath her chin.

Bee was standing at the end of the couch, fully dressed.

Amber lurched up. 'What's the time?' She didn't mean to sound so angry.

'Nearly eight. I'm going to work.'

Through the wall, the rush of the shower running. 'I'm late. Is someone in the bathroom?' Amber fell as she scrambled off the couch, picked herself up off the floor – Bee was walking away – 'I'm going to miss it – .'

'John's taking the kids to school. I've got to go. But listen we need to talk. Will you be home tonight?'

'Wait, can I get a lift?' Amber had laid her audition outfit over one of the matching nineteen-forties armchairs that squatted in the living room like mute grandparents. There would be people going all out, in full Victorian costume – this navy blouse and skirt was the closest thing she had. The clothes were streaked with thin white lines of cat hair from Poody, who was moulting. We need to talk. That would be hanging over her all day.

'I've got to go,' said Bee. 'I'm leaving.'

'Yes. I'm ready.' She was in the skirt, and turned her back to Bee while she pulled off the T-shirt she slept in and slung her arms through the straps of her bra.

In the hallway, Bee was calling goodbye to her family. A glimpse of dirty glasses on the kitchen table. Annabel, the youngest, sidled up to her mother for a hug. 'I love you, Mum' came from behind a closed door, and now Bee was pulling on her coat, calling '*Music*,' and, '*Milk*' and other cryptic instructions of family life and Amber had her shoes on, or at least one of them, her heel jamming on the other. Laces could wait. The hallway oppressed her. The picture rail, the black and white photographs of Bee and John's ancestors, a mother in a hat, their wedding, their children . . . that old-fashioned baby, an onion wrapped in lace, its knowing stare . . .

Trees were tossing in the wind. Bee pulled the car into the bus stop across from the station – it shook a little as they sat there, from the southerly. She was still talking. Amber gripped the door handle, poised to get out. Six minutes until the train. As soon as 'we need to talk' turned out not to mean 'we've discovered your shameful past,' she had been nodding on autopilot, listening only in a blur. Yes, these were fair points about how long she had been staying, and she definitely needed to get somewhere of her own. They all missed Tobias but. Yes yes yes. Morning traffic slowly, evenly streamed past.

'Oh, it's so hard for you!' Bee lunged forward and hugged her. Amber was surprised by her friend's grip, the way it held on for a couple of deep breaths so she was forced, somehow, to hug Bee back, and a tautness in her body began to relax – with the relaxation came a sort of pressing feeling and hotness in her eyes as though – well, she just wanted to get there, be on her way. 'Good luck. Do you know your lines?' Still hugging.

'Yes.' There weren't any lines. The casting call was for featured extras.

'You'll be brilliant. Here.' Bee wiped under Amber's eye. 'A little schmutz. Mascara.'

'Thank you, thank you!' Amber scrabbled in the coin tray for a mint, tugged at the wrapper as she extracted herself from the passenger seat. The air on the roadside was cold. A bus loomed and let its horn go at Bee. 'Sorry, sorry,' Amber mimed, searching for a break in the traffic.

She did the rest of her makeup on the train, sucking on the mint and rolling the shrinking, roughening disc around in her mouth until it was just a wafer, sharp-edged to the tongue. The cosmetic injection from the other day was taking effect and parts of her face had begun to feel caged. It was a relief to look in the small round hand-mirror, scowl, and see only minimal movement, a flashing in her eyes. The tightness was like being held. She smiled, and her top lip, which had been paralysed, stayed in place; straws and smoking would be difficult for a day or two. Amber checked over the curved rim of the mirror that none of the commuters were looking and mouthed a few words, testing speech. There were still a couple of small bruises, one below her left eye and the other on her cheek, from where the student beautician had injected filler. Powder covered the smudges nicely, though. No one would be able to tell.

The back gardens of suburban houses trundled by and disappeared into a tunnel. Through the other side came green banks scrubby with gorse, and the shining blue city. Graffiti progressed in unreadable chunks beneath a blaze of sky. Railway yards were comforting places, in their sameness around the world, their tangle of crossed lines and rusted connections, the possibilities of places to go. She joined the moving clots of office workers, civil servants, bankers, lawyers heading through the terminal towards glass and concrete offices and gathered energy from the crowd, inhaled with anticipation. The freedom of not being a wage slave! The hands on the giant round clock in the middle of the railway station pointed to eight thirty-five. She broke into a run.

In the taxi, she chatted with the driver getting her across town as fast as he could, a man with his own troubles, a bullied daughter and dyspraxic son. Minutes ticked over with the fare meter, and they talked, talked, drowning out the pouring time with words, her volume increasing when they stopped for lights as if loudness could make them *go*. Outside the warehouse Amber leaned forward in her seat, staring at the door across the parking lot while the receipt unspooled slowly from the machine, pushing down with her hands and almost lifting off but longing too to stay here with this man all day, watch the city and its funny rhythms through his windscreen . . . she snatched the receipt and boosted herself out and across the cold expanse of asphalt, past tidy colourful cars, the sort that belonged to real people.

She was too late for street scenes. The production people gave her a number anyway and told her they were collecting the extras into groups, there were several scenarios to fill, not only the street but a bar scene, a schoolhouse, the ports. A bar . . . the ports! She might get a line . . . the chaos might resolve into something better than she'd thought. Around the walls someone had pinned blow-ups of Victorian crowd scenes. 'We are looking for the right faces to go together. We are looking for authenticity.' Her head ached from smiling, which over the past months had become a reflex of hope rather than of happiness. She clicked her jaw and smoothed her hair.

Tobias had been a proper actor. His gift was precision; even she could tell that was what made him good. Hers was – had been – her looks. 'It must be much harder,' Bee said once, 'getting older when you've really been beautiful. Sorry!' Amber, checking her ghostly reflection in the window as she waited with Group D to be called up, thought that her face perhaps didn't quite look real – was not authentic – it was the face she needed, the face she used to be able to afford, but it was not the face she would have had if she were a Victorian woman. Hers was not the body, either – her breasts too enhanced, her skin too refined, her muscles lean and taut. In her last three, unsuccessful, auditions, there had been a green screen and the acting had to be done in front of it. 'You're running through the jungle . . . you're coming to a cliff. What are you going to do? . . . hesitate . . . leap over! Here comes a monkey and it's after your wallet . . . look out!' Standing afterwards in mutual exasperation with the director, near tears, her arms limp and useless by her sides. Now Amber played with the top of her blue shirt. It looked more old-fashioned buttoned up. She practised an authentic face, thinking hard of hand washing and the words *mangle, corset* and *coal.* Massaged the skin between her eyebrows, trying to frown through the stiffness. On the wall, a sepia woman threw her head back and laughed.

The sun moved across the warehouse space, and unemployed people who had the whole day to wait around for work that would involve spending the whole day waiting around did crosswords, read books or their phones, swapped stories, shared out the snacks they'd brought with them. Amber hadn't eaten since the mint in the car, and she was starving, but had nothing to offer back. Group C had only just gone in, so she nipped outside for a quick, appetite-suppressing cigarette. There was a slim joint in the bottom of her handbag. She straightened it out as she walked down the stairs, and saw that the paper had a hole in it. Unless she found someone with papers, or managed to reconstruct the joint from the papers that weren't torn, and frankly it looked a little dry and sad, she would have to give up on the idea. This was a sign, wasn't it? Shouldn't she get better at reading the signs?

She smoked it anyway, the pad of a finger over the hole, and checked her phone. There was a message from a new number. *Looked again for sexy pics – found more of u ;-) S.* Her finger burned. The sun was past the midpoint of the sky now, and a group of women in business clothes emerged from a ground-floor office and crossed the car park, laughing. Amber turned her phone off as violently as she dared, in a flare of rage at the whole digital world. She was so confused about her public self, a self she didn't own. It was a kind of shame, this confusion – to be in her thirties and still not know what to do, not have the right impulses, not be an adult the way people around her were adults. If she could get to a computer maybe she could track down the site, write a letter, get a lawyer, make them stop. No . . . she shrank from the idea of drawing attention to it, having people she knew in this life, now, look at her in some uncomprehending way. And this production person was holding them here so long. She would leave – she would tell them all to take their miserable job and shove it where the sun didn't shine! With a feeling of great release she ran up the concrete stairs and into the waiting area, just as the last few people from her group, Group D, were filing into the audition room through the far door. An older woman with too much makeup on, perfect casting for a raddled Victorian prostitute, held the door open for Amber, smiling. 'Come on, dear. It's our time.'

The auditions were brief. One by one, they filed in front of a camera, name, date of birth, and filed off. Amber was drawn into the slipstream, towards the lights, the machinery, the seamless flocked white backdrop. What did it matter – she was here now – what was there to lose? When it came to her moment in front of the camera, she felt its pull and smiled down the barrel with genuine warmth, even loving it, as if there were a friend behind the lens. She would never go through this again! For the first time in years she gave her true age. A casting director shuffled them into groups and asked them to pose straight on, in profile, standing, sitting, chat amongst yourselves. Amber found herself next to a young man with facial hair that might have been grown for the auditions or which might have been the look that twenty-somethings were into now. His name was Ted. He thought he recognised her. She named a bank commercial where she was one of several women dancing in a supermarket aisle. He frowned. 'I don't think so.'

The casting director moved them on. 'Thank you . . . Ted and . . . Amber!'

'Oh – yeah – .' He spoke as if something was dawning on him. 'I know – .'

'What?' His moustache had fascinating curls. 'You know where you know me from?'

His face shut down. 'Never mind.'

'You do or you don't?'

'I don't. Never mind.'

Amber held out a hand. 'Well, see you. Good luck.'

'That's it? Are we finished?' He was staring at her still.

She felt like a creature in a zoo. 'Boo!' She lunged at him, and he tripped backwards. She called to the casting woman. 'Is that us?'

'Yes, thanks. We'll call you!'

'Whoa,' said Ted. 'You're strange.'

'You're staring. It's rude.' Ordinarily she'd smile, but now she didn't. She liked this feeling.

'Wait,' the casting woman said. 'Amber?'

She was drawn over to a side of the room. 'I'm Rachel,' said the casting director. 'I just wanted to say, I recognised you from a couple of times with Tobias, and my girlfriend Lila, she's in camera, and I, we knew him a bit, and I just . . . '

'Oh,' said Amber. The sweet glee fell from her, or she fell from it, as though she was dropping, dropping like a stone in a well. 'Hi.'

'I just wanted to say, I'm sorry.' She tapped Amber's arm. 'It's so awful.'

'Thank you.' Tears came. Amber blinked, and felt the hot relief on her skin, as though the last piece of the protective shell had been stuck here all along, and it was being melted away. Her face, her throat, her whole body ached. She had been so afraid of this ache. But it was the loveliest feeling. 'Sorry. Thank you.'

Rachel tapped her arm again, and nodded, and turned to her assistant. 'Right. Group E.' Ted lurked by the door, taking a very long time to look for something in his bag.

In the women's washroom Amber startled a little dog that was standing by the bin, the end of its lead untethered, and it growled, staring at her feet. It was the old-fashioned sort of poodle that no one really had any more – pinkish white, with red-rimmed eyes and a nose she didn't want to look too closely at. As she stepped past its unexpectedly long body, the dog lunged at the air near her ankles. 'Oh my goodness,'

Amber said, but no response came from the dead green cubicle door. She checked her messed-up face in the wall mirror, her gaze sliding off the big picture until she unbuttoned her collar and shook out her hair. She growled. The dog growled again. The older lady from Group D emerged from the cubicle and Amber stepped aside to give her space. The woman kicked the snuffling dog out of the way and pumped soap onto her hands. She wouldn't meet Amber's eye.

The southerly cut across the parking lot. Amber rolled down the sleeves on the blue shirt and waved goodbye to Ted, who still lingered, as though he wanted to say something to her but lacked the courage. She put her head down into the wind and felt in her skirt pocket for the bus money as she pressed on towards the road.

REPORTS

Katherine Mansfield and J. W. N. Sullivan: A Speculative Reassessment[1]

David Bradshaw

J. W. N. Sullivan is an ever-present figure in Mansfield's letters from mid-1917 onwards, but he has been consistently overlooked by her biographers. She had distinctly mixed feelings about him, and it seems his behaviour, at times, could be boorish, but that hardly explains why Sullivan seems to have been so conscientiously ignored by commentators on Mansfield's life and work. According to Jeffrey Meyers, for example, whose source is Sydney Schiff (also known as 'Stephen Hudson'), Mansfield:

> resented Murry's friendship with the chain-smoking Sullivan [. . . and] criticised his lack of sensibility, which she considered far more important. 'A queer fish, a true Bohemian', she told [. . .] Schiff. 'He has written a Life of Beethoven and a book about Einstein. He likes beer, a lot of it [. . .] Sullivan has brains but no intuition, no sensibility. I like him but he sets my teeth on edge.'

As recalled by Schiff, Mansfield's assessment of Sullivan continued:

> 'He eats oranges and bananas and aims the peel and the skins at the fireplace. When he turns up I always start by liking his society and end by longing for him to go because of his antipathetic habits. I hate myself for this, but I can't help it.'[2]

However, although it appears that Sullivan did have a gargantuan thirst for beer and a tendency to fling orange peel into the Villa Isola Bella's fireplace, Mansfield cannot have made these precise remarks to Schiff, as Sullivan's *Beethoven: His Spiritual Development* did not appear until 1927 and he did not publish 'a book about Einstein' before Mansfield's death in 1923.

Mansfield's alleged comments are certainly consistent with what she (and others) said about Sullivan elsewhere, but they are also characteristic of the imprecise hearsay that has attached itself to his name. Charismatic to some, rebarbative to others, few in his lifetime thought Sullivan was a bit-part non-entity and neither should we. But he does not even rate a mention in the *Oxford Dictionary of National Biography*, never mind his own entry, and for this reason alone we need a more reliable profile of the man. He may have played only a supporting role in Mansfield's story, but he was undoubtedly one of her closer acquaintances and he may well have cherished hopes of a more intimate relationship.

Sullivan is often glossed as an 'Irishman', but he was not. In fact, as Charles Singer pointed out in 1937,

> his surname notwithstanding, he had only remote Irish connections. He was essentially a Londoner and was born at Poplar [. . .] on 22nd January 1886, the only son and eldest of three children of an official of a well known Protestant Mission.

It became apparent at school that Sullivan was a gifted mathematician and by 1900 he had joined the Telegraph Construction and Maintenance Company, who paid for his education at the Northampton Institute (forerunner of City University) in London, where he spent the next eight years studying mathematics and physics as well as working for his company. Sullivan also enrolled in classes at University College, London, in 1908–9, before working in the USA for a few years and then returning to England. During the First World War he drove an ambulance in Serbia before suffering a nervous collapse.[3] It was not long after he returned to London to convalesce that Sullivan joined the staff of Watergate House and got to know Murry and Mansfield.

Earlier that year, 1917, Sullivan had published his first novel, *An Attempt at Life*, and had married Sylvia Manooch. By Christmas, Mansfield was describing him as 'particularly nice' in a letter to Murry and mentioning that she and Sullivan had 'talked mainly about music – Beethoven chiefly'.[4] It is just possible that Sullivan had already taken a shine to Mansfield, as she reported to Murry that at 10.00 a.m. on Christmas Eve:

> the lad *Sullivan* turned up – He was playing the wag I think for he said he had not got a holiday – but might he spend part of the day with me. All this *dead* serious as though there were already a posse of police in the front garden. He was awfully nice to me and made up the fire and all that and went out for a bottle of wine. At four o'clock (I sent him away for lunch) he went back to Watergate House. He really is immensely anxious to join us, and I rather think he will – that we will let him. But I was so tired after he had gone that I fell asleep.[5]

By the beginning of 1918 Sullivan was introducing Murry and Mansfield to 'one of his Russian friends [. . .] one of these strange people who think our Dostoevsky is one of the words of profound wisdom'.[6] Mansfield told Murry she thought Sullivan was 'a good chap' in February,[7] and by the middle of that year they had clearly discussed such subjects as entropy with him. 'It is another day the spit of yesterday,' Mansfield told Murry on 1 June 1918. 'I think it is the end of the world – but not a Sullivan end. No, the planet will fry rather than grow cold.'[8] But it is also around this time that we see the first sign of Mansfield's tendency to become irritated with Sullivan. On 16 June she wrote to Murry, who seems to have been inconvenienced by Sullivan in some way, to 'confess' that she had '"turned" against Sullivan & couldn't greet him. Hes a coward and utterly abominably selfish. Feel inclined to write to him: "you do your share of the work, my lad, & don't worry about the planet getting cold".'[9] By August, however, Mansfield had 'turned' back in favour of their mutual friend. 'Sullivan comes & talks & is particularly nice,' she informed Murry. 'I have forgotten all about the quarrel.'[10] This fluctuation in Mansfield's attitude to Sullivan would come to typify her relationship with him.

Sullivan was slowly gaining a foothold in the higher journalism and had already attracted the attention of a major modernist writer, although his responsibilities at Watergate House were putting an increasing strain on his health.

> Many thanks for sending on Joyce's play [*Exiles*][11] [he began a letter to his publisher, Grant Richards, on 3 June 1918]. Can you send me his Switzerland address? He wrote to me, but I have lost his letter [. . .] As for my own activities I am at present incapable of any work and am going away shortly, by doctor's orders, for 'brain fag'. I cannot think and I cannot even understand what I read.[12]

Although, on 13 January, Murry had told Mansfield that he would 'sooner cut [his] hand off'[13] than introduce Sullivan to Lady Ottoline Morrell, part of Sullivan's convalescence from 'brain fag' would include a holiday at Garsington that came about after Murry intervened on his behalf. He wrote to Lady Ottoline in late May 1918:

> Sullivan, of whom I have told you, is suffering from brain-fag. It is very necessary that he should take the sick-leave he has in the country. On the other hand he has a wife – a very nice little person – and he can't afford to go.
>
> Would you do Katherine and me, and art, and Sullivan the good turn of letting him live for three weeks in the cottage? [. . .] He is, as I have told you, a very good man indeed and a dear friend of mine.[14]

Lady Ottoline was happy to oblige and in her memoirs she recalled Sullivan as:

> first a Mathematician, interested above all in Science, very fond of music, especially Beethoven [. . .] He was a delightful and sympathetic talker, and [. . .] he and I spent many hours talking, talking of life and Russian literature, and discussing the lives of our mutual friends and their various oddities.
>
> His wife, Sylvia, was a restless, erratic and erotic little creature, whom I called the Starling [. . .] I had arranged that a party of wounded officers should come out from an Oxford hospital every week and spend the afternoon with us. I naturally asked Sylvia Sullivan [. . .] to come and help entertain them, which she did most delightedly; but to my embarrassment I saw her sitting on the ground at their feet, pushing up their trouser legs and stroking their legs and ankles – perhaps her method of entertaining them was more successful than our more sedate way of giving them tea and showing them round the farm.[15]

As the War drew to a close, relations with Murry and Mansfield were cordial and increasingly intimate. 'We have had some powerful talks with Sullivan who continues to be very cheerful. (The result, I believe, of bacon sans ticket.),'[16] Mansfield told J. D. Fergusson in September 1918, though on 17 November she mentioned to Lady Ottoline that the Sullivans were among a number of visitors having tea at 2 Portland Villas while she was upstairs: 'I keep wishing that they never need climb so high as this little bedroom. I hope the rock cakes will sit very heavy on them.'[17] By March 1919 Mansfield was referring to their mutual friend as 'Sullivanoff' and telling Murry that he seemed to be anxious about his 'personal life'.[18] The following month, Mansfield mentioned to Woolf that Murry and Sullivan were 'downstairs discussing the theory of relativity [. . .] . I feel they are being a trifle portentous.'[19]

By this time, of course, Sullivan, alongside Aldous Huxley, was assistant editor of the *Athenaeum*, and after reading an article by Sullivan in the 24 October 1919 issue of the journal, Mansfield was dismissive of his writing.

> Sullivan is alright dont you think but undistinguished [she observed]. I always feel hes on the point of choosing the Idylls of the King as his great poem – But its serious & interesting and the wires are quite well laid. Which is, I think, his part in the job of literature.[20]

Mansfield was rather more gracious about another of Sullivan's contributions to the *Athenaeum*, deeming 'Science and Culture', which appeared in the 14 November number, 'very readable [. . .] An occasional *simple* article like that is very good for catching new readers I am sure.'[21] But Murry was never entirely happy with his two assistants. 'I went down to the office this morning to feel how things were going,' he told Mansfield on 5 January 1920:

> I think they are really all right; but I feel very much that when the cat's away the mice begin to play. There's always a general sense of irresponsibility. The paper is filled up just anyhow, and no-one dreams of looking a week ahead [. . .] You and I with our heads together – are the only editors of this paper. It's a mistake to have let anyone else have control. They are splendid, Sullivan & Huxley, at their jobs – but outside them useless.[22]

'Please ask Sullivan to review my story if it is not too late,' Mansfield wrote to Murry on 10 March 1920.[23] The 'story' in question was the first, unexpurgated version of 'Je ne parle pas français', and Sullivan's initialled review of it appeared in the *Athenaeum* on 2 April, where he favourably compared Mansfield's writing to that of Chekhov and Dostoevsky before drawing to a close by declaring that her story 'possesses genius'.[24] Unsurprisingly, Mansfield was delighted with this puff, which appeared under the heading 'The Story-Writing Genius', and she wrote to thank Murry 'for [her] bouquet in the A[thenaeum] [. . .] It was a very nice one.'[25] Yet despite his public admiration of her work, Mansfield's private attitude to Sullivan remained broadly contemptuous. 'Hes queerly insensitive [. . .] I feel I don't ever want to speak to him again,' she let Murry know two months later. 'Such disgusting indifference. He is a *clumsy* creature. I think Im terribly intolerant of *clumsiness* [. . .] Don't ever ask Sullivan here – will you?'[26] Mansfield took another dig at him in a letter to Murry of 1 December 1920:

> I do wish S[ullivan] would eat his dinner for once without a bottle of G.K.C. on the table. Even if he doesn't dash his viands with it he always points to the bottle [. . .] Let me be as bad as I can. Es gibt etwas inferior in Sullivan [There is something inferior in Sullivan]. His shoes will always carry a trace of *Fleet Street* & he's too proud of the trace to have 'em cleaned.[27]

Nevertheless, when Murry travelled to Menton in January 1921, Sullivan accompanied him. Relations between Mansfield and her complimentary but '*clumsy*' friend were now poised to enter a more turbulent phase.

Very soon after arriving in the South of France, Sullivan must have headed north for Paris, probably in order to facilitate a divorce from Sylvia.[28] One 'Monday', around late March 1921, after he had returned south, Sullivan wrote to Sydney Waterlow from the Villa Isola Bella and gave him an overview of his recent experiences:

> I have had a truly extraordinary time. On arriving in Paris I became completely stupid for some days. I then became very nervous and depressed. I have been able to do practically no work of any kind. After nearly three weeks of this I learned that my wife had acted as a free individual and had rather definite ideas as to what she wanted to do next. We have discussed matters with great mutual regard and are now separated. She is probably going off to Sicily: I have come down to stay awhile with Katherine and Middleton. My plans for the future are rather vague; my old plans are altogether upset. I am resolved, however, to live abroad as much as possible. I shall probably live in the neighbourhood of Katherine and Middleton, but I shall be returning to England pretty soon in order to dispose of my house in Sussex and generally straighten up my affairs.[29]

Behind this letter lies a tale that is indeed quite 'extraordinary'. While in Paris, Sullivan had been introduced by Nina Hamnett to the notorious occultist Aleister Crowley, otherwise known as 'The Beast'. 'They got on very well together,' Hamnett recalled, 'as they both were very good chess-players and very good mathematicians as well.'[30]

> Sullivan had no interest in the occult but, when he responded to the Beast's discussions of *The Book of the Law* by seeing numerical theorems in its passages, Crowley excitedly invited him to the Abbey [his base in Sicily] to write a mathematical proof of *Liber AL*,

one of Crowley's biographers has written.[31] According to another, Sullivan was so taken with Crowley's work that Crowley 'extracted a promise from Sullivan that he would do his best to discover his True Will'.[32] In his *Confessions* (Sullivan is one of the three dedicatees),[33] Crowley recalls meeting Sullivan in Paris and refers to him as '"a fellow almost damned with a fair wife" named Sylvia. They had been married some time and she had developed a pain in the old place.'[34] Almost immediately, Crowley and Sylvia became involved in a relationship, and this turn of events may well be what Sullivan is alluding to when he says in his letter to Waterlow that Sylvia 'acted as a free individual'. 'Absorbed in his work, [Sullivan] had no taste in common with Sylvia bar music,' Crowley continues, 'and he had begun to find it rather a nuisance to have to trail her along at his heels. He asked me point-blank to take her off his hands for a time . . . I was glad to oblige. He could have her back when he liked by whistling for her':

> We talked day and night for a fortnight. On his part, he showed me a great many mysteries in *The Book of the Law* that I had not suspected till then [. . .] Our conversation was uninterrupted except for the tyranny of sleep and Sylvia. She became pregnant [. . .] It was agreed she should return to Cefalu with me, he to join us and work out fully the mathematical theories

> of *The Book of the Law* as the convenience of his editor permitted. After Sylvia's confinement, we would confer more about the proper course of action. He then went off to Mentone [*sic*] to bid god-speed to the girl he really loved, a woman writer who was living with one of his editors so long as her lungs would let her (they lasted till 1922).[35]

Despite misremembering the year of her death, the 'woman writer' Crowley has in mind, of course, is Mansfield, who in late March 1921 told Waterlow that 'Sullivan, having drunk 2 bottles of wine and a wineglass of brandy has gone off to Marseilles'.[36] Sullivan was on his way to rendezvous with Sylvia and Crowley, as 'The Beast' recalled in his *Confessions*:

> We were to meet Sullivan at Marseilles, sailing for Palermo with or without him as his editor might permit. The few days of absence had wrecked him mentally and morally. We had no sooner sat down to lunch than he burst into a torrent of maniacal ejaculations.
>
> All this was spouted by a whale answering to the name of 'I want Sylvia back'. When his breath failed, and he fell back panting like a mad dog, I remarked between mouthfuls, 'Righto! I'll have to get the cabin changed and take a few of Sylvia's things out of my trunk. I think there's nothing else, provided, of course, Sylvia wishes it'. The poor man was flabbergasted and Sylvia flew into a royal rage. My contempt for him was one thing; my indifference to her quite another [. . .] They were reduced to shamefaced stammering [. . .] Sullivan, selfish and stupid, actually proposed to hurry back that night to Paris, though Sylvia was obviously fagged out with the journey of the day before, to say nothing of her having set her heart on enjoying the beauties of the Riviera – it was her first escape from England.[37]

After a few more days in Marseilles, during which Crowley persisted in his attempts to enlist Sullivan into his occult investigations, the Sullivans left by train, with Crowley seeing them off with little regret for Sylvia and a great sense of a missed opportunity with Sullivan: 'I could have made him the evangelist of Thelema; with his abilities he might have been more important in history than St. Paul.'[38]

The lingering unsavouriness of Crowley's reputation aside, it is curious that this material has left practically no mark on Mansfield studies. 'The Beast', appropriately enough, comes across as grotesquely obnoxious in his dealings with the Sullivans, but does this mean his testimony is entirely unreliable? After all, his version of events dovetails neatly with what we know of Sullivan's movements at this time from both his own and Mansfield's correspondence. Is it possible, therefore, that Sullivan arrived in Marseilles 'wrecked [. . .] mentally and morally' after his sojourn in Menton less because he was in turmoil over Sylvia, and more because he had been rebuffed by Mansfield? Incidentally, according to two of Crowley's biographers, Sylvia would 'die shortly afterwards of typhoid',[39] but this information, unlike Crowley's account of the events of early 1921, is completely without foundation. She died, in fact, in 1974.[40]

Sullivan was certainly back in Menton by April 1921,[41] and around the 18th of that month Mansfield wrote to Schiff with these 'extraordinary' goings-on and Sullivan's central role in them almost certainly in mind:

> I am simply staggered there's no other word for it, by your analysis – heaven knows its infinitely more – of Sullivan. Perfect! From the first word . . . to the last. And that 'he has less imagination than he thinks', that 'his future lies in the development of his powers of application'. My dear Sydney. That is divination indeed.
>
> I am fond of Sullivan – and I am his friend – but with *reservations* [. . .] His lack of what we mean by sensitiveness is hard to bear, so too is his lack of self discipline. I mean that in every sense [. . .] He wants to live somewhere near me for the next few years &, privately, I shrink from the idea. But he's a vague creature. Perhaps Ill never see him again. At the moment this thought is pleasing. How hateful I am! My excuse is he has been staying here – here all day long until 10 o'clock at night – and Sydney – one is so *infernally watchful*. His habit of going into the dining room, taking an orange, bringing it to the salon, tossing the peel into the fireplace. Oh! Oh! But thats only one 'obvious' small horror [. . .][42]

Do we deduce from this that Sullivan may have made plain his feelings for Mansfield, without sufficient 'self discipline', during one of his recent visits in Menton? If so, such a scenario may lurk behind Mansfield's comments to Murry of 15 May:

> I was not surprised at Sullivan. He's so *uncertain* at present I mean in his own being that it will come natural to him to pose. I don't know how far you realise that you *make* him what he is with you – or how different he is with others. Also at present S. has no real self respect and that makes him *boast*. Like all of us he wants to feel important & that's a *right* feeling – we *ought* to feel important – but while he remains undisciplined & dans le vague he *can't be* important. So he has to boast.[43]

On 19 May 1921 Mansfield asked Murry: 'Sullivan has "gone" for the time being – hasn't he? I confess I do not want to see him here – not now.'[44] Furthermore, on 27 May Murry told Mansfield that he was 'freed from the nightmare of having [Sullivan] near us – it was becoming really oppressive'.[45] A couple of days later, however, he mentioned that Sullivan was a fellow guest at the Waterlows,

> and though I am convinced that it wouldn't be any good if Sullivan were to live near us, I am nevertheless glad that he – with all his absurdities & lack of refinements – is alive and our friend. And it's the same with old Sydney. My affection for them both is very real.[46]

By July, Mansfield was telling Brett: 'Sullivan I am sure will wax very prosperous and shine with fatness. He has become a humorous character to me.'[47]

There must have been a temporary *rapprochement* between the Sullivans, as Mansfield told Brett on 4 August 1921 that it was:

> not v. nice to see Mr and Mrs Sullivan a-lapping up the cream & licking of their paws somehow. I think Sullivans obsession is all a fake – a make up [. . .] Its *not* pretty! Now I shall be indiscreet & trust to your discretion. S. has a very vivid imagination. Beware of it! But perhaps you have discovered it already. Before listening take a very large grain of salt & let it dissolve slowly in the mouth (without swallowing) as they say. That is *dead private*![48]

But what, precisely, was '*dead private*'? Is Mansfield alluding to Sullivan's 'vivid imagination' and boastful 'obsession' with himself or his feelings for herself? Does she have in mind some ardent, '*clumsy*' declaration of his feelings for her that he may have blurted out in Menton earlier that year?

Sullivan published 'an appreciative, unsigned review [of *The Garden Party and Other Stories*] in the *Nation and Athenaeum*'[49] on 25 March 1922, in which he was especially complimentary about 'At the Bay' (though I wonder if Harry Kember in that story was conceived wholly without reference to him), and four days later Mansfield told Richard Murry:

> Yes, I too was very interested in Sullivan's review, though I didn't agree with it all [. . .] If I were to agree with Sullivan Id have to believe that the *mind* is supreme. But I dont – not by a long long chalk. The mind is only the fine instrument its only the slave of the soul.[50]

Sullivan's 'mind', however, was increasingly prized by other contemporaries and he found himself more and more in demand between the wars as an exponent of the new physics. In this expository role he would discuss contemporary science with the likes of Murry, Huxley, Pound,[51] T. S. Eliot,[52] Ottoline Morrell, Mary Butts[53] and, almost certainly, Mansfield, while the impact of his exegetical writings beyond avant-garde modernist literary circles was just as considerable. His *Aspects of Science*, published in 1922, 'was an unqualified success [. . .] [and] established his reputation at once',[54] but it was only the first of a series of 'masterly volumes'[55] that explained the rapidly expanding field of scientific knowledge to the reading public. Sullivan would build on its success with *Atoms and Electrons* (1923), *Three Men Discuss Relativity* (1926) and a second series of *Aspects of Science* in 1926.[56]

On 30 June 1922, a couple of weeks after Mansfield had written to Brett to say she suspected it could have been a 'drunk' Sullivan who had recently 'scared' Brett's servant,[57] Sullivan told Lady Ottoline:

> I have read The Garden Party. It is very good, I think. Thank-you very much for lending it to me.
>
> And I want to tell you how much I enjoyed the weekend; it was a very pleasant rest for me.
>
> I saw Eliot when we got to London and had a most interesting conversation with him about his poetry. It appears you were more right than I in your general impression.

This letter's most intriguing disclosure, however, is contained in its postscript: 'I should like to know whether you agree with my "Medallion" of Katherine. It will appear tomorrow (Saturday) or early next week.'[58] The 'Medallion' in question actually appeared in *The Times* on 27 July 1922, and, since it has not been linked with Sullivan hitherto, it is worth quoting liberally:

> **Medallions V**
>
> MISS KATHERINE MANSFIELD: JANE AUSTEN'S PUPIL
>
> It is certainly true that most of us seem to go through life with our eyes half-shut. But is this because we actually lack sensitiveness or because we are paying attention to something else? The question is not a trivial one, and it is one we cannot help thinking about when we read Miss Katherine Mansfield's stories. Indeed, they make the question extraordinarily prominent. Miss Mansfield, more than any other modern writer, leaves us wondering, 'Am I half-blind, or half-alive, or what?'
>
> [. . .] It is rare, indeed, for us to find a writer who *includes* us, who sees all that we see, and something more. Yet, up to a certain point, we must admit that Miss Mansfield is such a writer. And she sees everything much more vividly than we do. Reading her stories is like wandering at dusk through a garden we vaguely know, accompanied by a guide carrying a little searchlight. We know everything the guide points to, but we never saw it so clearly before.
>
> [. . .] Miss Mansfield distorts nothing. Her light is the same as ours, but it is more intense. This statement is not absolutely true; there are moments when Miss Mansfield's objects seem to us not perfectly in focus.
>
> At those moments we are aware that Miss Mansfield has not only light but heat. Her 'objectivity,' her artist's coolness, is not quite perfect. She is sometimes a little hard, sometimes a little sentimental, and sometimes, just for a flash, her vision fails her altogether and we see nothing whatever. These are purely momentary flickers; they grow more and more rare, but

even in her latest volume these moments occur. At the very end of her extremely sensitive story, 'At the Bay,' for instance, we are disconcerted, bewildered, by just one sentence which permits us to see nothing at all.

[. . .] She shows us the world and the people in it – the world we know and the people we know. That is to say, she shows us these people in relation to one another. This takes us a long way, particularly with women, for their life is chiefly the life of personal relations. But there is an inner life of which Miss Mansfield gives us only the most transient glimpses. She permits us to say of her observations and feelings, even when we are most ready to applaud, 'How feminine!'

[. . .] Why is this? Is it because Miss Mansfield does not trust herself to deal with a man who really has something in him? If that is so then we congratulate Miss Mansfield on her artistic rectitude. With her gifts, which have made her the best woman short story writer in the country, she could have been the smartest of the smart, the most brilliant of the brilliant. She has preferred not to belittle what she knew she did not fully understand. She has been as careful as Jane Austen not to say more than she knew.

It is customary to say that Miss Mansfield has been greatly influenced by the Russians. We see no evidence for it. Indeed, it seems to us that they are chiefly concerned with what Miss Mansfield largely neglects. Her art is of a more finite, and even domestic, order [. . .] It is a purely English as well as a purely feminine art. It is a finite art but, because it is finite, it can be made perfect. There are stories by Miss Mansfield which are not only perfect in themselves, but perfect in their *genre.*

Perfection is a great thing. It is not the greatest thing, and Miss Mansfield cannot be ranked amongst the greatest writers. But it is a quality which has a peculiar claim to immortality, and we know of none amongst Miss Mansfield's contemporaries whose claims are as good.[59]

Is it possible Sullivan has himself in mind when he writes that 'Miss Mansfield does not trust herself to deal with a man who really has something in him'? Does Sullivan's finely calibrated, slightly pernickety, essentially slight but fulsome praise of Mansfield amount to a kind of critical reprisal after his rejection by her the previous year? These, of course, are highly speculative questions and we have no way of answering them. Nor do we know how Mansfield responded to Sullivan's anonymous article. But she must surely have seen it and asked herself and others who wrote it. And if she did discover it was Sullivan, she may well have been perplexed, in particular, by his apparent failure to see any Russian influence in her fiction, because in his review of *The Garden Party* Sullivan had stated quite categorically that 'Miss Mansfield has learnt a great deal from the Russians, as all intelligent writers should, and far too few do'.[60]

Ironically, during the final months of her life, Mansfield's spiritual outlook and Sullivan's world view came into close alignment. Sullivan's name was becoming increasingly synonymous with scientific mysticism, and on 19 September 1922 Mansfield told Murry, in terms that Sullivan would have found entirely sympathetic, that 'the wave of mysticism prophesied by Dunning is upon us.' Mansfield goes on to recount 'a most interesting after-lunch talk at Beresford's' involving, among others, Orage and Sullivan:

> Sullivan came back for supper & he & I talked of all these ideas afterwards. It was, as he said, a 'simply stunning evening'. I do hope you see Sullivan for a longish time . . . Is this interference. Its hard not to interfere to the extent of wishing you found life as wonderful as it seems to me. Even the least idea – the fringe of the idea – of 'waking up' discovers a new world. And the mystery is that 'all' of us in our unlikeness and individual ways do seem to me to be moving towards the very same goal.[61]

The following month Mansfield journeyed to Gurdjieff's Institute for the Harmonious Development of Man at Fontainebleau, conscious, surely, of the fact that Sullivan had been a 'convert' to Gurdjieff's philosophy and involved with the Gurdjieff Institute in Hampstead.[62] Yet her caginess about Sullivan's non-mystical and non-musical sides remained acute. On 27 October she wrote to Murry: 'I was so glad to hear of your Sullivan excursion. But doesn't his chess obsession bore you dreadfully? It did me. But Beethoven and the stars & the baby all sounded nice.'[63] And on Boxing Day 1922, with Murry and Sullivan now sharing a cottage in Sussex, Mansfield told Murry:

> I heard from Brett yesterday. She gave me a very horrid picture of the present Sullivan and his views on life and women. I don't know how much of it is even vaguely true but it corresponds to Sullivan the Exhibitionist [. . .] I always feel Sullivan refuses to face the fact of his wastefulness.[64]

With 'Sullivan [. . .] away', Murry replied on New Year's Eve 1922:

> I don't a bit like the glimpse of Sullivan's activities I got through your letter *viâ* Brett. In some ways he's very restive. While he's down here, and towards me, he is *very nice indeed.* I'm not exaggerating. He makes a real effort to be considerate, and to try to get rid of the horrid, uncouth, masculine intellectual pride that is the worst thing in him: it's so utterly unworthy of himself at his best moments. But then it seems he rebels against his efforts, and when he goes up to London sometimes (not always) breaks into a real unregenerate Adam. But you mustn't imagine those moments are typical of him. I know of them only by what comes round to me. In all our direct relations he's very different, believe me.[65]

Ten days later, Mansfield was dead. Kathleen Jones, in noting who travelled to France for her funeral, remarks that Sullivan was one of those present. 'It is a strange mixture of people who knew Katherine only slightly and are there because John has invited them, and those for whom her death is a personal tragedy.'[66] Jones seems to suggest that Sullivan was there as a representative of the former category, but I wonder if he saw himself as bearing witness to something more akin to a 'personal tragedy'?

In the years that followed, Sullivan matured into one of the pre-eminent scientific commentators of his day and a leading authority on the music of Beethoven. In both capacities Sullivan had a clear impact on the development of Huxley's fiction, with his conversation and ideas about the connections between the new physics and philosophical idealism in particular helping to shape *Little Mexican* (1924), *Those Barren Leaves* (1925) and especially *Point Counter Point* (1928), in which Sullivan appears as the Dostoevskyan Maurice Spandrell.[67] Spandrell is both devoted to Beethoven and a dedicated libertine, and Navin Sullivan once told me it was family lore that when his father 'received his complimentary copy of *Point Counter Point* from Huxley he glanced through it, grunted, and hurled it in the wastepaper basket'.[68] But however unjust or irrelevant Sullivan considered Huxley's portrait to be, it is clear that his conduct in the 1920s had led to him acquiring a certain notoriety. In April 1924, for example, Sullivan told Waterlow that he had received a letter from 'Marge', Waterlow's wife, to say that he was not welcome at Oare, the Waterlows' house near Marlborough, 'as Miss Strachey is there, and I apparently am taboo by the Stracheys. Also, Marge says she is unhappily not in sympathy with me.'[69] Moreover, a long and intimate letter that Sullivan wrote to Mansfield's old schoolfriend, Vere Bartrick-Baker, in 1927 helps us to understand why a number of women, including Woolf, found some of his opinions and his behaviour towards women objectionable. Having begun by telling Vere (with whom he had been involved for some time and whom he would go on to marry the following year) that her 'beautiful letter' was 'full of the love that [he] crave[d] for', Sullivan proceeds to tell her about Jessie, a 'young and juicy' woman whom he had picked up and seduced 'out of vanity'. Having discovered he was impotent with Jessie, however, he had stopped seeing her. But he had recently met up with her again:

> I am convinced that I can still fornicate when nothing but the physical element is involved. I earnestly ask you not to oppose me in this. A sort of vanity is involved in this which is perhaps not unimportant [. . .] Your position, it seems to me, is utterly unaffected by the affair [. . .] The girl

is a nice girl but to me she is simply a representative of a class, and I want to prove that that class is still within my hunting range. As for you, you are my woman [. . .] You are my tested and very deliberately chosen wife, and will be in name as well as fact [. . .] Now come, Vere, make an effort. Let me have another go at this girl, not with your blessing but with your indifference. I've nibbled at my chocolate, but I haven't eaten it. Perhaps you find such purely physical desire rather disgusting. Perhaps it is. My desire is not even particularly strong, but to bring things off properly with this girl would really satisfy something in me.

Sullivan goes on to describe a fellow guest of the Huxleys (with whom he was then staying) as 'an ardent feminist, but not otherwise silly. I told her I approved of feminism and anything else that woke women up a bit and made them more interesting companions for men', and he concludes his letter by telling Vere about how the young women staying at the Huxleys are not at all '"provoked" by the prominent bulge in front of' his swimming shorts:

If the Jessie affair really and truly causes you the most excruciating and life-long torture, I may consider dropping it before finishing it. But I hope you'll let me finish it. It is curious, but I don't think I should mind very greatly letting you suffer just a little about such things. What I would never do would be to let you go [. . .] You are *organically* related to me. You are MINE. I shall pick you up and throw you down, kiss you, slap you, strip you and copulate with you, bath you, comb your hair, make you pee, slap your bottom, pull your nose and bite your ear – in fact, do anything I like with you.[70]

To reiterate, Sullivan would go on to marry Bartrick-Baker in 1928 and their son would be born the following year, so it is unlikely she was wholly outraged by the contents of this graphic letter, but alongside its candour and intimacy it also resounds with an almost monstrous self-regard. Is this the voice of the 'unregenerate Adam' whom Murry deplored? Does this letter offer us a glimpse of 'Sullivan the Exhibitionist', to borrow Mansfield's phrase? It almost certainly does.

From around 1932, Sullivan's health deteriorated and 'for the last four years of his life [he] was an invalid'.[71] He died on 11 August 1937, and although he had refused to act as a character witness for Crowley in 1933,[72] when 'The Beast' learned of Sullivan's death he was sufficiently affected to pen a brief obituary and to give it to Tom Driberg, who either drew on it substantially or, more probably, published it in full in his 'William Hickey' column:[73]

No one-track man was J.W.N. SULLIVAN, who has died, aged 51, of a painful disease [. . .] Sullivan was in youth a powerful heavyweight boxer.

> Another of his many interests: beer. He was a great drinker (I use 'great' admiringly). Once at the Dôme in Paris, noted Bohemian café, he drank 44 steins of light beer. He was not drunk. Once, in Berlin, he found that 14 heavy beers *had* affected him slightly. So he ate a lot of goulash, rested for 2 hours, was then able to drink 17 more. He might not have died [if] he had undergone treatment rigorously. But he hated doctors as much as he hated all other professional hierarchies; rarely kept appointments with them. Years ago he spent some time at the 'Abbey' in Sicily run by magician Aleister Crowley; came round to some extent to the view that some phenomena cannot be explained by 'pure science'. He is bracketed with Jeans & Eddington.[74]

Rather more soberly, *The Times* reported in its obituary that Sullivan had been 'A Gifted Interpreter of Science', who had 'won his way to the same rank as Sir James Jeans and Sir Arthur Eddington',[75] and, whatever we think about his unenlightened sexual politics, it is about time Sullivan's intellectual achievements and cultural role as an inter-war populariser of science were as widely acknowledged as theirs have been. But whether Sullivan really travelled to Crowley's Sicilian Abbey or whether this was merely wish fulfilment on Crowley's part must remain more open to question. In his *Eight Lectures on Yoga* (1939), Crowley speaks warmly of 'my old and valued friend the late J. W. N. Sullivan'.[76]

As the narrator of W. J. Turner's *The Duchess of Popocatapetl* (1939) puts it, Sullivan, to his admirers, was 'a man of powerful mind, capable of sharp penetration, rapid co-ordination, and lucid exposition altogether removed from the ordinary [. . .] one of the most lovable, brilliant, and uncomplaining of men'.[77] This assessment of his qualities was not shared by all the women he encountered, as we have seen, but Mansfield did warm to him intermittently and it is just possible that Sullivan was not just 'Murry's admirer', but also her own.

Notes

1. This article is a slightly revised and much shorter version of *Katherine Mansfield and 'the indiarubber faced, mobile lipped, unshaven, uncombed, black, uncompromising, suspicious, powerful man of genius in Hampstead', J. W. N. Sullivan,* Katherine Mansfield Birthday Lecture No. 4 (Bath: Katherine Mansfield Society, 2013).
2. Quoted in Jeffrey Meyers, *Katherine Mansfield: A Biography* (London: Hamish Hamilton, 1978), p. 150; repeated in Meyers, *Katherine Mansfield: A Darker View* (New York: Cooper Square, 2002), p. 150. Meyers is quoting from Stephen Hudson, 'First Meetings with Katherine Mansfield', *Cornhill*, 170:1017 (Autumn 1958), pp. 202–12 (pp. 209–10).
3. Charles Singer, 'Memoir', in J. W. N. Sullivan, *Isaac Newton 1642–1727* (London: Macmillan, 1938), pp. ix–xx (p. ix).
4. Vincent O'Sullivan and Margaret Scott, eds, *The Collected Letters of Katherine Mansfield,*

5 vols (Oxford: Clarendon Press, 1984–2008), Vol. 1, p. 358. Hereafter referred to as *Letters*, followed by volume and page number.

5. *Letters* 1, p. 360.
6. Murry to Mansfield, quoted in *Letters* 2, p. 47.
7. *Letters* 2, p. 84.
8. *Letters* 2, p. 208.
9. *Letters* 2, p. 242.
10. *Letters* 2, p. 265.
11. Published in 1918 by Grant Richards.
12. Unpublished letter, Harry Ransom Research Center, University of Texas at Austin, 3 June 1918. Hereafter referred to as HRRC. All letters quoted in this article that are held in this repository are unpublished unless stated otherwise, and all quotations from J. W. N. Sullivan's unpublished writings are made with the permission of Mrs Barbara Sullivan.
13. C. A. Hankin, ed., *The Letters of John Middleton Murry to Katherine Mansfield* (London: Constable, 1983), p. 100.
14. HRRC, n.d. [c. late May 1918]. I am grateful to the Society of Authors as the literary representatives of the Estate of John Middleton Murry for permission to quote from this letter.
15. Robert Gathorne-Hardy, ed., *Ottoline at Garsington: Memoirs of Lady Ottoline Morrell 1915–1918* (New York: Alfred A. Knopf, 1975), p. 259. Sylvia Sullivan later told her daughter that she and Sullivan 'were both amused by Lady Ottoline's rather blatant attempts to achieve a tête-à-tête' with Sullivan and that this may explain her negative portrayal of Sylvia: unpublished letter, Navina Ridley to David Bradshaw, 14 September 1994.
16. *Letters* 2, p. 275.
17. *Letters* 2, p. 291.
18. *Letters* 2, p. 306.
19. *Letters* 2, p. 314.
20. *Letters* 3, p. 54.
21. *Letters* 3, p. 104. Sullivan's initialled article is 'Science and Culture', *Athenaeum*, 4672 (14 November 1919), p. 1190.
22. Cherry A. Hankin, ed., *Letters between Katherine Mansfield and John Middleton Murry* (London: Virago, 1988), p. 245.
23. *Letters* 3, p. 244.
24. *Athenaeum*, 4692 (2 April 1920), p. 447.
25. *Letters* 3, p. 266.
26. *Letters* 4, pp. 112–13.
27. *Letters* 4, p. 130.
28. Unpublished letter from Navina Ridley to David Bradshaw, 14 September 1994.
29. Alexander Turnbull Library, National Library of New Zealand, Wellington, New Zealand. Hereafter referred to as ATL. All letters are unpublished unless stated otherwise.
30. Nina Hamnett, *Laughing Torso: Reminiscences* (London: Constable, 1932), p. 174.
31. Richard Kaczynski, *Perdurabo: The Life of Aleister Crowley* (Tempe, AZ: New Falcon, 2002), p. 289.
32. John Symonds, *The Great Beast: The Life and Magick of Aleister Crowley* (St Albans: Mayflower, 1973), p. 292. On 'the very next page to the one which contains the oath

of the husband', Symonds continues a few lines further on, 'is recorded the Beast's act of sex-magic with the wife'.

33. John Symonds and Kenneth Grant, eds, *The Confessions of Aleister Crowley: An Autohagiography* (London: Routledge & Kegan Paul, 1979), p. 27.
34. Symonds and Grant, p. 869.
35. Symonds and Grant, p. 869.
36. *Letters* 4, p. 202.
37. Symonds and Grant, pp. 869–70.
38. Symonds and Grant, p. 871.
39. Colin Wilson, *Aleister Crowley: The Nature of the Beast* (Wellingborough: Aquarian, 1987), p. 124. The same claim is made in Kaczynski, *Perdurabo*, p. 289.
40. Unpublished letter, Navina Ridley to David Bradshaw, 11 October 1994.
41. ATL, Sullivan to Waterlow, 9 April 1921.
42. *Letters* 4, pp. 205–6.
43. *Letters* 4, p. 224.
44. *Letters* 4, p. 228.
45. Hankin, p. 339.
46. Hankin, p. 341.
47. *Letters* 4, p. 255.
48. *Letters* 4, p. 260.
49. *Letters* 5, p. 134, n. 1. See 'Miss Mansfield's New Stories', *Nation and Athenaeum*, 30:26 (25 March 1922), pp. 949–50.
50. *Letters* 5, p. 133.
51. See Timothy Materer, *The Selected Letters of Ezra Pound to John Quinn, 1915–1924* (Durham, NC, and London: Duke University Press, 1991), p. 216.
52. See Michael Whitworth, '*Pièces d'identité*: T. S. Eliot, J. W. N. Sullivan and Poetic Impersonality', *English Literature in Transition*, 39 (1996), pp. 149–70.
53. See Nathalie Blondel, *Mary Butts: Scenes from the Life* (Kingston, NY: McPherson, 1998), p. 139.
54. Singer, p. xiii.
55. Singer, p. xlv.
56. For an authoritative account of Sullivan's writings and their broader cultural context, see Michael H. Whitworth, *Einstein's Wake: Relativity, Metaphor and Modernist Literature* (Oxford: Oxford University Press, 2001).
57. *Letters* 5, p. 203.
58. HRRC, 30 June 1922.
59. *The Times*, 27 July 1922, p. 13.
60. 'Miss Mansfield's New Stories', *Nation and Athenaeum*, 25 March 1922, p. 950.
61. *Letters* 5, p. 267.
62. Kathleen Jones, *Katherine Mansfield: The Story-Teller* (Edinburgh: Edinburgh University Press, 2010), p. 447.
63. *Letters* 5, p. 309.
64. *Letters* 5, p. 341.
65. Hankin, pp. 402–3.
66. Jones, p. 36.
67. For a detailed account of Sullivan's relationship with and influence on Huxley, see David Bradshaw, 'The Best of Companions: J. W. N. Sullivan, Aldous Huxley, and the New Physics. Part One', *Review of English Studies*, 47:186 (May 1996), pp. 88–106;

'The Best of Companions: J. W. N. Sullivan, Aldous Huxley and the New Physics. Part Two', *Review of English Studies*, 47:87 (August 1996), pp. 352–68.
68. Unpublished letter from Navin Sullivan to David Bradshaw, 17 September 1996.
69. ATL, 14 April 1924.
70. J. W. N. Sullivan to Vere Bartrick-Baker., n.d. 'Thursday' [envelope stamped 5 August 1927]. Formerly in the possession of Navin Sullivan; original now missing, photocopy in the possession of David Bradshaw. Navina Ridley recalled meeting in the late 1930s 'a strange woman who said 'I'm Jessie! I'm Patrick's mother! [. . .] it seemed that she had been acquainted with my father and that Patrick was his son.' Unpublished letter from Navina Ridley to David Bradshaw, 19 September 1990.
71. Singer, p. xix.
72. Symonds, p. 434.
73. See www.lashtal.com/wiki/Portal:Aleister_Crowley_Timeline/On_this_Day/August [accessed 26 November 2013].
74. William Hickey, 'These Names Make News – Master of Maths', *Daily Express*, 14 August 1937, p. 6.
75. *The Times*, 13 August 1937, p. 14.
76. See www.spiritual.com.au/2011/07/yoga-for-yellowbelllies-aleister-crowley-second-lecture/ [accessed 26 November 2013].
77. W. J. Turner, *The Duchess of Popocatapetl* (London: Dent, 1939), pp. 242, 248.

The Influence of Katherine Mansfield in the Work of C. K. Stead

Gerri Kimber[1]

This report will examine how the life and work of New Zealand's most iconic dead writer, Katherine Mansfield (1888–1923), is reflected in the critical writing and fiction of C. K. Stead, New Zealand's most eminent living writer, with a career spanning more than 50 years. Stead set his novel *Mansfield* during the three years spanning 1915 to 1918, the period when Mansfield connected with members of the Bloomsbury group for the first time, found her true voice as an author and was still in 'reasonably good health'; it was, as he points out, 'the time of her most intense engagement with an extraordinary cast of characters on the English literary scene'.[2] This essay will also consider two poems by Stead: 'Jealousy I' and 'Jealousy II',[3] based on episodes in Mansfield's life. The three tables which accompany this essay provide examples of how Stead uses Mansfield's writing to construct his novel and that of Woolf and Mansfield to construct the two poems above.

In 1972, thirty-two years prior to the publication of this novel, Stead became the recipient of the Katherine Mansfield Memorial Fellowship, offered annually to enable a New Zealand writer to work at the Villa Isola Bella in Menton, once the home of Mansfield. Stead was the third Fellow, following Owen Leeming in 1970 and Margaret Scott in 1971. During the eight months he spent in the South of France on this visit, Stead took the opportunity of rereading all the Mansfield primary texts published at that time, which led directly to the publication of the *Letters and Journals of Katherine Mansfield: A Selection* in 1977.[4] And Stead's immersion in all things Mansfield as a consequence of his Fellowship would reverberate through the rest of his life; his fascination, fostered on this trip, would lead not only to his critical volume on the letters and journal, but also to other more personally creative endeavours such as poems and ultimately to the novel, *Mansfield.* As Stead points out:

'Mansfield has remained an important part of my intellectual furniture – otherwise it wouldn't have been possible to write the novel'.[5]

In 1973, following his Katherine Mansfield Menton Fellowship, Stead wrote his first major critical article on Mansfield, which would eventually become the introduction to his edition of her letters and journals.[6] It is replete with facts and figures concerning Mansfield's literary output, many not widely known at the time, together with an appraisal of the editorial role of her husband, John Middleton Murry, in the publication of her writing after her death. Stead's article is generous in its praise of the wife, whilst for the most part coolly critical of the husband.

Stead's commentary confirms Murry's manipulating editorial role: 'He transcribed, edited, and wrote commentaries tirelessly but in a way which encouraged a sentimental, and sometimes falsely mystical, interest in her talent' (21). He notes Murry's hagiographic tone, which tended to stress Mansfield's spirituality, her beauty, her suffering and other-worldliness, a misleading emphasis found since in articles, biographies and memoirs of Mansfield in France;[7] and this same sycophantic tone is to be found in the London literary journal, the *Adelphi*, edited by Murry from 1923 to 1930. In the immediate aftermath of her death, Murry started printing several pieces of Mansfield's work in every issue, and this editorial policy continued for two years. As Stead wryly notes: 'his late wife was for some years the most regular contributor' (21).

As the months went by, the sycophantic line became ever more pronounced, and the amount of space given over to the Mansfield publicity machine became ever greater, until even her closest friends and admirers turned away in disgust. As Frank Lea remarks, Mansfield 'became the presiding genius of the paper – till even the friendly Bennett was forced to remonstrate, whilst with the unfriendly it became an article of faith that Murry was "exploiting his wife's reputation"'.[8]

During her lifetime Mansfield had three collections of short stories published. At the time of her death she had almost become a celebrity, receiving fan mail and good reviews for her work. Then she died. Without Murry, her star would not today shine so brightly, for three small volumes of short stories would not have been enough to maintain an iconic status over the next hundred or so years. However, following her death, Murry collected together all her papers, diaries, letters and unpublished stories, and gradually, over a number of years, created many volumes from these loose papers and notebooks, the detritus of a writer's life.

Stead discusses Murry's moral right to publish so much, 'ignoring her instruction to "tear up and burn as much as possible"' (21), but acknowledges the ambiguity of Mansfield's final instructions concerning her papers: 'destroy all you do not use' and 'destroy [. . .] all you do not wish to keep' (22). There is almost an implication that Mansfield *did* wish her papers to be published. She famously had a habit of going through her papers before every journey – and there were a great many of these in her short nomadic lifetime – as if 'preparing for death', destroying all those she did not want to keep. Why, then, did she not do the same with the papers she bequeathed to Murry? Stead believes that '[i]n these ambiguities, Murry might have found a sort of justification for his own procedure' (22).

Ian Gordon's comments in 1959 that the *Journal* was as much Murry's work as Mansfield's, is one step too far for Stead. Although agreeing with Gordon that Murry's editing was a 'brilliant [. . .] editorial patchwork' (23), Stead nevertheless maintains that Mansfield's writing is of such a quality that her own voice shines through, regardless of editorial manipulations.

Stead's own choice for his selection from the journals and letters was to be 'guided principally by the wish to represent Katherine Mansfield's writing at its best rather than to give a balanced biographical portrait' (24). He defines this 'best' as when 'the writing is least deliberate, when it flows easily and naturally, governed by feelings and observation rather than by any apparent calculation of its effect' (24). He notes his own resistance to passages of 'sensibility': 'her emotion is often less genuine when she is being "sensitive" than when she is being [. . .] satirical, or bullying, or simply plain and factual' (24).

Mansfield was a born mimic, raconteur and performer, all attributes useful in a fiction writer; in a letter writer, these same attributes manifest themselves – in Murry's own words, in a tendency 'to assume a personality to please a correspondent [. . .] in her it was very pronounced' (25). As Stead notes, 'She is always confidently herself, but it is a subtly different self for each friend' (25). Stead's favourite Mansfield is 'robust' and 'anarchic', with an ingrained comic talent, 'deeply committed to no social forms and niceties (in this she remained indelibly the colonial), seeing Nonsense everywhere (Male Nonsense especially), and enjoying her ability to represent it inflated to bursting point' (26). As he astutely notes: 'There was nothing mystical about her that antibiotics would not have cured' (27). In this first, early piece of Mansfield criticism by Stead, his admiration for her, both as a personality and as a writer, is evident, although he is never unaware of her faults and weaknesses. Her early death meant her talents were largely unfulfilled but they were, he believes, nevertheless 'superior to those of all her contemporaries except Lawrence' (27).

In Stead's next major article on Mansfield, entitled 'Katherine

Mansfield: The Art of the Fiction',[9] he makes his own personal assessment of Mansfield's fiction and comes up with new terminology with which to assess it. Her experiments 'taught us the fiction as distinct from the narrative, and it is in that sense that she is an innovator' (30). She would forego 'narrative' as such, and in its place would develop something altogether more modern, a coherence without the need for conventional narrative links, beautifully realised and executed in her stories 'Prelude' (1917) and 'At the Bay' (1921). Even Frank O'Connor, one of her fiercest critics, called these stories 'masterpieces and in their own way comparable with Proust's breakthrough into the subconscious world' (34). In the short story 'Je ne parle pas français' (1918), Mansfield discovered the more technically complex method Stead calls 'circumlocution' (41), where she 'establishes a central point of reference and then moves in circles about it, going back and forward in time' (42). This method would be repeated in 'The Daughters of the Late Colonel' (1920) and 'A Married Man's Story' (1921).

In this article Stead also addresses the question of Mansfield as a 'colonial' and/or a 'New Zealand' writer. For Stead, her childhood physical environment manifests itself constantly in her writing, as does the fact that her New Zealand background – her 'colonial' heritage – marks her out as a writer. She is detached, unmarked by established convention, caring little for social niceties and with 'only intelligence and instinct to guide her' (30). From her earliest writing, once she was established in Europe, would come the collection *In a German Pension* (1911), in which Stead sees a mixture of violence and humour, not so much anti-German, as anti-male.[10] At the age of 22, Mansfield's satirical and analytical skills are impressively developed.

In 1985, Stead writes a review[11] of a biography of the Hon. Dorothy Brett, an artist and friend to both Mansfield and Murry.[12] Brett, the hard-of-hearing daughter of Lord Esher, had a problematic childhood, resulting in a somewhat emotionally stunted adult. She became devoted to Mansfield, especially towards the end of the writer's life, and indeed Mansfield dedicated her last short story, 'The Canary', to her. After Mansfield's death she had an exceedingly brief physical affair with Murry, which she found 'overwhelming and confusing', and then an equally brief physical affair with D. H. Lawrence (174). As Stead recounts: 'Part of the problem was Murry's unwillingness to be just an average cad. He had to be sanctimonious as well' (174). Brett is most famous now for being the friend of Lawrence and Mansfield, rather than for her own talents as an artist.

The publication of Claire Tomalin's biography of Mansfield in 1987[13] brings Stead to the defence of Mansfield as a colonial – and, for him, more significantly – a New Zealand writer, in a review essay entitled 'Katherine Mansfield's Life'.[14] Stead points out: 'Mansfield spent half her life in New Zealand. Tomalin gives one tenth of her book to those years' (43). He views Tomalin's focus on Mansfield's adult and literary life as unsatisfactory, in that it removes attention from those things in her origins which explain much of her œuvre: 'She always saw herself as an outsider – "the little colonial"; and a large proportion of her most highly regarded stories are set in New Zealand' (43). Stead looks squarely at the question of whether she is 'a New Zealand writer' at all, and comes to the conclusion that she must be, by default, since 'she is not any other kind of writer'. He continues:

> She had no regional or metropolitan attachment, nor class allegiance, nor dialect, to place her among British writers. Yet the New Zealandness is hard to pin down. It has been laid over, concealed – deliberately. This is an essential part of Mansfield which I think Tomalin doesn't appreciate; but it has been neglected by other biographers as well. (44)

Taking the subtitle of Tomalin's biography, 'A Secret Life', Stead suggests that Mansfield's New Zealand heritage and inspiration is part of this secret life, not always foregrounded in her fiction, but nevertheless present as a topographical and inspirational undercurrent. He goes on to discuss one of Mansfield's early and less well-known New Zealand stories, 'The Woman at the Store' (1912), which demonstrates one of her principal narrative themes – that of the woman as victim – combining this with 'a harsh regional realism' (44), which foreshadows a specific genre of New Zealand realist fiction of the 1930s and 1940s. Stead quotes Elizabeth Bowen, asking 'Did she, by leaving her own country, deprive herself of a range of associations, of inborn knowledge, of vocabulary?' (45), and is disturbed that this subject is not raised anywhere in Tomalin's biography.

Stead has no time for the feminist view of Mansfield as lesbian or bisexual, discussed at length in Tomalin's biography, stating, 'I feel quite sure she would be distressed and angered to discover herself casually described as "sexually ambiguous", with a husband and a wife, and lovers of both sexes' (40). He remains convinced that there is no evidence to suggest that Mansfield continued any bisexual activity once out of her late teens and that to suggest otherwise reeks of sensationalism. For Stead, Mansfield is simply 'one of the most brilliant and extraordinary of modern women' (46).

Also in 1987 appears the second volume of Mansfield's *Collected Letters*,[15] edited by Vincent O'Sullivan and Margaret Scott, which Stead reviews in *The Dominion* in October 1987.[16] For Stead, a rereading of this comprehensive collection, which spans the years 1918–19, when the symptoms of Mansfield's tuberculosis would become more pronounced and her wanderings abroad in search of a cure would intensify, leaves him with an altered view of Mansfield. 'Previously, I was aware chiefly of her positive qualities – cleverness, inventiveness, humour, and high courage. I'm more aware this time of the dark side, and even of an element of falseness which I don't feel in the least inclined to condemn' (169). In this time of separation from Murry, her letters home speak volumes about her emotional state, her desperate sense of loneliness and isolation, which fed her insecurity and her fears.

Stead's critical response to the centenary of Mansfield's birth in 1988 is an essay entitled 'Katherine Mansfield and T. S. Eliot: A Double Centenary'.[17] As he points out, these two writers were born within three weeks of one another, so it is also Eliot's centenary, and their lives, as expatriates, occasionally overlapped.[18] It is easy for Stead to conjure up the similarities in their personalities, both, for him, encapsulating 'a curious combination of theatricality and secretiveness' (150). Their families were well-to-do, their fathers financially supportive, their mothers sensitive, if distant. 'For both, the landscapes of childhood remained more vivid and significant than those of their adopted country' (150). Stead also defines their differences, which are striking: Eliot being elusive, unadventurous and timid, turning to orthodox religion as he grew older, whereas Mansfield was a bold adventurer, 'a high-spirited pagan for whom the notion of art had replaced traditional religion as the source and receptacle of the highest truths and the finest achievements of mankind' (151). The most marked differences for Stead, however, are in their literary output, both enormously gifted, but whereas Mansfield's achievements grew consistently with the passage of time, cut short only by her untimely death, Eliot's early brilliance 'became progressively frozen under layers of Catholic-puritan angst' (151). In addition, literary history binds them in the sense that 1922, which produced James Joyce's *Ulysses* and Eliot's *The Waste Land*, was also the year of Mansfield's most significant story collection, *The Garden Party and Other Stories.*

In 1989, Stead gives the John Garrett Lecture at the University of Canterbury, New Zealand, taking as his theme 'Katherine Mansfield as Colonial Realist',[19] evidently harking back to concerns from his review of Tomalin's biography: namely, the notion of Mansfield as a 'colonial' writer. Stead acknowledges that '[t]he balance between maintaining living contact with the literary tradition, going back in our case at least to Shakespeare, and "making it new" on our own ground, has been the difficult task of New Zealand writers' (38). In Mansfield's writing, he feels, there are easily overlooked moments, which catch 'the sense of a gap between the local reality and the imported model, which is what so much of the post-colonial experience is all about' (40). One such story is 'The Doll's House' (1921), where the toy house and its toy occupants represent the artificiality of the colonial society, while the little lamp seems 'real'. So the child Else's last words, 'I seen the little lamp',[20] are a recognition that has 'symbolic significance for the development of post-colonial literature' (41).

Thus far, Stead's approaches to Mansfield have all been literary-critical and quite separate from his ongoing work as poet and fiction writer, but in 1996 the two come together for the first time in the poems 'Jealousy I' and 'Jealousy II'.[21] In 'Jealousy I', Stead's voice is Mansfield's voice – as she plays over in her mind the events of a dinner party which had in reality taken place on the night of 14 May 1920 – T. S. Eliot and his wife had just been to dinner with the Murrys (see Table 1).[22] Stead is here intertwining his two favourite literary personalities, and creating a poem from Mansfield's own impressions of the evening, recorded in a letter to Sydney and Violet Schiff. Many of Mansfield's original words are replicated in the poem, and this is the technique Stead would go on to employ in his novel *Mansfield*, using diary entries and letters, even an actual story, 'Psychology' (1920), to recreate events, to give his novel a 'ring of truth'. The jealousy in this poem is multi-layered: Mansfield's jealousy of Murry for having been in England when she was away ill in the South of France; jealousy, too, of Murry's ease with Eliot and especially with his wife, Vivien; and jealousy of Vivien herself, and the horror that she had been in Mansfield's bedroom before and that there might be more to her relationship with Murry.

'Jealousy II' is written from the point of view of Virginia Woolf, Mansfield's literary sparring partner, and again, a similar technique is used, though in this instance there is more conjecture, and several different Woolf sources are employed (see Table 2). Here it is Woolf who is jealous of Mansfield's writing, her personality, her vibrancy. Mansfield is recorded by many of her contemporaries as having a gift for impersonation, which she incorporated into her work through the myriad of characters presented there. Ida Baker, Mansfield's schoolfriend and companion, remarks, 'There was a bell-like quality in her rich low voice and her singing was a high, pure soprano [. . .] She was a born actress and mimic, and even in her ordinary everyday life took colour from the company she was in.'[23] Leonard Woolf concurs:

> By nature, I think, she was gay, cynical, amoral, ribald, witty. When we first knew her she was extraordinarily amusing. I don't think anyone has

> ever made me laugh more than she did in those days. She would sit very upright on the edge of a chair or sofa and tell at immense length a kind of saga, of her experiences as an actress [. . .] [T]he extraordinary funniness of the story was increased by the flashes of her astringent wit. I think that in some abstruse way Murry corrupted and perverted and destroyed Katherine both as a person and a writer [. . .] Her gifts were those of an intense realist, with a superb sense of ironic humour and fundamental cynicism.[24]

This description of Mansfield by a contemporary who knew her well, underlines how her humour attracted Woolf's husband and how this in turn led to Woolf's insecurity and jealousy (seen in Stead's poem) at the very mention of her name, not just as a writer, but as a woman and a potential rival.

In 2004, Stead returns once more to Mansfield for inspiration in his creative endeavours, this time producing the acclaimed novel, *Mansfield*, spanning three years from 1915 to 1918 during the Great War, chronicling the lives of Mansfield and her circle at this critical time. Reviewing the novel in England, Hermione Lee states:

> C. K. Stead is trying to do to Katherine Mansfield what Colm Toibin has just done to Henry James in *The Master* or Michael Cunningham to Virginia Woolf in *The Hours*: to take a short section of a great writer's life, extrapolate its essence from biographical information and primary sources, and turn it into a vivid, immediate fictional narrative which daringly enters into the famous subject's inner life.[25]

In his 2004 article, 'Men and Mansfield in *Mansfield*',[26] Stead explains his choice of time parameters for the novel: first, because it was during this period that Mansfield began to see clearly the sort of fiction she wanted to write – which would take her back to New Zealand and her family for inspiration; second, her tuberculosis had not yet been diagnosed and she was still in reasonable health; and third, during this period the cast of characters actively in her life reads like a who's who of the early-twentieth-century literary scene. After 1918, when she starts to become ill and spends more and more time away from England, her interaction with these people diminishes, and is mainly conducted through letters. Finally – and most importantly – these are the war years and, Stead says, '*Mansfield* is really a war novel' (135).

The novel follows closely what we know of Mansfield's movements during this time. Stead's modus operandi was that 'nothing in the novel should conflict with what is known. What I was interested in exploring, however, was the area beyond what is known' (132). Each chapter is written from the point of view of one of the main characters and is titled with that character's name. Of thirteen chapters, seven are written from Mansfield's point of view, with the symmetry of two at both the beginning and the end of the novel. Other characters represented with a chapter are Leslie Beauchamp (Mansfield's brother), John Middleton Murry, Dora Carrington, Frieda Lawrence and Frederick Goodyear (significantly given two chapters). Both Leslie Beauchamp and Frederick Goodyear would be killed in action in France, and Stead centres much of the book on their individual stories and experiences as they interact with Mansfield's.

In addition to the main war theme, Stead notes,

> *Mansfield* is a novel about relationships. It's about Katherine's struggle to find love and companionship; and about her effort to balance the duties and demands of human attachments against the consuming ambition to write what she called 'a new kind of fiction'. (133)

Five male characters are foregrounded: the brother Leslie, the loved friend Fred Goodyear, soon-to-be husband Murry, the lover Francis Carco and the intellectual Bertrand Russell. The novel represents Mansfield's relationship with each.

For Stead, there is the 'whiff of incest' (135) about the relationship between Mansfield and her brother, which he depicts as intense during the brief time Leslie is over from New Zealand, preparing for war and staying with his elder sister. Mansfield is obsessed with him whilst alive and even more so once he is dead. His death eventually becomes the catalyst she needs to turn her thoughts back to New Zealand, searching for creative inspiration in her homeland and memories of their childhood.

Stead accords Murry only one chapter. Discussing the novel, he says Murry was 'well meaning but not really up to the task. She was too brilliant for him to match, and too demanding for him to satisfy' (137). With Bertrand Russell, Stead employs Mansfield's own story 'Psychology', written at almost exactly the same time as their short-lived intimacy, and transforms it into part of the book's plot, since 'the incident it describes is a perfect illustration of what the newly fashionable Freudian psychology would have called repression and sublimation' (141). Concerning Mansfield's relationship with Frederick Goodyear, Stead has very little to go on in the way of factual record, so he relies on 'hints' and letters, and then uses guesswork. The use of Goodyear as a character reinforces the theme of war, and Lee admires Stead's choice:

> It was a cunning move to bring her friend Fred Goodyear (a minor figure in the biographies) into the centre of the picture. Goodyear, an English

> friend of Murry's, seems to have been in love with Katherine, and wrote her some critical letters about her contempt for other people and her need to 're-unite' with humanity. Stead imagines him in the horrors of the Front (where he lost both legs, and died) receiving a long letter from Katherine which spells out her need not to let 'false notes' creep in, 'better honest about what I see around me'. It's the novel's most interesting invention, bringing the realities of the war right into the centre of the story, and emphasising the tough self-knowledge, as a writer, which underlay all Mansfield's contradictory, often wilful performances.[27]

Stead is careful not to use much direct quotation from Mansfield's letters and journals, which he has said would allow her voice to take over, replacing his own. But he allows himself to invent a long letter from her to Goodyear,[28] which is in itself a clever exercise in ventriloquism.

Mansfield's affair with the writer Francis Carco (1886–1958) forms an important episode in the novel. Carco, who was born in Noumea, always liked to claim his 'South Sea' connection with Mansfield. During the First World War he became Corporal Carco (holding the same rank as 'le petit caporal' in Mansfield's story, 'An Indiscreet Journey' [1915]), working as a postman to a military baker's unit, near the front. Mansfield was disaffected with Murry during the winter of 1914–15. At the beginning of 1915 her brother Leslie, now in England as a soldier, lent her money, which enabled her to visit Carco in the war zone in north-eastern France. After three nights she suddenly returned to London and Murry, disillusioned, but with plenty of copy. Nevertheless, she retained the Carco relationship – long enough to make use of his apartment in Paris, on the Quai aux Fleurs overlooking the Seine, where she wrote 'An Indiscreet Journey',[29] an account of her visit to Gray (see Table 3).

There is a mystery here: why the affair and then its abrupt termination? Stead has Mansfield fall briefly in love with Carco, a love not reciprocated and therefore the reason for the departure. Claire Tomalin suggests Carco had given her more than just 'copy' for her stories, and that possibly she 'had contracted syphilis after her visit to Carco at the front'.[30] On this matter Stead, in his commentary on his novel, brings the crucial question back from medical speculation to psychological probability:

> Katherine was living the 'free life' and that meant 'free love'. Lacking the pill and antibiotics which protected the new free women of the 1970s and 1980s, she suffered damaging consequences – unintended pregnancies, venereal disease (which in turn lowered her resistance to TB). But one thing that neither the pill nor antibiotics could have protected her from – any more than they protected the new free women of the pre-AIDS

> era – was falling in love. As I represent her, the adventure with Carco had engaged deeper emotions and this had not been part of the plan.[31]

The novel *Mansfield* is dominated by Mansfield's relationships with men. Stead reveals that in her letters she reacts very differently to men than to women, and that there are nearly always sexual overtones in her correspondence with the former. She was an incorrigible flirt – a fact which attracted both men and women, including Virginia Woolf (as Stead notes in the poem 'Jealousy II'). The connection between Mansfield and Eliot, as outlined above, is an important one in Stead's creative writing. Significantly, *Mansfield* begins with an encounter between the two authors, walking home together after a dinner party. In his 2001 novel, *The Secret History of Modernism*, Stead has one of his characters, Samantha, write about the same encounter.[32] In conversation, Stead recalls that whilst writing *The Secret History of Modernism*, he thought, as he prepared this section on Mansfield and Eliot, that 'there was a whole novel in there'.[33]

Concluding her review of *Mansfield*, Lee considers it not altogether successful, since she feels that Mansfield's own voice – in her letters and journals – is so much more powerful than anything recreated as a fictional account. Alberto Manguel, however, writing in *The Spectator*, views the novel differently:

> Cannibal chef C. K. Stead has served us the most delicious, exquisitely prepared, delicately spiced Katherine Mansfield *dans son jus* that one could ever wish for, and the gourmet in me is immensely grateful. If we are to have biographies, fictional biographies at that, let them all be like this three-star novel, done to a turn. I came away from Stead's Mansfield (precisely subtitled 'A Novel') feeling that I now understood something of 'how it's done', or at least of how Mansfield succeeded in doing that which made even the lofty Virginia Woolf jealous: 'the only writing I have ever been jealous of,' the author of Mrs Dalloway once confessed.[34]

What is certain is that Stead understands the inner workings of Mansfield's craft more than most. As Miguel notes,

> [Stead] does not copy or merely report: he translates that which we know or intuit of her thoughts and feelings into the language of story, so that the jottings of her documented voice in journals and letters become a moving, comprehensible, convincing fictional narrative.[35]

Mansfield knew, or was acquainted with, so many people now regarded as stars of twentieth-century literature that Stead's problem must surely have been who to leave *out*. In Miguel's words, we have 'the timid and yet priggish T. S. Eliot, the inspired and violent D. H. Lawrence, the kind and scatterbrained Lady Ottoline Morrell, the randy and politically engaged Bertrand Russell, the lovesick and intelligent Carrington', to name but a few.[36]

It might have been thought that one whose interest in Mansfield had been mainly academic and literary-critical would end up writing little more than a thinly disguised biography. But although Stead has been a notable critic, poetry and fiction have always taken precedence, and *Mansfield* reads fluently as a novel, to be appreciated just as easily by someone with no previous interest or knowledge of Mansfield, while also holding the attention of the most critical of Mansfield scholars.

Stead's most recent collection of poems, *The Yellow Buoy* (2013), contains two Mansfield poems, 'Isola Bella' (previously published in *The New Yorker*) and 'Cornwall, May 1916',[37] which suggest it is not a subject he is yet ready to put behind him, that we may perhaps look for more, and if so, certainly with keen anticipation.

Table 1

'Jealousy I' (C. K. Stead, 1996)	[All spelling mistakes/errors *sic*]
(Katherine Mansfield, April 1920) Tonight the T. S. Eliots to dine – John has just gone down to see them off. Tom's an angel – but Vivien how I detest her! 'My husband' She brays – 'Oh don't be sorry for *him*!' And when John dropped the spoon: 'You are *noisy* tonight my dear. What's wrong?' (Tom leaning towards her attentive admiring.) Later in my room sprawled on a sofa she drawled 'This furniture's *changed* since you came back.' I shivered. When had she been here before? When John returns and defends her I feel I've been stabbed. How could it be? and with that *teashop* creature!	The Elliots have dined with us tonight. They are just gone – and the whole room is *quivering*. John has gone downstairs to see them off. Mrs E's voice rises 'Oh dont commiserate Tom; he's *quite* happy.' I know its extravagant; I know, Violet, I ought to have seen more – but I dislike her *immensely*. She really repels me. She makes me shiver with apprehension . . . I don't dare to think of what she is 'seeing'. From the moment that John dropped a spoon and she cried: 'I say you are noisy tonight – whats wrong' – to the moment when she came into my room & lay on the sofa offering idly: 'This room's changed since the last time I was here.' To think she had been here *before*. I handed her the cigarettes saying to myself: 'well you won't find it changed again'. Isn't that extravagant. And Elliot, leaning towards her, admiring, listening, making the most of her – really minding whether she disliked the country or not . . . I am so fond of Elliot and as he talked of you both tonight I felt a deep sympathy with him. You are *in* his life like you are in mine. Don't think that it Is impertinent. Oh, I could explain and explain that. But this teashop creature. M. comes up after they are gone, and he defends her. He tells me of a party he gave here & how she came & was friends with him & how he drank to get over the state of nerves she had thrown him into. 'I like her; I would do the same again.' I feel as tho' I've been stabbed. **Vincent O'Sullivan and Margaret Scott, eds, *The Collected Letters of Katherine Mansfield*, 5 vols (Oxford: Clarendon Press, 1984–2008), Vol. 4, p. 11. Letter to Sydney and Violet Schiff, 14 May 1920**

Table 2

'Jealousy II' (C. K. Stead, 1996)
(Virginia Woolf, January 1923)

Katherine believed I despised her
as a colonial
or so she told Ottoline –
and it's true I wrote
after our first supper together
'She stank like a civet cat
that had taken to street-walking.'

It wasn't just the perfume –
there was something hard
clever
inscrutable.
Later I was in love with her
but she would have none of that.
Now she's dead
and I can confess in my journal
'Hers was the only writing
I was ever jealous of.'
Oh yes but there's more
and I won't write it.
She was the one
who could make Leonard laugh.
I caught us once in a mirror –
Katherine with her mask-face
dark eyes
quick wit
Leonard on fire
admiring
and I
long-faced
lugubrious
superfluous.
No
that I couldn't forgive –
not ever.

The dinner last night went off: the delicate things were discussed. We could both wish that ones first impression of K. M. was not that she stinks like a – well civet cat that had taken to street walking. In truth I'm a little shocked by her commonness at first sight; lines so hard & cheap. However, when this diminishes, she is so intelligent & inscrutable that she repays friendship. **(1: 58)**

I've plucked out my jealousy of Katherine by writing her an insincere-sincere letter [. . .] So I've had my little nettle growing in me, and plucked it as I say. **(2: 80)**

K. M. (as the papers call her) swims from triumph to triumph in the reviews; save that squire doubts her genius – so, I'm afraid, do I. **(2: 87)**

I have been dabbling in K. M.'s stories, & have to rinse my mind – in Dryden? Still, if she were not so clever she couldn't be so disagreeable. **(2: 138)**

So what does it matter if K. M. soars in the newspapers, & runs up sales sky high? Ah, I have found a fine way of putting her in her place. The more she is praised, the more I am convinced she is bad. After all, there's some truth in this. She touches the spot too universally for that spot to be of the truest blood. **(2: 171)**

Katherine has been dead a week [. . .] When I began to write, it seemed to me there was no point in writing. Katherine won't read it. Katherine's my rival no longer [. . .] And I was jealous of her writing – the only writing I have ever been jealous of. This made it harder to write to her; and I saw in it, perhaps from jealousy, all the qualities I disliked in her. **(2: 227)**

If she'd lived, she'd have written on, & people would have seen that I was the more gifted – that wd only have become more apparent. **(2: 317)**

But K.M. always said affectionate admiring things to me, poor woman, whom in my own way I supposed I loved. **(2: 318)**

Anne Olivier Bell, ed., *The Diary of Virginia Woolf*, Vol. 1 – 1915–1919, Vol. 2 – 1920–1924 (London: Hogarth Press, 1977, 1978)

When we first knew her she was extraordinarily amusing. I don't think anyone has ever made me laugh more than she did in those days.

Leonard Woolf, *The Autobiography of Leonard Woolf* (London: Hogarth Press, 1964), p. 204

Table 3

They spent the night talking (a great deal), making love (effortlessly, cosily), and, she supposed, sleeping, though it was never more than a half-sleep. She had not been mistaken about Carco. He was so at ease, natural, clever, entertaining. There was something feminine about him – not just his small neatly rounded body, his long curly eyelashes and soft wavy-brown hair, his particularity about washing and scenting himself and doing his hair, and the fine bangle he wore on his arm. In his personality he was not what she thought of as a 'Pa-man' – one whose strong masculinity could make her love him against all the odds including her better judgment. But he was a man, one who knew how to please her in pleasing himself.	There was a fire in our room and a tiny lamp on the table. The fire flickered on the white wood ceiling. It was as though we were on a boat. We talked in whispers overcome by this discreet little lamp. In the most natural way we slowly undressed by the stove. F. swung into the bed. Is it cold, I said. 'No, not at all cold. Viens ma bebe, don't be frightened. The waves are quite small.' His laughing face & pretty hair, one hand with a bangle over the sheets, he looked like a girl. But seeing his puttees, his thin black tie & the feel of his flannelette shirt – & the sword, the big ugly sword, but not between us, lying in a chair. The act of love seemed somehow quite incidental, we talked so much. It was so warm & delicious lying curled in each others arms, by the light of the tiny lamp le fils de Maeterlinck, only the clock & the fire to be heard. A whole life passed in the night: other people other things, but we lay like 2 old people coughing faintly under the eiderdown, and laughing at each other and away we went to India, to South America, to Marseilles in the white boat & then we talked of Paris & sometimes I lost him in a crowd of people & it was dark & frightening, & then he was in my arms again & we were kissing. (Here he is. I know his steps.)
C. K. Stead, *Mansfield* (London: Harvill, 2004), p. 31	**Margaret Scott, ed., *The Katherine Mansfield Notebooks*, 2 vols (Minneapolis: University of Minnesota Press, 2002), Vol. 2, p. 12**

Notes

1. This essay is a longer version of a chapter entitled: '"To Hell with the Blooms Berries": Katherine Mansfield in *Mansfield* and the work of C. K. Stead', in Elizabeth Wright and Paul Edwards, *Bloomsbury: Inspirations and Influences* (Cambridge: Cambridge Scholars, 2014).
2. C. K. Stead in conversation with Gerri Kimber, 29 August 2008. C. K. Stead, *Mansfield: A Novel* (London: Harvill, 2004).
3. C. K. Stead, *Collected Poems 1951–2006* (Manchester: Carcanet, 2009), pp. 281–2.
4. C. K. Stead, *Letters and Journals of Katherine Mansfield: A Selection* (London: Allen Lane, 1977).
5. C. K. Stead in conversation with Gerri Kimber, 29 August 2008.
6. C. K. Stead, 'Katherine Mansfield: The Letters and Journals', in *In The Glass Case: Essays on New Zealand Literature* (Auckland: Auckland University Press, 1981), pp. 20–8.
7. For a detailed analysis of Mansfield's reception and reputation in France, see Gerri Kimber, *Katherine Mansfield: The View from France* (Bern: Peter Lang, 2008).
8. Frank Lea, *The Life of John Middleton Murry* (London: Methuen, 1959), p. 113.
9. Originally published in *The New Review* in 1977. C. K. Stead, 'Katherine Mansfield: The Art of the Fiction', *In the Glass Case*, pp. 29–46. The article arose from a lecture delivered at University College, London, in January 1977.
10. Katherine Mansfield, *In a German Pension* (London: Stephen Swift, 1911).
11. C. K. Stead, 'Katherine Mansfield's Friend', in *Answering to the Language: Essays on Modern Writers* (Auckland: Auckland University Press, 1989), pp. 172–4. First published in the *Times Literary Supplement*, January 1985.
12. Sean Hignett, *Brett: From Bloomsbury to New Mexico: A Biography* (London: Hodder & Stoughton, 1984).
13. Claire Tomalin, *Katherine Mansfield: A Secret Life* (London: Viking, 1987).

14. C. K. Stead, 'Katherine Mansfield's Life', in *Kin of Place* (Auckland: Auckland University Press, 2002), pp. 39–48. First published in the *London Review of Books*, November 1987.
15. Vincent O'Sullivan and Margaret Scott, eds, *The Collected Letters of Katherine Mansfield*, 5 vols (Oxford: Clarendon Press, 1984–2008), Vol. 2, p. 205. Hereafter referred to as *Letters*, followed by volume and page number.
16. C. K. Stead, 'Katherine Mansfield's Letters', in *Answering to the Language*, pp. 169–71.
17. C. K. Stead, 'Katherine Mansfield and T. S. Eliot: A Double Centenary', in *Answering to the Language*, pp. 149–61.
18. Stead is also an expert on T. S. Eliot. See his books: *The New Poetic: Yeats to Eliot* (London: Hutchinson, 1964) and *Pound, Yeats and the Modernist Movement* (New Brunswick, NJ: Rutgers University Press, 1986).
19. C. K. Stead, 'Katherine Mansfield as Colonial Realist', in *The Writer at Work* (Dunedin: University of Otago Press, 2000), pp. 38–42.
20. Gerri Kimber and Vincent O'Sullivan, eds, *The Edinburgh Edition of the Collected Fiction of Katherine Mansfield*, 2 vols (Edinburgh: Edinburgh University Press, 2012), Vol. 2, p. 420.
21. Stead, *Collected Poems*, pp. 281–2.
22. *Letters* 4, p. 11. Letter to Sydney and Violet Schiff, 14 May 1920.
23. Ida Baker, *Katherine Mansfield: The Memories of LM* (London: Michael Joseph, 1971), p. 233.
24. Leonard Woolf, *The Autobiography of Leonard Woolf* (London: Hogarth Press, 1964), p.204.
25. Hermione Lee, 'Capturing the Chameleon', *Guardian*, 29 May 2004, p. 27.
26. C. K. Stead, 'Men and Mansfield in *Mansfield*', in *Book Self: The Reader as Writer and the Writer as Critic* (Auckland: Auckland University Press, 2008), pp. 132–46.
27. Lee, p. 27.
28. Stead, *Mansfield*, pp. 193–7.
29. The story was never published in Mansfield's lifetime, appearing in the posthumous collection *Something Childish and Other Stories* in 1924.
30. Tomalin, p. 226n.
31. Stead, 'Men and Mansfield in *Mansfield*', pp. 145–6.
32. C. K. Stead, *The Secret History of Modernism* (London: Harvill, 2001), p. 161.
33. C. K. Stead in conversation with Gerri Kimber, 29 August 2008.
34. Alberto Manguel, 'Leaving Fingerprints Behind', *Spectator*, 5 June 2004, p. 44.
35. Manguel, p. 44.
36. Manguel, p. 44.
37. C. K. Stead, *The Yellow Buoy: Poems 2007–2012* (Auckland: Auckland University Press, 2013), pp. 41–2.

'Woman of Words'

Robin Woodward

Virginia King's Katherine Mansfield monument, 'Woman of Words' (2013), is an outstanding work in the history of New Zealand sculpture and a unique work in the history of art. It is the only figurative work to have been commissioned by the Wellington Sculpture Trust, the only public sculpture of a female figure by a New Zealand sculptor, and the only statue of Katherine Mansfield in the world. What is more, this 3.4-metre figure is an exceptional work of art. One can almost hear the swish of Mansfield's skirts as she strides out of Midland Park, heading down to Lambton Quay. Even more distinctive is the form. In this work, Katherine Mansfield is literally a 'woman of words'. Her dress, hair and ribbon are all formed in text – single words, lines and passages from Mansfield's writings. Sweeping around the hem of her skirt trails the text 'do you know the heron has got beautiful blue legs?' Across the back of her head are shopping lists taken from her diaries. The ribbon that swirls off her arm sends a message to Middleton Murry.

This imposing figure was commissioned early in 2012 as the result of a closed-call competition in which nine artists were invited to submit concepts for a monument to Katherine Mansfield. The brief was exacting. The work had to be accessible to the public and resonate with its audience, and be educative and, if possible, interactive. Most importantly, the sculpture needed to be a monument that celebrated the life of Katherine Mansfield, rather than being a memorial to her. It should honour Mansfield's literary heritage, affirming her aspiration to be seen as 'a writer first and a woman after'. In response, sculptor Virginia King decided to create a work in the figurative form of a woman cloaked in phrases selected from Mansfield's writing. She focused specifically on Mansfield's references to New Zealand, aiming to present a balanced

Figure 3. Virginia King, 'Woman of Words'. © Virginia King. Figures 3 to 6 courtesy of Virginia King.

selection that would inform the public and convey the writer's humour, insight and perception.

Wrapped in her writing and defined by her own words, here in 'Woman of Words' Katherine Mansfield presents a mask-like face to the world. This references the line in her letter to Sylvia Payne, 'don't lower your mask unless you have another mask prepared beneath – as terrible as you like – but a mask.' The sculpted mask is all the more notable because it is cast in stainless steel as opposed to being an open form cut through with space, which is the style that characterises most of the sculpture. With the appearance of an impenetrable veneer, this visage has a particularly strong presence. So too do the slender, elegant hands, rather like those of a musician, which allude to Mansfield's early years as a cellist and her continued interest in the arts.

The importance of the hands is emphasised by King because hands and gloves are frequently remarked on in Mansfield's notebooks and short stories. In fact, the hands of 'Woman of Words' almost became gloves as King responded to the keenness of vision that distinguishes Mansfield's writing. She was particularly taken with Mansfield's sensitivity

Figure 4. 'Woman of Words', in progress. © Virginia King.

to nuances of gesture and movement in descriptions of women pulling on their gloves. Observations such as this were part of the writer's keen awareness of the finer points of women's fashion and her close observation of details such as fabrics, buttons and accessories. In her turn, Virginia King is just as meticulous in her minute attention to detail. Her 'Woman of Words' wears an ankle-length skirt in the style that was fashionable with society women in the 1920s. Teamed with a long-sleeved fitted bodice, the figure-hugging skirt flares from the hips in six panels. The cut of the cloth, the fullness of the skirt and the closely fitted sleeves are based on 1920s fashion plates. Most specifically, the sleeves reference Mansfield's short-story fragment, 'One great advantage' (1922),[1] with its expressed wish for romantic, long, pointed sleeves.

The complexity of cross-reference between Mansfield's writing and the visual form of this sculpture is mirrored in the physical process of the making of the artwork. Both the hands and the face are modelled from life. The delicate hands are based on those of Judy Craig, whose husband, Jon Craig, was the Wellington Sculpture Trust's chairman of the Katherine Mansfield sculpture project. The shape of the head and the outline of the facial features of 'Woman of Words' are based on those of Nathalia Lusardi, an Argentinian visitor to New Zealand, whom the sculptor met on Auckland's Waiheke Island during the summer of 2012. King sketched and photographed Lusardi before carving a plaster of Paris mask of her face and neck. A ceramic mould was made of this carving so that a prototype could be cast in wax; five models in wax were cast. By working up the model in this softer material, King could explore a range of expression and determine the finish to the mask-like face before casting it in stainless steel.

The process of creating the hands was just as labour-intensive – photographing, sketching and carving a pair of hands, making a mould, casting in wax. From there, King could finesse the hands, separating the fingers and carving the final details such as the fingernails, before making yet another mould for the stainless steel pour. To ensure that the quality of material in the solid-cast hands would be identical to that in the rest of the work, King collected together and melted down the scrap, or 'drop outs', of marine-grade stainless steel that she had kept from laser-cutting earlier works.

In contrast to Mansfield's mask and hands, the body of the sculpture is in written language – and the text, of course, is that of the 'Woman of Words' herself, Katherine Mansfield. When she died at the

Figure 5. Close-up, 'Woman of Words'. © Virginia King.

age of 34, Mansfield left a wealth of short stories, diaries and notebooks. As mentioned earlier, it is from these that King sourced the quotations that cloak the 'Woman of Words'. From the very inception of her idea to clothe Mansfield in her own words, the sculptor was occupied with selecting the text. She immersed herself in Mansfield studies for more than three years during the development of this artwork. It was a process that began well before she submitted her proposal to the selection committee, because although the sculpture was not formally commissioned until early 2012, the project was first mooted in 2009.

Throughout the competition process and during the fund-raising stage, King was already searching for text, selecting and experimenting with content as well as determining the length of each phrase and the layout of the text on the panels of the sculpture. This was long before any words could be placed on the panels, or any shaping, laser cutting and assembly could begin. Then, just as King was doing the final edit of her text, unpublished short stories surfaced, so Dr Gerri Kimber, Katherine Mansfield scholar at the University of Northampton, forwarded new lines for King's consideration and inclusion amongst the text of the sculpture.

The placement, as well as the selection, of text was a major aspect of the work. The words that swirl around the writer are governed by the size, shape and pattern of each panel. The side panels, for example, which are fairly narrow, carry the titles of short stories, many of which are succinct phrases or single words such as 'Bliss', 'Prelude', 'Poison', 'The Fly', 'Millie', 'Miss Brill'. Mansfield's bobbed hairstyle has been created from an assemblage of 50 single-word shopping lists culled from a notebook dated 1921. Even the ribbon that flutters from the right of her waist communicates a close connection with the author. Its message to Murry reads, 'don't play around'.

The proportionate size of the figure presented further technical challenges. At the design stage, two maquettes were developed in order to confirm the stance of the figure and the precision of the shaped panels for the placement of text. The first maquette was made of paper stretched over a movable wooden frame, and, in the search for anatomical accuracy, was designed on a 1:5 scale. The frame was covered with shaped paper panels which were then removed and trimmed individually, and any changes recorded. After that, the maquette was reassembled and sealed with polyurethane to hold its form. A second, larger maquette, created on a 1:3 scale, was laser-cut out of sheet stainless steel and the panels were pressed, formed and welded together. Final changes were transferred to computer drawings for the full-size figure,

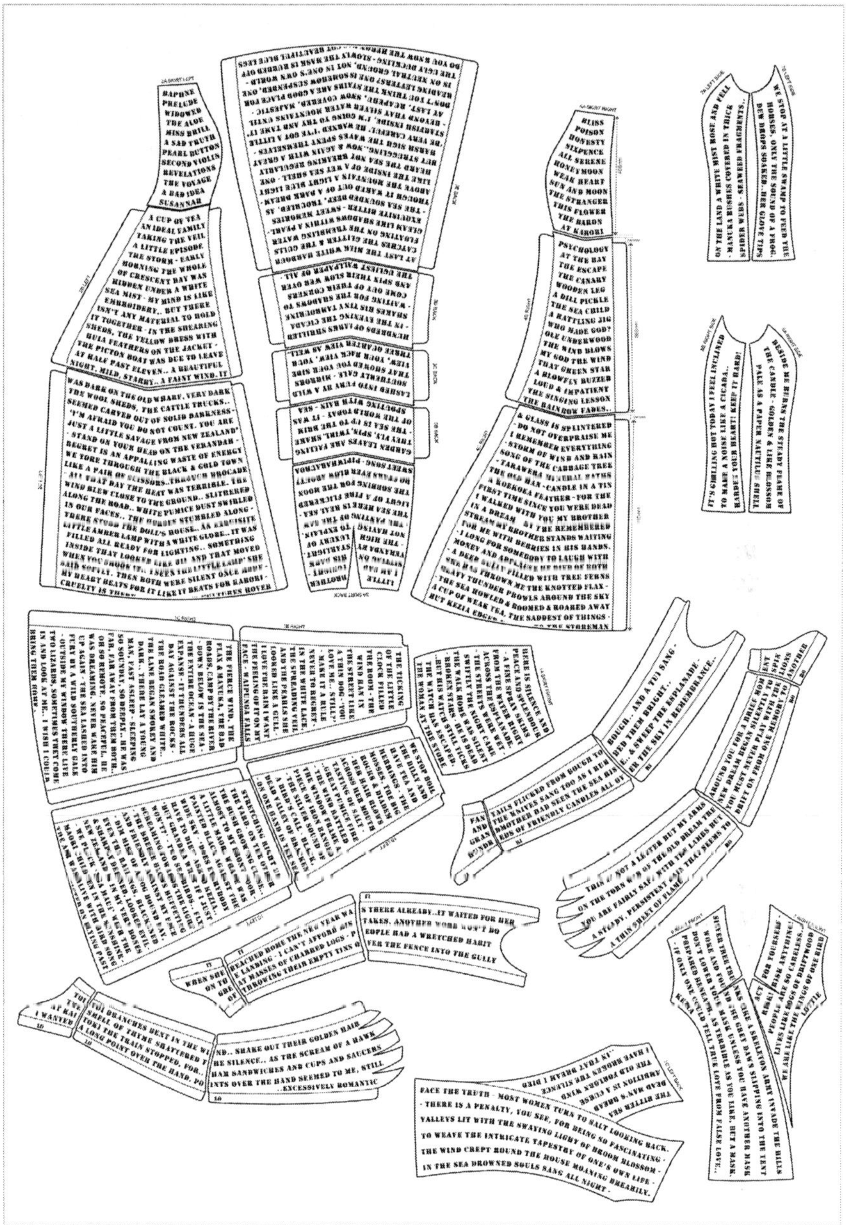

Figure 6. Artist's layout of 'Woman of Words'. © Virginia King.

so that the lines of text could be selected and placed on each panel, according to content and length.

Laser cutting the lettering into the steel was a painstaking process as the laser beam was moved only fractionally for each cut in the shaping of a letter. If the machine jammed in the formation of any of the letters and this went unnoticed, the entire panel had to be recut. For the skirt in particular, a key aspect of the technical process was the creation of soft fabric curves from flat sheets of stainless steel panels, which needed to be shaped after being laser-cut with quotations. The shaping and curving of the steel panels required a mastering of technology as the fabrication team made incremental pressings of the sheet steel using a foot-operated 20-tonne press to develop the soft flowing curves of the fabric. To develop the subtle compound curves of the torso, a more delicate Pullmax machine was used. During this entire process of pressing and shaping, the stainless steel panels were covered with a plastic film to protect the outer surfaces.

Although King marked the direction of each movement in pressing the panels, the overall form was developed by eye. Beginning at the skirt hem, each panel was shaped and fitted against its adjacent panel. When all the panels were formed, stitch welds were marked at 10-mm intervals. Then began the laborious process of making small welds along the junctions of the panels, marks made in a pattern designed to suggest a dressmaker's top stitching along the seam lines of a garment. Both the outside and the inside seams were joined, with some parts being fully welded to add further strength. Collectively, the filigree panels of laser-cut text have a structural purpose as well as an aesthetic effect, providing structural strength and visual movement while grounding and simplifying the form of the artwork.

Mansfield's birthplace and the setting for her earliest short stories, Wellington, was always going to be the place for this monument. Mansfield recalled running down Lambton Quay with her younger brother, whom she adored – and whose death in the Great War devastated her. The specific location of the work, however, came under careful scrutiny. A site within Midland Park was originally selected for the work, but the Wellington City Council had concerns about reducing Wellington's Central Business District's already limited 'green space'. So the 'Woman of Words' stands just outside the park, looking towards the sea, as if setting off at a brisk pace down Lambton Quay. At night, lights placed within the base of this lattice-like figure reflect off the inner surfaces of the perforated sculpture to create a shell of radiant silhouetted quotations. Virginia King's 'Woman of Words' has become an illuminated lantern on Lambton Quay.

Note

1. Gerri Kimber and Vincent O'Sullivan, eds, *The Edinburgh Edition of the Collected Fiction of Katherine Mansfield*, 2 vols (Edinburgh: Edinburgh University Press, 2012), Vol. 2, pp. 505–7. Published by John Middleton Murry as 'The Dressmaker', in the *Scrapbook*, pp. 231–3.

REVIEWS

Janet Frame, *In the Memorial Room* (Melbourne: Text Publishing, 2013), 202 pp., NZ$35, ISBN 978 1 9221 4713 4

The latest publication in what has become a virtual campaign by Janet Frame's literary executors to keep her name alive and her reputation bright before the public is a novel, *In the Memorial Room,* written in 1974 while Frame was holding what was then called the Winn-Manson Katherine Mansfield Fellowship in Menton. Here is what an unsigned foreword tells us about the work:

> In 1973, Janet Frame was awarded the Katherine Mansfield Fellowship, and she spent the following year in Menton on the Côte d'Azur. Beneath the Villa Isola Bella, where Mansfield lived and wrote for a time, is the Memorial Room, a small stone room commemorating her work and given to the Mansfield Fellow as a place to write.
>
> Though she struggled to work in the difficult conditions of the Memorial Room – with no running water or toilet facilities and delays in receiving her fellowship payments – it was in Menton that Janet Frame wrote *In the Memorial Room,* the story of Harry Gill, writer and recipient of the Watercress-Armstrong Fellowship.
>
> Frame did not allow publication of the manuscript during her lifetime – would certain people see themselves in the characters portrayed and, finding unflattering portraits, be offended? But she always intended the novel to be published posthumously, at the right time. Tucked away, to be looked at later, the Menton novel waited while Frame went on to write *Living in the Maniatoto,* a novel interlaced with some of the same characters, events and places.
>
> Now, almost forty years after Janet Frame wrote *In the Memorial Room,* on her second-hand typewriter, the wait is over.

The Fellowship, we are made to feel, was less a favour to Frame than just another set of difficulties to overcome, obstacles to be surmounted – slow remittances, no running water or toilet, second-hand typewriter. But now, for us, her readers, 'the wait is over'.

I was the holder of the Fellowship in 1972, two years before Frame, and I remember how disconcerted I was when the poet Anton Vogt, who had left New Zealand in a huff over I've forgotten what, vowing never to return, and who had taken up residence in Menton, wrote a scathing piece on Frame's behalf in the New Zealand *Listener,* condemning whoever was responsible for providing for her so inadequately during her tenure. I knew there was a struggle to keep the Fellowship going (it has continued almost year by year right up to the present), and this was the kind of publicity which could only have an adverse effect on its chances of survival. I wrote a piece, in effect an answer, for the same journal, explaining that one was not obliged to use the room as a workplace; that, having three small children, I had chosen to use it and had found it not without its charms and advantages; that there were plans to improve it; that meanwhile there was a public loo in the little Garavan railway station only two minutes' walk away – and so on.

Vogt had in fact provided Frame with accommodation in a villa attached to his own house; and he and his wife would have found themselves unflatteringly portrayed in this novel, as would several of the members of the Watercress-Armstrong (i.e. Winn-Manson) Fellowship committee, whose naive enthusiasm for the work of the writer they commemorated, Margaret Rose Hurndell (i.e. Katherine Mansfield), is mocked. Celia and Cecil Manson and their son Bill, in particular, are cruelly lampooned and would have been deeply hurt. Frank Sargeson, posthumously celebrated for the help he gave Frame at a crucial time in her life, used to say that helping Janet was a risky business; you were as likely as not to be punished for it in her fiction – and those who awarded her the Menton Fellowship would have had cause to agree.

As for the poet, Margaret Rose Hurndell, whose work is commemorated by the Watercress-Armstrong award, we are offered a couple of brief clips of her poems which seem (and Frame surely intends they should) extraordinarily pretentious and opaque. Harry Gill, the narrator and recipient of the award, reflects that Hurndell's poetry would probably be forgotten in a few years, and that the Watercress-Armstrong 'memorial gesture' might be destined for oblivion. It was a strange idea indeed to make the tenure of a literary Fellowship the subject of a fiction written while holding a similar one in the same town; and all the more so when it offers 'a horrifying vision' of the creators of the Fellowship 'feeding on the death' of the writer commemorated, 'nourishing themselves with the power of permanence which death has and which they so much desire' (65).

But none of this would matter too much if the novel, only now publicly revealed, were indeed, as the jacket blurb announces, 'a funny, nuanced and brilliantly witty masterpiece [. . .] Frame at her sparkling best'. Do we care if a brilliant novel or poem unfairly skewers some innocent and worthy victim? Think of Lawrence's fictional version of Lady Ottoline Morrell, Huxley's of Middleton Murry, Mansfield's of Francis Carco, or (this has a long history) Dryden's of Shadwell and Catullus' of Caesar. It's a matter of interest; something to be noted by scholars; a reason for tut-tutting and sympathy sometimes. But if the work is successful and important, the circumstances and people who occasioned it are not of primary concern – less and less so as time goes by.

In this case, however, the claims made for the novel are grossly exaggerated. It arouses interest because anything by Frame does. It certainly deserved preservation, and attention by scholars and critics. But I seriously doubt it was wise, or will serve her public reputation well, to have put it out in the commercial marketplace promoted in these extravagant terms.

* * *

Harry Gill is a 33-year-old writer who has been awarded the Watercress-Armstrong Fellowship in Menton. Differences between this fellowship and its recipient on the one hand, and the originals in real life on the other, are clear. Gill is male and younger than Frame was when she received the award; and the writer commemorated is a poet whose dates are quite a lot later than Mansfield's. Beyond those details, however, there is not a lot of space between the fiction and the reality.

Harry is met in Menton by Connie and Max Watercress, their son Michael, and other members of the Welcoming Committee. He represents himself as personally insignificant and is made to feel his work is unimportant and that he doesn't look or behave like 'a real writer' (30–4). The Watercress son, Michael, on the other hand, with a big beard, great confidence, and early signs of literary talent, exactly matches Connie and Max's idea of a perfect recipient of their award. At a reception the mayor supposes Michael *is* the Fellow, and has his photograph taken for next day's *Nice-Matin* shaking his hand. At a restaurant Michael is again mistaken for the Fellow and given free champagne, while Harry is overlooked. Later in the novel, when Harry goes deaf overnight, Connie and Max will attempt to persuade him to give up the Fellowship in Michael's favour.

The senior Watercress pair are both unsuccessful writers – 'Somehow their writing life had been separated from their ambition'– but the death and fame of Margaret Rose Hurndell had allowed them 'to bask [. . .] in reflected glory. They flourished in her fame' (40). This reverence is another cause for Harry's sense of his own inadequacy. The key to the Memorial Room is handed over to him with much emotion, and when he goes there alone, the room (unmistakably modelled on the Mansfield memorial close to the little Menton-Garavan station) is described as 'another grave for her, to keep alive her death rather than her work'. It is, Harry reflects bitterly, a 'unique memorial, to pay a writer to work within a tomb!' (45).

One of the problems throughout this novel is that it is at times a non-realist work of symbol and fable, at others a literal recounting of Frame's experience of the Fellowship and a vehicle for her personal grumbles and deeper anxieties. So immediately after the sentences quoted above come complaints about the 'sheer physical discomfort', the lack of 'running water or toilet, little light and little warmth', the 'roar of construction machinery [. . .] and the constant close passing of the trains' (45). Gill is not pleased, and neither was Janet Frame.

At quite another level of reality (or unreality/symbolism) Harry tells us he is going blind. When he informs local GP, Dr Rumor, of this he is told his eyesight is perfect and that he is displaying 'incipient signs of intentional invisibility'. 'You are trying to make yourself invisible [. . .] Like a child who shuts his eyes and thinks no one can see him.' Dr Rumor reminds him of the recent history of 'annihilation of races' and adds, 'There's another form of annihilation, obliteration if you will, of a psychological nature, practised by human being on human being.' And he goes on, 'you are co-operating with your assassins', and 'on the point of vanishing' (60–3).

Harry rejects this at first, but then seems to accept it as fitting his case.

> I found myself thinking again and again of psychological annihilation [. . .] I thought, if a person's psychological climate, which, I suppose, could be interpreted as his habitual method of dealing with his life, were of passive submission as mine in my short-sighted world had been, then a storm of unusual force, a combination of aggressive personalities, could wreck him, tear him to pieces like wolves descending from the mountains upon the timid sheep. (64)

We are clearly in Frame territory here, and it's difficult to see this quite as 'fiction' – rather a moment of more than half-serious self-inspection by Frame in her own person.

Harry has found himself a dingy, smelly one-room apartment – all he could afford on the 'rather meagre Fellowship' (33); but Elizabeth and Dorset Foster, members of the Welcoming Committee, now rescue him from this and set him up in their spare villa next door. The opportunity seems to exist for the mood of the novel to lift; but soon, from feeling overlooked and slighted, Harry finds himself swamped with attention, including further offers of accommodation he doesn't need. Feeling patronised, and armed with Dr Rumor's warning that he may be in danger of psychological annihilation, he begins to suspect and resent the attention even more than the neglect:

> Regularly the Watercresses claimed me, for a journey, for a visit, for a meal, to enlist my co-operation in annihilation of me and their replacement of me by their son. I realised this. I was no longer afraid. The Fosters were more to be feared. [. . .] Unfortunately I, in the little house, was in direct view, a captive. And so they descended upon me. Where could I, Harry Gill, hide? (80)

Elizabeth Foster is the older sister of Margaret Rose Hurndell (they were named after the royal princesses of Frame's childhood) and is part of the Committee which includes Liz Lee and her husband George, an Englishman whose speech is so astonishingly unintelligible that each time he says something, what Harry hears is, 'Angela will be livid' (31–2). As the novel goes on, and Harry gets to know him better, this becomes 'Angela will be livid – Old, retired' (105). This is the novel's best, and most characteristic, Frame joke – based on language, and with a delicate nuance of Kiwi versus posh-Pom antipathy.

Though he now has a place to live and write, the excess of attention impedes progress with his work – and with Frame's too, it seems. There is no narrative momentum – indeed, hardly any movement at all; and it's here that Frame/Harry introduces a new experiment. Harry has been reflecting on the idea, prevalent in Menton, of 'retirement', and how 'human beings' (Frame novels are prone to pronouncements of this kind) 'live their lives in a prison of images', trapped by 'the appalling deceit of language', in particular the metaphor of the journey (74). Harry has heard of an Englishman, an expert on Shakespeare, who retired to Menton vowing to speak only in nouns and verbs. 'All references to emotion were excluded because they could not be described accurately. There was no reference to things of the spirit: no abstract words [. . .] No thoughts.' His intention was to '[strip] his mind of the corruption of language' (77–9).

This is an idea that appeals to Harry. Wanting to hide from the Hurndellites who are besetting him,

> I retreated into my novel, I became the retired professor, and if you want to find me, you must look there, and [. . .] you will find Harry Gill, living his pure life, unadjectived, unadverbed, fully nouned and verbed and numbered; and you will read of the consequences of his decision: '*Quick now, here, now, always* – '. In the next chapter. (80–1)

This introduces what I'm sure must have been an accidental ambiguity about whether what we are reading has become the novel Harry is writing, or continues to be, as it began, only an account derived from the journal of his 'tenure'. That question apart (and I think it would be fruitless to labour it), the effect of this decision, which carries on through Chapter 8 and on into 9, has to be seen at some length for its full effect to be felt. On me it struck a seriously false note, somewhere between free-wheeling vacancy and pretentiousness. For example:

> They asked me was the heater working. I said yes the heater was working. The heater was a radiator with thirteen panels, filled with oil which heated when the heater was plugged into the electricity. The switch could be

> adjusted on a scale from one to ten, with a wattage from seven hundred and fifty to one thousand, a medium warmth. It was grey, with small grey rubber wheels making it portable as far as its flex of two metres would stretch without pulling the plug from the power point set five centimetres from the passageway into the hall upon a yellow-painted skirting board.
> – Keep the heat switched on, Elizabeth said as, noting that the temperature had risen, I bent to adjust the thermostatic control.
> Elizabeth's voice was loud.
> I straightened and stood up in a second.
> – I will leave it switched on, I said. – At night I will turn it off.
> – Leave it switched on at night too.
> Dorset's voice was several decibels louder than Elizabeth's, although I had no instrument to measure it. (83–4)

This experiment in literalness, which is perhaps (who knows?) intended to illustrate the unsatisfactoriness, the deadly-dullness, of realist fiction – in other words that there is no escape from 'the deceit' of metaphor, symbol, fable, myth – runs on for a dozen dire pages, but breaks down when Louise says to Harry, 'Your time is your own.'

'It isn't, you know,' Harry says (98), and his 'three thousand words without adjectives, without judgement, feeling, thinking' have been derailed by a 'time image from within the convention of the myth' (101).

The novel ambles on now with further lucubration on time, retirement, the discontents of Menton's inhabitants, the ferocious competitiveness of Margaret Rose Hurndell's devotees, and the necessary 'emptiness' of the novelist, whose consciousness must make space for his characters. By Chapter 13 Harry is able to describe his state in Menton as 'settled' (126); but the Fosters, keen to look after him even better, decide improvements must be made to the house, all for his benefit, and once again he is beset everywhere by noise and activity.

Harry is anxious about his larger role as writer: 'My fellow writers have called me a man of straw. I do not write political articles. I do not march in demonstrations. I do not make my voice heard against tyranny, injustice. In private life I turn the other cheek as I murmur, *I understand the motive*' (139). This may well have been an anxiety of Frame's, though I don't think any of her fellow-writers ever called her a woman of straw, because it was always accepted that she'd had a rough ride in her early years and was, so to speak, exempt from kitchen duties.

Just over two-thirds of the way through the novel, Harry's encroaching blindness is abandoned, or set aside, in favour of a new disability. He wakes to find himself stone deaf – a significant shift in the narrative's underlying metaphor; and the consequences of this disaster will account for the very little, in terms of action or event, that follows. Dr Rumor, to whom Harry now returns, describes his condition as 'Auditory Retaliation. [. . .] A sealing off, a closure. Auditory hibernation' (151–2). After a few more (written) questions from Harry he replies (also in writing), 'everything is favourable for your obliteration. You have been stifled, muffled, silenced. You cannot cry out because you cannot hear the cries of others.' He recommends that Harry 'Just wait and see. I think your condition will cure itself' (153).

So the ending of the novel occurs like a slow loss of vital functions, but with the following momentary snap to attention: 'Whatever the explanation I accepted my deafness with a passivity which, before the age of the raging clitoris, would have been looked on as feminine' (157).

Harry refuses to see a specialist and tells everyone (always in writing) that the condition is permanent and incurable. He does, however, resist the attempt of the Watercress parents to wrest the Fellowship away from him for their son, even discovering a kind of confidence, not so much in himself, as in, or through, the comparison with Michael, and the latter's lack of true literary substance:

> What a paragon of a writer he was! I simply couldn't deny it [. . .] and although I did feel a sneaking jealousy of his ability to play the role in costume of a writer [. . .] his talent did not match his appearance [. . .] His thoughts and the thoughts of others were constantly on what he would achieve, on what he would become. [. . .] Poor chap, I thought. He's already going to seed. Destroyed by his promising future. A man without a past or present. Was he not then a completely un-metaphorical man, deprived of time? (193–4)

Dialogue is now confined to what can be written on scraps of paper. There is a lack of conviction in the writing, and of substance in the story. One feels Frame's reluctance to continue and her resorting to what reads sometimes like vacuous self-imitation:

> I had not realized until then that we own the words we speak as we own the food we swallow or reject; we own the words, command them, shift them, re-emphasise them; they, powerful, have little power over our speaking them; the loneliness that came over me was caused, I think, by the degradation of the words, their descent from the pampered sheltered ones to the homeless outcasts that could not be spared an inflexion or a morsel of emphasis or a loving hesitation. (187)

And so on. She has lost the confidence that there is any story to sustain, and is only going through the motions. The novel concludes with variations of 'last words' of the kind put at the end of a formal letter, repeated over and over; and then passages that seem to be copied from a manual of 'rules for good writing', six or seven pages of them, going wearily nowhere, saying nothing.

This is a looking-in-darkly rather than a looking-out-bravely novel, with an exceptionally unappealing and self-disliking central character. It is also fiction which makes surprisingly little of the visual lift offered by its Côte d'Azur setting.

* * *

Half-way through the novel Margaret Rose Hurndell's sister explains to Harry, 'I'm here – we're here – more or less to guard Rose's interests, not in a material way, in a memorial way' (131). There is certainly an irony in the fact that a novel about the memorialising of a dead writer, which is in part a satire on such pieties, should be posthumously published as itself an act of memorialisation of (as the jacket reminds us) 'one of New Zealand's greatest writers'. I find it difficult to believe Frame could have thought the novel was finished, or that she would have wanted it published in this unsatisfactory state.

The joke about the man whose every statement is heard as 'Angela will be livid' was for me a small flashing reminder of what good company Frame could be, how clever and funny as well as serious – both in person and on the page. Of course there is intermittent but clear evidence of her great talent, and sometimes just the unmistakable ring of authentic Frame sentences. But there is too much unfiltered resentment and malice, too much unevenness of tone and uncertainty of direction – and in the end, no shape.

From the example of Mansfield and many others we know that the enthusiastic heirs of a writer's copyright, the 'keepers of the flame' as Ian Hamilton called them in his book on the subject,[1] are not always the best or wisest servers and preservers of a literary reputation. Much that has happened since Frame's death has repeated the lesson.

C. K. Stead

Note

1. Ian Hamilton, *Keepers of the Flame: Literary Estates and the Rise of Biography* (London: Hutchinson, 1992).

Isobel Maddison, *Elizabeth von Arnim: Beyond the German Garden* (Farnham: Ashgate, 2013), 298 pp., £60, ISBN 978 1 4094 1167 3; Jennifer Walker, *Elizabeth of the German Garden – A Literary Journey: A Biography of Elizabeth von Arnim* (Brighton: Book Guild, 2013), 484 pp., £20, ISBN 978 1 8462 4851 1

2013 is an excellent year for Elizabeth von Arnim, who, until recently, has had the strangest of critical receptions; to date, there have been only three biographies, a handful of scholarly articles and a couple of PhD theses. Now three books on von Arnim have been published all at once. Isobel Maddison's study *Elizabeth von Arnim: Beyond the German Garden* is the first scholarly monograph exclusively on von Arnim's novels and does much to rehabilitate her as a successful writer of complex satirical fiction. It is a wide-ranging introduction based on a tremendous amount of research. Scholars will appreciate Maddison's discussion of some of von Arnim's best novels as well as hitherto unknown texts. She works closely with von Arnim's letters at the Huntington Library and, very helpfully, includes the complete Finding Aid to the Collection in the book.

Maddison is critical of the epithet 'middlebrow' often applied to von Arnim and presents her subject as a progressive, political author whose best writing defies easy categorisation. The first half of von Arnim's career is discussed under the heading of 'The "German" novels' and culminates in a detailed investigation of von Arnim's epistolary novel *Christine* (1917) in the context of anti-invasion literature. Maddison then examines the Fabian philosophies that underpin some of the later marriage-problem novels such as *Love* (1925) and *Expiation* (1929). These discussions are interesting and illuminating, yet the elaboration of the historical context at times overshadows the analysis. Maddison offers valuable insights, but her book needs a stronger critical vision that would hold together chapters as diverse as an introductory biographical sketch, a lengthy summary of von Arnim's contemporary reception, explorations of the political, biographical and feminist implications of various books, the film adaptations of von Arnim's novels and, last but not least, her friendship with Katherine Mansfield.

The latter is one of the most interesting chapters in Maddison's study. Following Kathleen Jones's lead, Maddison explores the personal and literary relationship between Mansfield and von Arnim. It is salutary to see von Arnim discussed as a significant literary influence on Mansfield's *In a German Pension* (1911) and as an important friend in the last years of Mansfield's life. Maddison does not deny the occasional tensions caused by the changeable tempers of both cousins but is right when she insists that, in spite of Mansfield's unflattering portrait of von Arnim in 'A Cup of Tea', both writers were attached to each other. Quoting from Mansfield's reviews of von Arnim's novels, Maddison lists a number of talents both writers possess: 'wit and whimsy', 'an instinct that keeps it true to experience', a sense of detachment coupled with a 'touch of worldly wisdom' and a keen eye for psychological nuance (102). Maddison discusses the shared anti-German sentiment in the early works of both cousins and notes the fashionable propagation of vegetarianism Mansfield may have picked up from von Arnim. Both writers associate the German appetite for meat with the political voraciousness of the Kaiser, and Maddison reads Mansfield's gluttonous Baron as a response to von Arnim's Baron von Ottringel in *The Caravaners* (1909). She concludes her textual analysis with a comparison of Mansfield's 'The Black Cap' (1917) and the finale of von Arnim's *The Pastor's Wife* (1914). Maddison carefully works out the structural and thematic similarities between both texts and notes their shared preoccupation with marriage and female frustration. Influence ran both ways between Mansfield and von Arnim, according to Maddison, who speculates that von Arnim began writing *Vera* (1921) after 'long talks with Mansfield' (122) and implies that the psychological acuity of *Vera* is at least partly inspired by Mansfield's modernist preoccupation with the human mind.

In her biography of von Arnim, *Elizabeth of the German Garden,* Jennifer Walker also highlights the relationship with Mansfield and offers the most detailed account of their friendship to date, quoting at length from their correspondence and choosing passages that show the depth of their affection for each other. Walker presents Mansfield and von Arnim as two considerable creative forces on an equal footing. Her indifference to elitist critical taxonomies enables her to look at von Arnim's life and works unhampered by any academic diffidence about von Arnim's status as a bestselling celebrity author. Less interested in questions of literary influence, Walker focuses on the personal relationship between the cousins and presents von Arnim as a warm, generous and loyal friend who supported and encouraged Mansfield in the final years of her life. We learn how von Arnim's visits became a lifeline for Mansfield during her isolation in Switzerland. Mansfield's irritation over von Arnim's unfortunate comment that 'At the Bay' was a 'pretty little story', which allegedly inspired 'A Cup of Tea', is carefully contextualised and loses much of its sting. Both cousins, as she rightfully points out, were fascinated with masquerades, role play and the exploration of different selves, making the assessment of their relationship challenging and fascinating in equal measure.

Walker is the first biographer to capture the force of von Arnim's personality and amalgamate the contradictions of her character into a coherent whole. Refusing to be bogged down by detail, her writing is perceptive, imaginative and often of great insight. Von Arnim's enigmatic attraction to her abusive second husband, Sir Francis Russell, loses much of its mystery and Russell himself is portrayed as a charming but deeply troubled man incapable of empathy. Walker is also the first biographer careful to maintain the difference between the author (Mary) and her famous literary character (Elizabeth). This biography has a double focus. The first is von Arnim's relationships with the men in her life. Her stormy affair with H. G. Wells and subsequent lifelong friendship with him are traced in some detail. However, Walker's claim that their passionate connection remained platonic is doubtful. Sometimes she seems to arrive at conclusions by suppressing contradictory evidence and hence her excellent portrait of von Arnim lacks in shade. The way she downplays the tensions between von Arnim and Mansfield is a case in point. Likewise, von Arnim's fraught relationship with several of her children and the depressed phases of her later life are glossed over, as are von Arnim's own less amicable qualities; the autocratic and domineering aspects of her character are less examined than her loyalty, generosity and deep love of nature, humans and dogs.

Walker's second focus is music. She is the first biographer to pay adequate attention to von Arnim's outstanding musical talent as an organist and her love of Wagner. She discusses her musical education and explores the musicality of von Arnim's writing. Beyond that, Walker's comments on the novels are largely biographically motivated in tracing real-life inspirations for characters and plot elements. Not all her analyses are equally convincing and, in praising each book as a little masterpiece, she does not pay enough attention to the significant differences in quality between them. With the exception of Wells, Mansfield and E. M. Forster, Walker does not discuss von Arnim's many literary connections, but for a better understanding of von Arnim's works Walker's biography is indispensable and fascinating reading.

Maddison and Walker both deserve praise for opening up new perspectives on von Arnim, whose works are finally beginning to receive the critical recognition they deserve. Both scholars and general readers of interwar fiction will find Walker's and Maddison's studies rich in material, interesting and inspiring to further research.

Juliane Römhild
La Trobe University

Ann-Marie Einhaus, *The Short Story and the First World War* (Cambridge: Cambridge University Press, 2013), 219pp., £55, ISBN 978 1 1070 3843 1

Set in the late 1920s when there was a major surge of Great War books, Patrick Hamilton's *Mr Stimpson and Mr Gorse* (1952) has as its protagonist an impostor masquerading as a 1914 war hero. Among his fellow frauds is a hapless Major who has seen no active service and yet specialises in the poetry of remembrance:

> Mention of Passchendaele, he felt, would be most inspiring . . . It furnished almost as many rhymes as '[Flanders] Field'. There was 'fail' ('Shall we then . . . ?'). There was 'bewail' ('Who shall . . . ?'). There was 'gale' ('Midst War's great . . .). And 'pale', and 'dale', and 'veil', and 'hail', and 'quail', and 'flail', and 'nightingale', and 'grail' (holy, naturally), and 'vale', and innumerable smashing ones.[1]

Great War poetry has turned into a compendium of floridly archaic clichés.

In view of the lasting dominance of trench poetry as the authentic voice of the First World War, it is refreshing to turn to Einhaus's recovery of perhaps the least known of literary forms through which contemporary readers understood their war experience. Einhaus shows that the topical short story was a tremendously popular medium in wartime, notwithstanding its near-total invisibility in our literary memory of the war. As evidence of its marginal status she cites the memorably perverse tendency of anthologies with some version of the phrase 'war stories' in their title to incorporate virtually no short stories whatsoever; meanwhile, hundreds of actual war stories languish in back issues of the defunct magazines in which they briefly flourished. The side-lining of the popular Great War story is exacerbated, Einhaus argues, by our critical tendency to return to the same examples, such as stories by canonical modernists like D. H. Lawrence and Katherine Mansfield. This is doubtless why their works, alongside other well-known war stories by Joseph Conrad and Rudyard Kipling, are not discussed in any significant detail here, although there is a brief reading of Mansfield's 'The Fly' alongside a intriguingly lurid-sounding magazine story of wartime bereavement (Ben Ray Redman's 'The Enduring Image') in which a grieving woman falls from a cliff, lured by the apparition of her lost lover's death in flight (74–5).

The book's introduction and first three chapters are a metacritical account of what is to be gained by recovering these forgotten works in terms of enhancing our understanding of Great War culture. The next two chapters work more closely with the primary material. Chapter 4 focuses on stories of death and disability, and these substantially confirm Jay Winter's influential revisionist argument in *Sites of Memory, Sites of Mourning* (1995) that traditional forms of consolation endured resiliently throughout what is axiomatically understood as the 'modernist' war. Chapter 5 tackles morality in popular fiction, much of which recklessly promises that war will make men both manlier and more moral, while other stories capitalise on the war as a place to explore ethical dilemmas. As Einhaus points out, however, the economic and political exigencies of popular magazine culture ensured that real problems like conscientious objection were seldom among those quandaries; indeed, even the beastly Germans seem to have proved easier than pacifists to write about sympathetically. The final chapter surveys Great War stories written long after the event and shows how the wounds of the war were reopened by the Second World War rather than superseded. The archive of texts here is fascinating, and this book will be of great interest to those seeking to supplement their reading of Mansfield via a fuller context from the golden age of the commercial as well as the experimental short story.

Marina MacKay
Durham University

Note

1. Patrick Hamilton, *The Gorse Trilogy* (London: Black Spring, 2007), p. 287.

Saikat Majumdar, *Prose of the World: Modernism and the Banality of Empire* (New York: Columbia University Press, 2013), 232pp., US$40, ISBN 978 0 2311 5694 3

Katherine Mansfield's autobiographical and fictional writings frequently rage against the banality of settler colonial existence. Her yearning for the metropolis, with its associations of avant-garde culture and sexual possibilities, features prominently in biographical narratives. The geography of empire creates an index of desire for the colonial subject that inevitably locates fullness or transcendence elsewhere. In *Prose of the World: Modernism and the Banality of Empire,* Saikat Majumdar takes as his subject the political and aesthetic import of boredom or banality in the work of a range of postcolonial writers. This chimes with a turn in modernist studies towards the everyday. Majumdar, however, takes this interest in new directions, given the transnational purview of his approach. To read colonial experience and its literary representation as forever marked by traumatic, sensational and cataclysmic events is to overlook great swathes of the experience of colonial modernity, not to mention the way imperial power can be felt in the banal routine of bureaucratisation. Furthermore, Majumdar breaks apart the association of boredom (or its elevated cousin, *ennui*) from 'its context of subjective singularity and material privilege' (15). He reads it, instead, as an affective response to exclusion and marginality, which again runs counter to metropolitan narratives of colonial experience as exotic, hyperbolic and adventure-laden.

In a richly textured introduction, Majumdar sets out the philosophical, anthropological and aesthetic parameters of his monograph. He roots notions of the banal in Enlightenment modernity and the rise of the novel. While realism relies on a functional sense of the ordinary, for modernist writers such as Virginia Woolf, the problem with the realism of Bennett or Galsworthy was not the inclusion of the everyday but its constraining or functional aspect. Modernist 'newness' arrives precisely in the transcendence achieved through the charged or heightened experience of everyday objects, sensations or moments. Colonial banality, then, is an oppositional aesthetic mode characterised by repetition and circularity, given that narrative is so often driven by the extraordinary or the event.

Prose of the World explores the work of four postcolonial writers: James Joyce, Katherine Mansfield, Zoë Wicomb and Amit Chaudhuri, all diasporic writers with a mobility often denied their characters. Majumdar reads Joyce's focus on the paralysed banality of Irish life as radical in its refusal of the conventions of literary aesthetics. Joyce's ethnographic interest in everyday objects constitutes a new narrative mode in its associations with the peripheral. It is born of and unsettles the relationship between imperial centre and colony. In Wicomb's writing, too, Majumdar finds a rejection of the literature of spectacle and trauma so often associated with South African writing. Chaudhuri, like Wicomb, eschews the narrative of national allegory, associated in his case with a Nehruvian vision of modern India, in favour of the everyday regional.

For our purposes here, however, the chapter on Mansfield deserves extended attention. Critics have troubled over where to locate or how to read a 'colonial' Mansfield. As Majumdar so eloquently documents, she has historically been seen as a writer whose aesthetic complexity emerged from, and in response to, Europe. He radically rethinks this narrative by turning to the New Zealand stories that bookend her career, focusing on her depiction of the boredom and frustrations of settler life, particularly for women. This conventional domesticity, however, works in dialectic with a submerged awareness of the violence and trauma that must be suppressed in order to sustain the bourgeois settler existence. Through this oscillation we can attend to the question of indigeneity in Mansfield's work. *The Urewera Notebook,* Majumdar argues, trades on an idyllic portrait of Maori culture as espoused by contemporary ethnographer, Elsdon Best. Unlike Best, however, Mansfield includes moments of submerged violence, shifts that chime with the changing discipline of anthropology itself. In her early New Zealand stories too ('Millie', 'The Woman at the Store', 'How Pearl Button Was Kidnapped'), Majumdar finds what James Clifford calls an 'ethnographic surrealism' which 'attacks the familiar, provoking the eruption of otherness – the unexpected'. Cultural difference becomes a site of 'eruptive mutual contact' (99), unsettling the conventional hierarchies of empire. It seems a missed opportunity that Majumdar's reading takes little account of the contexts of composition and publication of these early stories. They were written for and published in London's avant-garde magazines, and Mansfield was constructing herself as a New Zealand writer in response to the currency of the barbaric and 'primitive' in the pages of *Rhythm.* Majumdar's interest in the 'transitional sensibility' caused by the 'destabilisation of colonial empires' (99) accords with the ways Mansfield chose to 'bring' New Zealand to the empire's heart.

This is an ambitious and theoretically sophisticated book. It not only offers a startlingly original perspective on this body of writing but also reframes postcolonial writers' relationship to modernism and modernity. There is something slightly random in the chosen writers, but the coordinates of the approach are so lucidly laid out that the book is sure to generate scholarship that brings other writers into view. This is a field-changing monograph that has much to contribute to recent interest in the legacies or afterlives of modernism, and the relationship between modernism and postcolonialism.

Anna Snaith
King's College London

Kate McLoughlin, ed., *The Modernist Party* (Edinburgh: Edinburgh University Press, 2013), 240pp., £70, ISBN 978 0 7486 4731 6

In the film *Tom and Viv* (1994), a morose Eliot (Willem Dafoe) looks on in brooding silence as Vivienne (Miranda Richardson) dances with another male partner. We recognise in this scene how creativity originates in alienation from the festive crowd. The individual retreats from an oppressive sociality, cultivating a private refuge that rejects noise, clamour, motion, frivolity. But Tom himself makes a scene; he throws an adult tantrum, sulking in a way that gets him the fascinated attention of any spectator who has been trained by Austen's novels to pay close attention to the edges of the dance floor, where gossipy onlookers whisper *sotto voce* commentaries, or where longing gazes speak eloquently of unrequited desire. Tom's sulk is an old-fashioned, if not obsolete, version of modernism: the canonical modernist in geographic, cultural and personal exile, wrestling with alienation to produce a great art of authenticity and originality.

While this experience of the modernist party may seem unappealing, threatening to implode into grouchy individuals greatly preferring to go their separate ways, readers can readily join the festivities of *The Modernist Party*. This welcome collection of fascinating and timely essays reassesses the significance of social gatherings in a range of modernist literary texts and contexts. McLoughlin's introduction considers the modernist party's relationship to similar categories – the public sphere, the carnivalesque, the network, the salon – delineating at the outset a spectrum on which the party can serve at one end as 'a model for creativity' and at the other as 'the vehicle for nihilistic experiences of despair and self-effacement' (2). She synthesises a well-chosen guest-list of philosophers and theorists to introduce the collection, drawing on Kant, Bourdieu, Habermas, Bakhtin and Freud to construct a vocabulary for a 'party paradigm' (1). She also explains the collection's contribution to the exuberantly productive field of the New Modernist Studies, with its recent turns to materiality and the everyday.

Angela Smith's essay on Mansfield's 'party stories' provides illuminating interpretations of five key stories in her œuvre: 'Frau Brechenmacher Attends a Wedding', 'Sun and Moon', 'Bliss', 'Her First Ball' and 'The Garden Party'. Smith's subtle readings complicate, without rejecting, the receding model of modernist exile and alienation; Mansfield's fictional parties produce elusive revelations in which protagonists achieve partial, or precarious, heightened consciousness or insight. Thus parties are epistemological events, and the pleasures of parties have to do with new knowledge linked to the power of modernist formal experimentation to disrupt and unsettle. Smith's essay begins by treating us to an episode of Mansfield herself as a hostess who artfully created an 'unguarded and spontaneous' (81) atmosphere for her guests. This episode, and Smith's tantalising description of the 'sensuous attention to detail' (82) evident in the Alexander Turnbull Library's collection of Mansfield objects, are enticements to consider the materiality and embodied experience of modernist contexts. Parties both distract and cultivate 'sensuous attention'.

Readers interested in the material conditions of the modernist party scene will be especially interested to read Smith's essay alongside Margo Natalie Crawford's on the Harlem Renaissance and Black Arts Movement and Nathan Waddell's on the Cabaret Theatre Club. Mansfield attended the latter, by now a familiar *topos* of modernist mingling. Together, Smith's, Waddell's and Crawford's essays provoke further thinking about both cosmopolitanism and primitivism from a transatlantic perspective. Here are opportunities to probe the complexities of performance and spectatorship, as well as both the attentiveness and oblivion engendered by leisure and sociability. Mansfield scholars will eagerly accept the invitation to the modernist party, and will want to compare notes afterwards.

Rishona Zimring
Lewis & Clark College

Andrew Eastham, *Aesthetic Afterlives: Irony, Literary Modernity and the Ends of Beauty* (London: Bloomsbury, 2011), 272 pp., £54.00 hb, £24.99 pb, ISBN 978 1 4725 1210 9

Aesthetic Afterlives traces the lineage of Paterian aesthetics from its incandescent impact within English fin de siècle culture to its spectral 'afterimage' (3) in modernist and postmodernist writing. Eastham outlines the continuing 'cultural legacy' (1) of Pater's *Studies in the History of the Renaissance* (1873). Persuasively arguing that Pater 'set a model for literary modernity both in style and philosophy' (1), he examines Pater's legacy of 'disenchantment and persistence' (2) in writing ranging from Oscar Wilde, Vernon Lee and Henry James to its 'shadowy contemporary presences' (188) in Alan Hollinghurst and Zadie Smith.

While it is a critical commonplace that modernist writing emerged from 1890s Symbolism and Aestheticism, at the same time as it rejected them, there have been few recent studies that track these hereditary traces so thoroughly. Eastham focuses on the modernist and late modernist work of Katherine Mansfield, D. H. Lawrence, Evelyn Waugh and Samuel Beckett, but there is no reason why his general arguments, once unpacked, could not fruitfully be applied more widely to other modernist works. At the very least, Eastham's epigrammatic outline of the ways in which literary modernism 'covertly mediated' the 'central tropes' of Aestheticism can provide future scholars with a useful definition of the two movements' shared concerns:

> the refusal of habitual and conventional concepts of identity; the image of self-wrought, artificial beings; the development of a literary style that carried a new kind of sensuous consciousness, at the same [time] as it opened up a space of acute epistemological crisis. (173)

While High Modernism attempted through a pose of extreme ironic detachment to repudiate the self-regarding 'excesses of the 1890s' (96), it was nevertheless 'implicated' (173) in Aestheticism's twin legacies of beauty and irony, as Eastham demonstrates in the chapters on Mansfield, Lawrence and Waugh. The young Mansfield, returning to New Zealand from her adolescence in London, yearned for an 'ideal of a sensuous life to come' (86), in which the Aestheticism of Wilde and Pater figured centrally. As Sydney Janet Kaplan has argued, Wilde was for Mansfield a consciously cultivated artistic influence; however, influence necessitates both imitation and battle, and as Claire Tomalin has suggested, Mansfield's 1909 rejection of Wilde was a defining moment in her life. Yet, while this rejection holds a central place in scholarly accounts of Mansfield's *Bildung*, Eastham reads it as simply one (albeit a significant one) in a 'series of disavowals': first, of provincial New Zealand life in favour of fin de siècle Aestheticism, then of 'the mauve and yellow rhetoric' of Wilde in favour of modernist 'professional literary culture' (87). These disavowals haunt the *Notebooks* and, eventually, as Eastham suggests, lead to a 'reanimation' (117) of Mansfield's early Aestheticism in the Paterian-inflected prose poetics of 'Prelude'. Beholden to neither 'Romantic poetry nor [. . .] the modernist novel' (106), Mansfield's literary impressionism and ironic narrative mode work to bridge the 'divide between Aestheticism and modernism' (117).

Eastham's chapter on Mansfield is exhaustive, comprising close readings of 'Prelude', 'The Modern Soul' and crucial sections of the *Notebooks*, and is followed by an equally lengthy chapter on D. H. Lawrence, whose personal relationship with Mansfield in many ways mirrors the narrative of literary disavowal and disgust felt by Mansfield towards Wildean Aestheticism. Though Lawrence might have wished to 'put [. . .] to the flame' the remnants of the aesthetic, Eastham argues that he nevertheless 'recuperates the discourse of Romanticism in order to evoke the beauty of a germinal life which evades representation' (151). These chapters on Mansfield and Lawrence form the gem-like centre of Eastham's study, and though reminiscent of Pater's flame in their impressionistic hardness, nevertheless reward concentrated reading.

For scholars of Evelyn Waugh, the chapter on *Brideshead Revisited* represents a rare treat. Eastham astutely reads *Brideshead* as 'a novel of aesthetic education which attempts to orchestrate a translation of artistic to religious passion' (152). Of course, Waugh's novel explicitly announces itself in terms of Charles's 'aesthetic education' (Waugh 92), and scholars up to this point have been content with noting Waugh's various Aesthetic and Decadent allusions (Julia's jewelled tortoise, Charles's Arcadian skull), before dismissing these as marginal to a more serious Catholic schema. Eastham, however, reads Charles as a direct descendent of Pater, demonstrating his narrative inheritance of a verbal and formal 'Paterian style' (157) combining lush, paratactical, impressionistic syntax with a mode of 'aristocratic Epicureanism' (157) characterised by the competing claims of irony and consumption. As Eastham reads it, though the novel appears to make a final retreat into 'Catholic austerity' (152), this can only occur through a 'transposition' of Pater's 'hard, gem-like flame' to 'the flame of religious faith' (171), significantly manifested in Brideshead's over-determined, 'deplorable' Arts and Crafts chapel (Waugh 381). Without making reference to a single notable critic of Waugh, Eastham makes bravura, against-the-grain claims about the ends of beauty and irony in Waugh's magnum opus.

While a focus on Mansfield and Lawrence is most prominent, Eastham's study of Beckett 'brings the conceptual trajectory of *Aesthetic Afterlives* to completion' (15). Within the extreme negations of *The Unnameable*'s 'art and code of dying', Eastham identifies the 'attenuated and spectral form' of Aestheticism's Romantic subjectivity (177). Straining the limits of irony, Beckett paradoxically produces the sublime. Ambitious in scope, broadly researched and elaborately (if densely) argued, Eastham's book will prove of immense use to scholars anxious to reanimate an alternative line of influence in the history of literary modernity.

Naomi Milthorpe
University of Tasmania

Notes on Contributors

Erika Baldt is an English lecturer at Burlington County College in New Jersey. Her research interests include Anglo-American modernism and cosmopolitanism. She has published essays on the work of Katherine Mansfield, Virginia Woolf, Vita Sackville-West and Jessie Fauset.

David Bradshaw is Professor of English Literature at Oxford University and a Fellow of Worcester College. As well as a number of modernist novels and numerous articles on all aspects of modernism, he has edited *The Hidden Huxley* (1994), *A Concise Companion to Modernism* (2003), *The Cambridge Companion to E. M. Forster* (2007), *A Companion to Modernist Literature and Culture* (2006) and *Prudes on the Prowl: Fiction and Obscenity in England, 1850 to the Present Day* (2013).

Richard Cappuccio, a retired educator, is a member of both the Katherine Mansfield Society and the Katherine Mansfield Birthplace. His article, 'The Swinging Gate: Katherine Mansfield's Missionary Vision', was published in 2013. He and his wife, Dr Ann H. Marshall, live in Charlottesville, Virginia, and enjoy their garden there. He thanks both his wife and Dr Isobel Maddison for their help and patience in preparing the essay that appears in this journal.

Delia da Sousa Correa grew up in New Zealand and studied at the University of Canterbury before moving on to graduate study in London and Oxford. She is Senior Lecturer in English at the Open University and is co-editor of *Katherine Mansfield Studies*. Her research focuses on connections between literature and music in the nineteenth century and early modernist period.

Louise Edensor is Lecturer in the International Foundation Programme at Middlesex University in Dubai and is the Editorial Assistant for *Katherine Mansfield Studies*. She is currently a doctoral candidate at the University of Northampton, working on her thesis, 'Katherine Mansfield and the Construction of the Self'.

Melinda Harvey is Lecturer in English at Monash University. Her edited collection (with Sarah Ailwood), *Katherine Mansfield and Literary*

Influence, is forthcoming with Edinburgh University Press in late 2014. She is co-reviews editor of *Katherine Mansfield Studies*.

Seamus Heaney was born in County Derry, Northern Ireland, in April 1939. His first collection of poetry, *Death of a Naturalist* (1966), heralded the beginning of a literary career that would span almost fifty years and include over twenty volumes of poetry and criticism. Professor at Harvard and Oxford Universities, Heaney was awarded the Nobel Prize for Literature in 1995. He died in Dublin on 30 August 2013.

Kevin Ireland has published a collection of short stories, six novels, two memoirs, a discursive book on fishing and an account of growing old. His twentieth volume of poetry, *Selected Poems 1963–2013*, was published in 2013.

Alice Kelly completed her PhD on women's writing of the First World War in 2013 at the University of Cambridge, having previously studied at the University of Sussex, Reed College in Portland, Oregon, and the University of Oxford. She is currently a Visiting Scholar at Yale University. She is co-editing a volume of essays entitled *Shaping Modernism: Katherine Mansfield in Context*.

Gerri Kimber, Senior Lecturer at the University of Northampton, is co-editor of *Katherine Mansfield Studies* and Chair of the Katherine Mansfield Society. She is the deviser and Series Editor of the four-volume *Edinburgh Edition of the Collected Works of Katherine Mansfield* (2012–15). She is the author of *Katherine Mansfield: The View from France* (2008) and *A Literary Modernist: Katherine Mansfield and the Art of the Short Story* (2008).

Mirosława Kubasiewicz is a Lecturer at the University of Zielona Góra, where she teaches courses in the history of English literature, as well as in practical English. Her research interests focus on connections between literature and philosophy (in her PhD thesis she looked at the work of Katherine Mansfield from a Heideggerian perspective), and on the work of Katherine Mansfield and other women writers.

Marina MacKay is Senior Lecturer in English at Durham University. She is the author of *Modernism and World War II* (2007). She also edited *The Cambridge Companion to the Literature of World War II* (2009) and, with Lyndsey Stonebridge, *British Fiction after Modernism* (2007).

Isobel Maddison is a Fellow of Lucy Cavendish College, University of Cambridge, where she is a College Lecturer and the Director of Studies in English. She works primarily on female modernism and on the connections between modernism and popular fiction. She also has interests in women's writings of the First World War. She has published on the work of Dorothy Richardson and Katherine Mansfield, and is the author of *Elizabeth von Arnim: Beyond the German Garden* (2013).

Todd Martin is a Professor of English at Huntington University in Huntington, Indiana. He teaches twentieth-century British and American literature and has published on such varied authors as John Barth, E. E. Cummings, Clyde Edgerton, Sherwood Anderson, Julia Alvarez, Edwidge Danticat and Katherine Mansfield. He is the Membership Secretary of the Katherine Mansfield Society and the Liaison Editor for *Katherine Mansfield Studies*.

Naomi Milthorpe is a Lecturer in English at the School of Humanities, University of Tasmania. Her research interests centre upon interwar comic and satirical fiction, alternative modernisms and reading culture. Forthcoming essays will appear in *Affirmations: Of the Modern* and a new edited collection on Katherine Mansfield and influence. She is currently finishing a book on Evelyn Waugh, intertextuality and satire.

J. Lawrence Mitchell is Professor of English, Texas A&M University, and Director of Cushing Memorial Library & Archives. Besides Katherine Mansfield, his literary interests include Joyce, Kipling and D. H. Lawrence. He contributed to *Celebrating Katherine Mansfield* (2011) and his articles have appeared in such journals as *American Literary Realism, English Literature in Transition, The Hemingway Review, Journal of Modern Literature* and *Journal of New Zealand Literature*. His most recent article, on the Garnett family, appeared in *The Book Collector*.

Alex Moffett is Assistant Professor of English at Providence College, where he teaches twentieth-century British and Irish fiction. His essay on thermal tropes in Mansfield's short stories was published by the *Journal of Modern Literature* early in 2014.

Josiane Paccaud-Huguet is Professor of Modern English literature and Literary Theory at Université Lumière-Lyon 2. She has published extensively on modernist authors (Joseph Conrad, James Joyce, D. H. Lawrence, Malcolm Lowry, Virginia Woolf). Her latest publications include *Rewriting/Reprising in Literature: The Paradoxes of Intertextuality*, a co-edited volume (2009). She is currently finishing a monograph on the 'passion for the real' in twentieth-century fiction – *The Real Thing: The Modernist Moment of Vision* – which includes a chapter on Katherine Mansfield.

Emily Perkins is the author of four novels, including *The Forrests* (2012) and *Novel About My Wife* (2010), and a collection of stories, *Not Her Real Name* (2002). Her stories have been widely anthologised and broadcast, and her books have won awards in New Zealand, the UK and the US. She has lived in Auckland, London and Wellington, where she currently teaches creative writing at the International Institute of Modern Letters.

Juliane Römhild holds an Early Career Development Fellowship at the Department of Arts and Critical Enquiry at La Trobe University, Melbourne. Her research interests are English and German middle-brow fiction and women's writing. She has published on Elizabeth von Arnim and W. G. Sebald.

Helen Rydstrand is a PhD candidate at the University of New South Wales. Her thesis examines early-twentieth-century concepts of rhythm and their formal and thematic influence on the modernist short story in the work of Katherine Mansfield, Virginia Woolf and D. H. Lawrence. She is Assistant Secretary of the Katherine Mansfield Society.

Kathryn Simpson is Senior Lecturer in English Literature at Cardiff Metropolitan University. Her research focuses primarily on modernist women's writing and contemporary fiction. She has published on Virginia Woolf (including *Gifts, Markets and Economies of Desire in Virginia Woolf* (2008)), Katherine Mansfield and David Mitchell. She is co-reviews editor for *Katherine Mansfield Studies* and Vice-president of the International Virginia Woolf Society.

Anna Snaith is Reader in Twentieth-Century Literature at King's College London. She edited Virginia Woolf's *The Years* for the Cambridge University Press edition of Virginia Woolf (2012), and her monograph, *Modernist Voyages: Colonial Women Writers in London 1890–1945*, was published in 2014. She is currently editing *A Room of One's Own* and *Three Guineas* for Oxford World's Classics.

C. K. Stead edited the Penguin Modern Classics *Letters and Journals of Katherine Mansfield* (1977), and his novel *Mansfield* was published by Harvill-Secker (2004). He has published twelve novels, including *My*

Name was Judas (2006), and most recently *RISK* (2012). Arc has just published the UK edition of his fifteenth collection of poems, *The Yellow Buoy* (2013). He received a CBE in 1986, the Order of New Zealand in 2007, and the Prime Minister's Award for fiction in 2010. He is Professor Emeritus at the University of Auckland.

Robin Woodward is a Senior Lecturer in Art History at the University of Auckland. She is a specialist in New Zealand art, with particular expertise in contemporary sculpture and public art. In addition to her teaching and academic research, she works in an advisory role with arts trusts and civic bodies. Her approach addresses the artistic and historical context of the œuvre of individual artists and the visual analysis of specific works and sites. She has written monographs and thematic texts on aspects of modern and contemporary painting as well as sculpture.

Rishona Zimring is Associate Professor of English at Lewis & Clark College in Portland, Oregon. She is the author of *Social Dance and the Modernist Imagination in Interwar Britain* (2013), as well as numerous essays on the literature and culture of modernism and modernity.